THE EVOLUTION OF
OPEC

ALBERT L. DANIELSEN
University of Georgia

HARCOURT BRACE JOVANOVICH, PUBLISHERS
New York   San Diego   Chicago   San Francisco   Atlanta
London   Sydney   Toronto

To Eleanor, Bart, Lea, and Will

Cover photo: Copyright Barrie Rokeach 1982.

paperbound
ISBN 0-15-525080-9
clothbound
ISBN 0-15-129394-5

Library of Congress Card Number: 81-85395

Printed in the United States of America

Preface

The Organization of the Petroleum Exporting Countries (OPEC) is important, and will remain so, because its member nations have sovereign control over two-thirds of the world's most accessible petroleum reserves. Since 1973, OPEC has probably influenced the material well-being of more people worldwide than any other international organization. In fact, in its impact on real income, OPEC rivals domestic monetary and fiscal institutions in many countries, including the United States, Japan, and those in Western Europe. In this sense, to study OPEC and the international petroleum markets is a way to better understand the world's economic structure and how it functions.

The evolution of OPEC is not difficult to comprehend if the organization is viewed as an institution designed to improve the material well-being of its members. The modus operandi has been to substitute collective for individual action. The basic principles required to understand petroleum markets are easily within the grasp of those who have some familiarity with the elementary concepts related to purely competitive, monopolistic, and oligopolistic markets as found in a typical college economics course. Equally as important as the theory, however, are the institutions which have developed since oil became an important commercial product in the late 1800s.

This book is designed as a supplement to standard principles of economics textbooks. When used in introductory courses, it should be assigned late in the year, since it presupposes a knowledge of marginal analysis and supply and demand. Knowledge of capital theory will be helpful, although this topic is covered in Chapter 2.

The book is also suitable as a supplement to intermediate- and graduate-level courses in microeconomic theory, industrial organization, international economics, international politics, and economic development. It is designed to allow readers with diverse interests and backgrounds to gain better insight into their particular specialties. Chapters 2 and 3 may be emphasized in the more theoretical courses, whereas the material covering historical, current, and future developments in Chapters 4–6, 7–9, and 10, respectively, are appropriate for many other courses. Former students, corporate and government officials, as well as politicians who seek a better understanding of the evolution of OPEC and world petroleum markets, will find the book of interest. In fact, many current international and domestic events are difficult, if not impossible, to interpret without a sound understanding of the evolution of OPEC.

The efforts of many individuals have contributed to the writing of this book. I shall not enumerate any of my students or colleagues at the University of Georgia for fear of excluding someone who provided a useful insight into one or more of the issues considered in the book. The same applies to my former colleagues at the U.S. Federal Energy Administration and at the U.S. Department of Energy, where I worked while on leave during 1977 and 1978. Similarly, my associates in other academic institutions and in the International Association of Energy Economists, and those who reviewed my journal publications, have contributed immeasurably to my thinking about OPEC; but I will not implicate them in the present work. Those of you who know me will recognize your own contributions and be able to identify marginal differences in our interpretation of events. Only you can appreciate the magnitude of my debt.

I am also indebted to the reviewers of the book, who provided helpful comments on the organization and content of the original manuscript. They include: Professor Robert Campbell, Department of Economics, University of Oregon; Professor Thomas Clark, College of Business Administration, Department of Management, Georgia State University; Professor Nazli Choucri, Department of Political Science, MIT; and Professor Robert Deacon, Department of Economics, University of California at Santa Barbara.

Terence Retchless, Liana Beckett, and Barbara Rose at Harcourt Brace Jovanovich, Inc., provided excellent editorial assistance throughout the project, as did Geri Davis who coordinated the art work. I am also indebted to Arnold Balk at the University of Georgia Library, as well as to Barbara Daniel and Dolores Holt at the University of Georgia Cartographic Center for their original renderings of the more complicated figures and maps. Rough-draft typing was accomplished with patience and competence by Sylvia Graves, Judy Griffin, and Shirley Williams; Kathy Barber, Betty Futch, and Johnnie Edwards assumed the typing responsibilities for the second draft. The student assistants who contributed most to the project were Jack Berry, Jim Bosserman, and Susan Burns, while Gena Hampton, Gigi Mills, and Bryan Willis served shorter stints. I am indebted to all of these people, while bearing full responsibility for the remaining deficiencies.

Suggested Course Use

The book is divided into three parts: (1) theory, (2) history, and (3) modern structure. It is designed so that assignments can be made to cover all or only part of the subject matter. For example, Chapter 1 and Chapters 4 through 6, respectively, provide an introduction to the energy problem and to the evolution of OPEC; these may be assigned as outside reading for most students. Chapter 7 outlines the modern structure of petroleum markets and should be read by everyone. Chapters 8 and 9 on policy options and Chapter 10 on the outlook for the future may be assigned or made optional to the interested reader. Since the material in Chapters 2 and 3 is theoretical, the appropriate ideas may either be assigned in their entirety or introduced into lecture sessions on an "as needed" basis. The "cartel problem" and the "base-point pricing" sections in Chapter 3 contain perhaps the minimum theoretical material which will be required for most students. Neophytes often find this material an exciting supplement to the standard fare offered in most economics courses. Following are suggested assignments for specified courses.

Principles of Microeconomics

The evolution of OPEC provides a fascinating case study for budding economics students. This book uses a minimum of technical terms so that even beginning students can comprehend the material through individual reading. An optimal strategy for most classes will be to assign the introductory and historical chapters—1, 4, 5, and 6—as outside reading about five weeks into the semester. An interesting lecture about the formation of OPEC and its modern structure can be developed from the material contained in Chapters 6 and 7. Chapter 7 should be assigned immediately after the oligopoly chapter in the principles text. The reactions to OPEC and the policy options for consuming countries in Chapter

8 may also be taken up at this time. Chapter 9, which considers the options available to OPEC, is probably too detailed for beginning students; but specific sections, such as indexing of natural gas to oil prices, may be worked into the lecture sessions. The same may be said about the theoretical chapters, 2 and 3. I would not recommend assigning these chapters to the average beginning student. However, for honors classes and for superior students, Chapter 2's discussion of depletable resource theory may be assigned after the monopoly chapter in the principles text. Similarly, Chapter 3's discussion of cartel theory may be assigned along with the oligopoly chapter.

Intermediate Microeconomic Theory

A frequent criticism leveled against the intermediate micro course is its lack of applications. The analysis of OPEC provides an excellent opportunity to apply and illustrate microeconomic theory. This book can be fully integrated into the micro course, or it can be used selectively. I suggest that the introduction and historical chapters—1, 4, 5, and 6— be assigned as outside reading when market structure is first introduced. The theory of depletable resources in Chapter 2 should be discussed after monopoly; and Chapter 3, on cartel theory, will complement the textbook chapter on oligopoly. Having established a firm historical and theoretical basis for the analysis of OPEC, the student is reasonably well prepared to comprehend the modern structure of petroleum markets as presented in Chapter 7, the policy options available to the consuming countries in Chapter 8, and the policy options available to the producing countries in Chapter 9. In my own classes, I devote a full week to Chapters 7 through 10, and students invariably rate this among the most enjoyable segments of the micro course.

Other possibilities for course utilization include selective assignments from Chapters 2, 3, 8, and 9. For example, the material contained in the section on spatial pricing in Chapter 3 is rarely found in an intermediate textbook, but it conveys an important set of economic ideas. On the other hand, some of the material in Chapter 3 may duplicate that found in the main textbook; in addition, sections such as the one on SDR pricing in Chapter 9 are probably too technical even for most students of microeconomics; these sections can be omitted without detracting from the central ideas contained in the book.

Industrial Organization

The oil industry is far and away the most important industry in the world as measured by sales volume. Appendix B to this book shows that 20 of the top 44 U.S. corporations in terms of sales are oil companies. This book is essentially an industry analysis and, as such, it provides a case that can be used in its entirety in an industrial organization (IO) course. On the other hand, it may be useful as a supplement to illustrate basic principles found in the IO literature. For example, the importance of resource availability, the size and share of the market, cost conditions, organizational structure and performance, quota and allocation schemes, as well as many other concepts, literally permeate the study.

Courses in industrial organization vary in scope and even subject matter, so it is difficult to prescribe an optional strategy for using this book in the "typical" course. The variety of courses found in this field reflects both the students' background and the instructors' proclivities and research interests. If students want a refresher on depletable resource and/or cartel theory, they can find the information they need in Chapters 2 and 3. Of special interest to IO students is the material covering the early development and modern structure of the world petroleum markets as specified in Chapters 4 through 7. Chapter 9, which deals with the policy options available to OPEC, may also be considered in detail in this course. Chapter 8, on consumer-country reactions and policy options, and Chapter 10, on the outlook for the future, may be assigned as outside reading.

International Trade and Development

It is amazing to me that so many international economics courses place such little emphasis on the analysis of OPEC and world petroleum markets. Oil accounts for half the tonnage, two-thirds of the ton miles, and about one-quarter of the value of all goods and services entering internation trade; and the value of oil is over ten times that of wheat, corn, or soybeans. Yet oil markets are scarcely mentioned in many international economics textbooks. Instead, wheat, corn, wine, and cloth remain the favorite classroom examples, even though they are trivial in importance when compared with oil. Oil provides a classic example of immiserizing growth; cartelization of oil markets can be used to illustrate the "terms of trade" argument for restricting trade; and oil makes an ideal case in point for the futility of selective embargoes.

Students of international economics generally have had sufficient training such that none of the material in this book should be beyond their grasp. Since course orientation varies from the highly theoretical to the institutional, professors will want to assign chapters on the basis of their individual needs. The entire book could be assigned as outside reading. However, for most students, I suggest that the introduction and historical chapters—1, 4, 5, and 6—be assigned as outside reading fairly early in the course. Emphasis may then be placed on the modern structure of petroleum markets found in Chapter 7, on policy options, in Chapters 8 and 9, and on the outlook for the future, in Chapter 10. Students who have escaped exposure to depletable resource theory and the theory of spatial pricing—both of which typically are omitted in undergraduate programs—should be required to read appropriate sections from Chapters 2 and 3.

Resource and/or Energy Economics

The world petroleum market is only a part of the total resource and energy picture; but it is the largest, and by many criteria, the most important part. Oil is the "swing fuel" in energy markets, and OPEC is the "swing producer" in the oil market. Furthermore, the prices of all other energy resources are dependent on the current and prospective price of oil. Like courses in industrial organization, those in resource and energy economics vary in scope and even subject matter, so it is difficult to prescribe an optimal strategy for a "typical" course. Similarly, variety reflects different student backgrounds as well as individual instructor preferences. I suggest that at least a full week be devoted to this book. The introduction should be assigned with Chapter 1 of the regular textbook. Students may be assigned the historical chapters—4, 5, and 6—as outside reading at the same time that material on basic resource endowments and alternative energy sources is presented. Sections of the theoretical chapters—2 and 3—may be assigned to suit individual student needs. In many cases, assignments from these chapters will prove to be preferable to assigning comparable material from the textbook. Emphasis should be given to the modern structure of petroleum markets, as presented in Chapter 7, and to the policy options available to the consuming countries, as offered in Chapter 8. Students with special interests in Africa and the Middle East may wish to focus on the policy options available to the producing countries, as presented in Chapter 9. The final chapter may be assigned to supplement the concluding chapter of the regular text.

Contents

Part Three   Modern Structure   157

7 Modern Structure of the World Oil Market   159

8 Consuming Country Reactions and Policies   201

9 Exporting Country Options   235

Part One

Foundations of International Petroleum Analysis

Petroleum accounts for half the tonnage, two-thirds of the ton miles, and one-fourth of the value of all commodities exchanged in international markets; it is by far the most important internationally traded commodity, as measured by volume and monetary value. These statistics on market shares stand in sharp contrast to the ones observed prior to the expansion of petroleum trade in the 1960s and before the sensational price increases of the 1970s. Why have these trade and price patterns emerged? What might we expect in the next twenty years? A primary purpose of this book is to provide answers to these questions.

Part One presents an introduction to the basic theory required to understand the evolution of the Organization of the Petroleum Exporting Countries. Chapter 1 explains why the rise of OPEC was almost inevitable and discusses OPEC's role in effecting a redistribution of income, within and among countries, that is without precedent anywhere in the world. The chapter also provides an overview of the entire book.

Chapter 2 outlines the theory of depletable resources as developed by Harold Hotelling and others. This theory, which is rarely covered in a principles course or even in more advanced courses, is a relatively new, highly specialized field that is still being developed. It is particularly relevant to long-term analyses, and is important to any serious consideration of resource utilization.

The theory of cartel behavior is the subject matter of Chapter 3. It is applicable to short and intermediate time periods, and it, too, is currently undergoing modification and reevaluation. The spatial theory of base-point pricing is also included in this chapter. Some of this material can be found in textbooks on intermediate microeconomic theory and industrial organization; however, simple duopoly models, such as the Cournot and Edgeworth models, are not developed here. A clear distinction is made between the concepts of cartel formation and those of cartel stability. The background material and theories developed in Part One are used in assessing the historical developments and policy options considered in the remainder of the book.

READER'S GUIDE TO PART ONE

In this part we introduce OPEC as a formal organization and present the basic ideas required to understand its structural evolution and performance. Chapter 1 provides the setting for subsequent analyses found throughout the book. Chapters 2 and 3 should be within the grasp of the reader who has mastered the material in a college-level principles course. Readers with more advanced economics training can skim the section headings to identify the specialized concepts which will require closer examination. The headings "Net Price" and "Backstop Technology," found on pages 30 and 31, respectively, are two such concepts. Readers with little or no training in economics will probably find Chapters 2 and 3 difficult, but well worth the effort.

Introduction 1

Basic Considerations:
The Members of OPEC; Brief History of OPEC; Non-OPEC Energy Producers; Consuming Countries.

Market Structure.

Production and Price Trends:
Oil Production; Price Trends.

Plan of Study.

READER'S GUIDE TO CHAPTER 1
This chapter provides an overview of OPEC and world petroleum markets. Although the day will come when petroleum no longer serves as an energy resource and OPEC ceases to exist, petroleum is now the primary energy resource, and OPEC is the most important institution determining its availability and price. This chapter stresses the importance of OPEC, defines some basic terms, introduces the principal actors involved in energy markets, and outlines the long-term production and price trends.

3

Basic Considerations

The formal confederation of thirteen sovereign nations into the group now known as the Organization of the Petroleum Exporting Countries (OPEC) should be viewed as a natural development evolving out of the geographic distribution of petroleum reserves. Basically all that was required was that the leaders of the oil-rich nations discover the potential value of their resources. After that, they simply needed to devise institutions which would enable them to appropriate a larger share of that value for themselves.

The time frame over which OPEC evolved may be seen as either very long or extremely short, depending on one's point of view. In fact, it required a half century for the various leaders to discover what was at stake, and another quarter century for them to implement plans for cooperation. After that, developments occurred more rapidly. OPEC was formally organized in 1960, and only thirteen years later it was—and still is—the primary instutition determining all energy prices. OPEC does not literally control oil prices, but it is the central institution in the modern structure of energy markets. OPEC is sometimes referred to as a *cartel*—a term implying the opposite of competition in that it describes an arrangement among producers to cooperate. OPEC is not a perfect cartel, but it is an organization designed to promote cooperation among independent oil producing nations.

The Members of OPEC

OPEC officially came into existence as a result of a conference held in Baghdad, Iraq, September 9–14, 1960. OPEC's *founding members*—five of the principal oil exporting countries that attended the Baghdad conference—include Saudi Arabia, Iran, Kuwait, Iraq, and Venezuela. Eight other countries have since been admitted as *full members*, bringing the total membership to thirteen (see Table 1–1). The founding members have veto power over admission of new members, but otherwise all full members have equal rights within the organization. Any country which is a "substantial net exporter" and whose petroleum interests are "fundamentally similar" to those of member countries is eligible to join. (Trinidad and Tobago, Syria, and Congo have applied for membership but have not been accepted.)

OPEC derives its power from the fact that its members own two-thirds of known petroleum reserves and that their extraction costs are minuscule. Thus, oil from OPEC can effectively compete with alternative energy resources in almost every market. Members of OPEC export 85

TABLE 1–1

Oil Reserves, Population, and Land Area of Member Countries of OPEC, 1980

Type and Year[1]	Reserves (billion barrels)	Population (millions)	Land Area (thousands of sq. miles)
FOUNDING MEMBERS			
Saudi Arabia* (1960)	165.0	8.1	873
Iran (1960)	67.5	36.9	636
Kuwait* (1960)	64.9	3.0	8
Iraq* (1960)	30.0	12.8	172
Venezuela (1960)	17.8	12.7	352
FULL MEMBERS			
Qatar* (1961)	3.6	0.2	4
Libya* (1962)	23.0	2.6	680
Indonesia (1962)	9.5	142.0	788
UAE* (1967)[2]	30.4	0.8	32
Algeria* (1969)	8.2	18.0	920
Nigeria (1971)	16.7	84.5	380
Ecuador (1973)	1.1	7.3	109
Gabon (1975)	0.5	0.6	103
TOTAL	438.2	329.5	5,057

*Arab country.

[1]Date of admission shown in parentheses.

[2]United Arab Emirates includes Abu Dhabi, Dubai, Sharjah, Ras Al-Khaimah, and Umm Al Qaywayn. The largest of the Emirates, Abu Dhabi, joined in 1967.

SOURCE: *International Petroleum Encyclopedia, 1981,* Tulsa, Oklahoma: PennWell Publishing Company, 1981.

percent of all oil moving in international trade, primarily because their reserves are large and extraction costs are low. If they desired, OPEC members could set prices near their extraction costs and capture an even larger share of energy markets. However, establishing prices near extraction costs and driving alternative fuels from the market is not perceived to be in their best interests. Instead, through OPEC, member countries have adopted cooperative policies to hold prices well above costs and to reduce production while increasing their current and potential income. It is an old adage in the petroleum industry that "less is more," meaning that less production will yield more revenue for all producers combined.

Brief History of OPEC

It is difficult to overemphasize the importance of OPEC's long evolution. Leaders of the member countries began their learning process as early as 1872, when the shah of Persia (now Iran) granted Baron Julius de Reuter a seventy-year concession to exploit all Persian energy resources. The shah was to receive £40,000 and a 15–20 percent profit share for the concession. But the shah soon learned he had struck a bad bargain and cancelled the concession and confiscated de Reuter's £40,000. This pattern was to become the modus operandi of company–country relations, and today is embodied in the terms *renegotiation* and *changed circumstances*.

The history of world petroleum market institutions shows there were two fairly resilient cooperative arrangements among producers prior to the formation of OPEC. The first was a cartel of major international oil companies, and the second was composed of oil producers in the United States (the leading oil producing country during the first half of the century). Both cartel-type institutions were effective for several decades.

The *international corporate cartel* was formed by the Red-Line Agreement in 1914 and reinforced by the As-Is Agreement in 1928. The former specified that Middle Eastern reserves would be developed through one company, the Turkish Petroleum Company, which was wholly owned by three international oil companies, British Petroleum (BP), Royal Dutch-Shell, and the French Compagnie Française des Petroles (CFP), to use their current names. The As-Is Agreement divided the sale of oil in world markets between BP, Royal Dutch-Shell, and Exxon. The other major oil companies were worked into the agreements during the 1930s. In the early 1950s, the corporate cartel consisted of CFP and seven giant international corporations, Exxon, Mobil, Texaco, Socal, Gulf, Shell, and BP, referred to in the more imaginative literature as the "Seven Sisters." It admitted new entrants from time to time, and functioned on a world scale from 1914 until about 1955.

The second cartel-type arrangement was created by several state governments in the Unites States for the purpose of limiting production. The system they devised, known as *market demand prorationing*, was a quota and allocation scheme that proved extraordinarily effective in limiting output and maintaining prices from 1935 to 1970. The institution was sanctioned by the federal government in 1935, and it still exists as a latent force capable of withholding production and maintaining oil prices above competitive levels. However, its role as the principal determiner of oil prices has been usurped by OPEC.

The OPEC nations further evolved during the 1940s and 1950s under the umbrella of market demand prorationing in the United States and in opposition to the Seven Sisters' unilateral domination of international operations. Of greatest importance in the evolution of OPEC was the practice of *profit sharing*, a system that was introduced in Venezuela in 1944 and that spread to the Middle East during the early 1950s. This period marked the beginning of the emergent OPEC's takeover of production and pricing decisions.

Earlier it was stated that OPEC is not a perfect cartel. The reason is that, despite its remarkable efforts toward cooperation, there are inherent conflicts of interest among its members. Nor is OPEC an Arab organization, as is sometimes mistakenly believed. Only three "founding" and four "new" members are Arab. In all, they are geographically dispersed over three continents and an island, and vary considerably both in population and land area (again, see Table 1–1). It is not even true that all member countries are wealthy; per capita output and petroleum reserves vary enormously among them, and some are really quite poor (see Table 1–2). This extreme diversity that characterizes the OPEC

TABLE 1-2
Per Capita GNP and Oil Wealth
Member Countries of OPEC Compared to the United States, 1980

Country	Per Capita GNP[1] (dollars)	Per Capita Oil Wealth[2] (thousands of dollars)
UAE	24,360	1,216
Kuwait	18,390	692
Qatar	29,900	676
Saudi Arabia	9,500	652
Libya	6,960	283
Iraq	2,730	75
Gabon	5,250	27
Iran	2,170	58
Venezuela	3,370	45
Algeria	1,720	15
Nigeria	620	6
Ecuador	1,100	5
Indonesia	350	2
United States	10,719	5

[1] 1979 data.
[2] Oil reserves valued at $32 per barrel.
SOURCES: Table 1-1 and Central Intelligence Agency, *The World Factbook, 1981,* Washington, D.C.: April 1981. Council of Economic Advisers, *Economic Indicators,* August 1981, pp. 1, 6.

membership is a continual impediment to the achievement of cooperation in pricing and production policies. Yet, despite a lack of unity, OPEC has managed to effect the most colossal commercial redistribution of income in history.

Non-OPEC Energy Producers

An important constraint on the member countries' quest for greater revenue is competition from non-OPEC energy producers. Holding oil prices far above production costs serves to increase the value of *all* energy resources and leads to increased production outside OPEC. Conventional energy resources are abundant, and those who own them benefit from policies which restrict oil production and raise prices.

The two largest energy resource owners and producers outside OPEC are the USSR and the United States (see Table 1-3). China, Mexico, Canada, and the principal North Sea countries—the United Kingdom and Norway—are potential major oil producers. Of these, Mexico is the only prime candidate for admission to OPEC, although it prefers to remain outside for now. Norway might also qualify, but its interests are more "fundamentally similar" to the other European countries than to OPEC's. Canada has large reserves relative to its population and could become a major oil and natural gas exporter; but it has chosen to reduce exports because of internal political conflicts between national and provincial authorities over the distribution of energy-related income. The United Kingdom and the United States are net oil importers, but North Sea oil is expected to make the UK energy self-sufficient within the decade. The USSR is self-sufficient in energy. It is a net exporter of oil to other Eastern bloc countries and of natural gas to Western Europe.

An examination of energy resource utilization among countries shows that choices vary widely. Some countries produce more energy than they consume, whereas others consume more than they produce. A country which produces as much energy as it consumes is said to be *energy self-sufficient*. A net importer is one that has chosen to utilize *foreign* energy resources and is said to be *dependent* on foreign energy. Although it can be misleading, this terminology is pervasive in much of the energy literature. Terms such as *dependent* will be used sparingly in this book because they imply the absence of choice. However, a useful measure for making international comparisons is the more technical term *degree of dependence,* defined as the ratio of imports to total consumption and expressed as a percent. A negative *dependency ratio* indicates the country is an exporter; a value of zero indicates self-sufficiency; and a value of 100 means 100 percent of domestic consumption is imported.

TABLE 1-3
Proved and Probable Reserves of Crude Oil, Natural Gas, and Coal, January 1, 1981

Country or Region	Crude Oil (billion barrels)	(percent total)	Natural Gas (trillion cu. ft.)	(percent total)	Coal (billion short tons)	(percent total)
MAJOR PRODUCERS						
OPEC	435	67.1	1,003	38.0	4	.4
USSR	63	9.7	920	34.9	257	26.4
United States	26	4.0	191	7.2	247	25.3
Mexico	44	6.8	65	2.5	2	.2
China	20	3.1	25	1.0	109	11.2
MINOR PRODUCERS						
United Kingdom	15	2.3	25	1.0	50	5.1
Canada	6	1.0	87	3.3	7	0.7
Norway	6	0.9	43	1.6	—	—
OTHER (EAST) EUROPEAN	1	.02	9	0.3	90	9.2
OTHER FREE WORLD	32	4.9	268	10.2	209	21.4
TOTAL	648	100.0	2,639	100.0	975	100.0

SOURCE: U.S. Dept. of Energy, *International Energy Annual*, September 1981, Washington, D.C.: pp. 82–84.

Dependency ratios can be calculated for any commodity, including a particular energy resource such as oil. The *oil dependency ratio* is interesting because oil is the principal internationally traded commodity. Another important figure is the *energy dependency ratio,* derived by calculating the BTU-equivalent value of alternative energy resources. The *degree of energy dependence* is not a perfect measure, since alternative resources are imperfectly substitutable. But for gross comparative purposes it reveals that countries are in greatly differing positions in terms of energy self-sufficiency.

Consuming Countries

An important constraint on OPEC is the tendency for consuming countries to reduce overall energy consumption and substitute alternative energy resources for oil. Natural gas, coal, and nuclear energy are all good substitutes for oil. As presently constituted, the demand for crude oil is derived from the demand for refined products—gasoline, diesel fuel, home heating oil, jet fuel, residual fuel oil for generating electricity, and other, more specialized oil products. Elementary economic theory teaches that consumers alter their behavior when relative prices change. They buy fewer units of goods whose prices have increased, they work harder, or they reduce savings to maintain previous levels of consumption. Choice and substitution of other goods, leisure, or future consumption are always involved. In essence, consumers are harmed by higher oil prices and react by changing their behavior patterns.

The principal energy consuming countries, as opposed to the oil consuming countries, are also the leading energy producers, although oil imports are closely related to total energy consumption. Table 1-4 shows the levels of consumption, production, and imports of primary energy expressed in thousands of barrels per day oil equivalent, for the principal consuming and importing countries. Nearly all energy trade is oil trade, but Canada, the Netherlands, and the USSR export natural gas; and Japan imports coal as well as oil. The United States is by far the leading energy consumer, and the USSR is a clear second. The United States is also the leading oil importing country, followed by Japan and West Germany. Japan, Italy, and West Germany produce almost no oil and are highly dependent on oil imports. However, the terms "energy consuming" and "oil importing" are obviously not synonymous.

Cooperation among the consuming countries is difficult to achieve because the countries are highly diverse in terms of their status as consumers and producers of energy, as distinguished from consumers and producers of oil *per se*. The United States has strong producer interests

TABLE 1-4
Primary Energy Consumption, Production, and Net Balance
OECD (Organization for Economic Cooperation and
Development) and Communist Countries, 1978
(thousand barrels per day oil equivalent)[1]

	Primary Consumption	Primary Production	Primary Imports[2]	Energy Dependence Ratio[3]
OECD				
United States	37,572	30,843	(6,729)	17.9
Japan	7,315	990	(6,325)	86.5
West Germany	5,510	2,306	(3,204)	58.2
United Kingdom	4,288	3,665	(623)	14.5
Canada	4,384	4,822	438	—
France	3,897	957	(2,940)	75.4
Italy	2,859	510	(2,349)	82.2
Netherlands	1,513	1,669	156	—
Belgium	1,033	155	(878)	85.0
Norway	453	807	354	—
Total OECD	68,824	46,724	(22,100)	32.1
COMMUNIST COUNTRIES				
USSR	21,620	25,400	3,780	—
Eastern Europe	8,073	6,240	(1,833)	22.7
Total Communist	29,693	31,640	1,947	—

[1]Based on BTU-equivalent energy in natural gas, coal, nuclear, and hydropower.
[2]Excess consumption over production is shown as a deficit in parentheses.
[3]Ratio of primary imports to primary consumption.
SOURCE: Central Intelligence Agency, *Handbook of Economic Statistics, 1980,* Washington, D.C.: pp. 118–119.

compared with Japan, West Germany, France, and Italy. Thus, there are inherent conflicts as well as harmonies of interest among them.

Market Structure

The world oil market is extraordinarily complex. It consists of buyers and sellers of crude oil, refined products, and a vast array of contractors engaged in service activities ranging from exploration and drilling, to marketing fuel oil to residential consumers, and to selling gasoline at the pump. These diverse activities make up the market structure in which buyers and sellers interact.

A distinguishing characteristic of the market is the existence of large and integrated corporations. Six of the ten largest corporations in the United States, as measured by dollar volume of sales, are integrated international oil companies, or "majors" (see Appendix B). Exxon, for example, employs 175,000 workers and has greater sales than any other corporation in the world. The other major oil companies include Shell, British Petroleum, Mobil, Texaco, Gulf, and Standard Oil Company of California (Socal). The majors are fully integrated, both vertically and horizontally. *Vertical integration in the oil industry* refers to companies engaged in nearly all phases of oil-industry operations—exploration, drilling, production, transportation, refining, and marketing. *Horizontal integration in the energy industry* refers to budding operations in oil shale, coal, and nuclear or solar energy.

Literally thousands of nonintegrated oil and energy companies exist to complement and compete with the international majors. Complementary activities include exploration and drilling, which are generally undertaken by independent contractors. Consumer cooperatives and small private corporations frequently own pipelines, refineries, and distributorships for refined products; and there are dozens of partially integrated firms which would be classified as giants in most other industries. Over thirty oil companies import more than 500,000 barrels of oil per month into the United States. Figuring the average market price of refined products at $1 per *gallon*, this represents annual sales of $250 million. Thus, even small oil importers, or "independents," are very large enterprises. Relations between the majors and independents is complicated by the practice of joint ventures commonly undertaken in exploration, drilling, and pipeline construction.

The international majors and independents are naturally engaged in selling refined products. In addition, the national oil companies and oil ministries representing the member countries of OPEC are an important part of the market. The oil ministries generally operate through long-term service and sales contracts with both large and small international oil companies. Saudi Arabia and the Arabian American Oil Company (Aramco) exemplify producing-country and joint-venture relationships. The Aramco partners—Exxon, Mobil, Texaco, and Standard Oil of California—are among the largest companies in the world; and Saudi Arabia is by far the leading oil exporter.

Most of the oil exporting countries have "national" companies, such as the "National Iranian Oil Company," which are becoming increasingly competitive with the international majors and independents for crude oil and for "downstream" operations, such as oceangoing transport, refining, and marketing. Some of the oil importing governments have fully or partially nationalized their own oil companies. British Petroleum (BP), for example, operates like a private international major; but 40 percent of its stock is owned by the British government. No international oil company is totally independent. Legal and financial interests, which extend across national boundaries, necessarily bring them in contact with government officials who both influence and are influenced by their behavior. In short, the market structure is complex and should be thought of as an evolving blend of competitive and cooperative inter-relationships.

Production and Price Trends

Energy from the sun, uranium, and coal is abundant; but the world is mostly fueled by oil and natural gas (see Figure 1-1). Coal was the most important fuel a half century ago, but it has gradually been displaced by petroleum for reasons that are basically economic. Liquids and gases are difficult to locate; but once found, the costs of extraction, distribution, and utilization are relatively low. Oil and natural gas are both inexpensive to transport by pipeline, but oil costs only one-sixth as much as natural gas to ship by tanker. The major reason oil has become

FIGURE 1-1
World Primary Energy Consumption, 1925–1975
(in quadrillion BTU and percent)

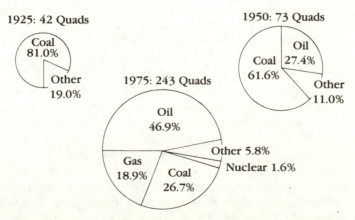

SOURCE: Central Intelligence Agency, *Handbook of Economic Statistics*, 1976, Washington, D.C.: September 1976, p. 76.

the principal energy resource is that reserves of both oil and natural gas are abundant in the Middle East, and oil transport costs in oceangoing vessels are relatively low. Natural gas and coal are also abundant, but transport costs from the major producing countries to the major consuming regions are high.

This book is about OPEC, and therefore it is primarily about oil. However, it is important to remember the potential substitutability of energy resources. Substantial substitutions have already occurred within a relatively short time span. In fact, the present and next generations will witness nearly a complete transformation to the more abundant energy resources, such as oil shale, uranium, and geothermal and solar power. But for now, the world is fueled primarily by oil and natural gas (that is, petroleum).

Oil Production

Before his death in 1976, J. Paul Getty was considered the richest man in the world. His career began at the age of 17 in the oil fields of Oklahoma in 1903. According to his autobiography, one of the first things he learned was to think in terms of millions—millions of barrels and millions of dollars. Today, the international oil companies and member countries of OPEC also think in terms of millions—millions of barrels *per day* and millions of dollars *per day*. On an annual basis, the larger companies and even the small countries think in billions.

OPEC accounts for half the total world production and 60 percent of free world oil production (see Table 1-5 and Figure 1-2). However, the USSR produces more oil than any other country in the world. Saudi Arabia, producing 10 million barrels per day, is the second leading producer, followed by the United States. Saudi Arabia is of course the leading oil exporter by a wide margin. The United States was an early leader in oil production and until 1953 produced more oil than all other countries combined. Oil production in the Soviet Union lagged behind that in the United States until well into the 1970s, despite the fact that the USSR has much larger reserves. In general, since 1950 oil production has become more closely related to recoverable reserves in most of the producing countries, and expansion has proceeded at a particularly rapid pace in the USSR and in member countries of OPEC.

Compound annual rates of growth in production reveal many interesting relationships. Oil production in the USSR grew more rapidly than that in the United States and in OPEC nations during the period 1950–1980 (see Table 1-6). It was particularly rapid during the 1950s and 1960s. These decades may be regarded as transitional, since the USSR was "catching up" with the West in oil exploration and end-use technology. The growth rate in the United States and in OPEC nations

TABLE 1-5
Average Daily Oil Production, U.S., Soviet, OPEC and Total World, 1860–1980
(million barrels per day)

Year	United States	USSR	OPEC	Total World
1860	.000	.000	.000	.001
1870	.014	.001	.000	.016
1880	.072	.008	.000	.082
1890	.126	.079	.000	.210
1900	.174	.208	.006	.409
1910	.574	.193	.030	.898
1920	1.214	.070	.084	1.887
1930	2.460	.349	.659	3.868
1940	3.707	.610	1.004	5.890
1950	5.407	.748	3.432	10.419
1960*	7.055	2.943	8.800	21.026
1970	9.648	6.976	23.408	43.210
1980**	8.597	11.720	26.890	59.455

SOURCES:
1860–1950, American Petroleum Institute, *Petroleum Facts and Figures, 1971 ed.,* pp. 548–557.
*1960–1970, Central Intelligence Agency, *Handbook of Economic Statistics,* Washington, D.C.: 1979, p. 135.
**1980 (1979), U.S. Department of Energy, *Monthly Energy Review,* August 1981, pp. 88–89.

was less during the 1950s than it was in the 1960s, because output was restrained during the 1950s by regulation of production imposed by state authorities in the United States and by the international majors in the member countries of OPEC. Market demand prorationing was much less effective in restraining output and maintaining prices during the 1960s. The growth rate declined markedly during the 1970s, as output was once again restrained and demand slackened in response to higher prices. The growth rate in production was negative in the United States because of both geological and regulatory constraints on production. The growth rate in OPEC was lower than for the world as a whole and much lower than in the USSR. But for OPEC, this was a deliberate choice based on a desire to increase prices.

Price Trends

Prices paid for oil in world markets prior to 1959 were determined by oil prices in the United States. The break between U.S. and world prices after 1959 came about as the result of U.S.-imposed oil import quotas under the Mandatory Oil Import Control Program. A more detailed

FIGURE 1-2
Average Daily Oil Production
U.S., Soviet, OPEC and Total World, 1860–1980

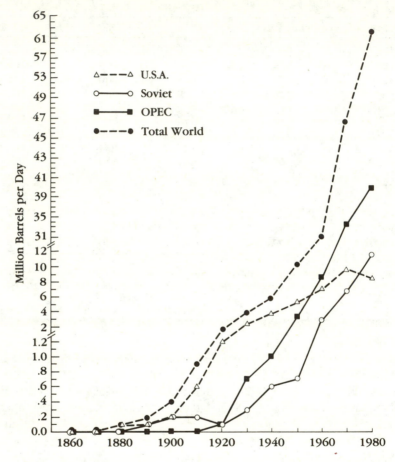

account and explanation of these trends and events will be presented in Chapters 4 through 7. However, a brief overview of the long-term trend may add perspective at this point.

Oil prices before 1935 were highly variable but generally within the $1–$2 per barrel range (see Figure 1-3). Prices rose sharply during and after World War I, when there were fears of oil depletion. But these fears were soon allayed by new discoveries in Texas and in the Middle East. The depressed prices of the late 1920s and early 1930s are attributable to new and hitherto unknown reserves, especially the supergiant East Texas field.

TABLE 1-6
Compound Annual Growth Rates in Oil Production by Region,
1950–1980
(in percent)

Time Period (*decade*)	United States	USSR	OPEC	World
1950–1960	2.7	13.7	9.4	7.4
1960–1970	3.1	8.6	9.8	7.2
1970–1980	−1.2	5.2	1.4	3.2
1950–1980	1.5	9.2	6.9	5.8

SOURCE: Table 1-5.

Prices were relatively stable from 1935 until 1945 because of state-level production quotas and federal price controls imposed during World War II. State quotas held prices up and federal controls later held them down. Meanwhile, the international oil companies were developing foreign reserves slowly, so that U.S. prices were not much influenced by competition from abroad. In fact, foreign competition was severely constrained and the United States remained a net oil exporter. Although prices more than doubled when they were decontrolled in

FIGURE 1-3
U.S. and World Crude Oil Prices and Percentage Changes in (Nominal) Prices, 1913–1980

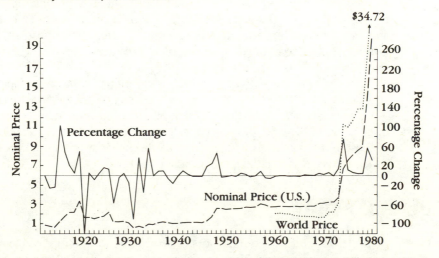

1946, they generally remained in the $2.50–$3 per barrel range until 1969. This remarkable stability of prices is attributable to market demand prorationing and to the Mandatory Impact Control Program of 1959.

The U.S. and the world oil prices diverged after 1960. Domestic prices were stable, but the world price declined as oil production by OPEC member countries increased at a rate of 9.8 percent per year. There were subtle institutional reasons for the rapid growth in production and the low world prices. These will be explained in Chapter 6; but, in essence, OPEC was not very cohesive at the time, and conditions outside OPEC were not yet ripe for the kind of market control that would be observed in the 1970s.

Sharp upward movements in the world oil price occurred in 1971, 1973, and again in 1979; these price increases were associated with internal revolutions in Libya (1969) and Iran (1979) and with the Fourth Arab–Israeli War (1973). However, the first upward movement occurred in 1970, after the overthrow of King Idris in Libya and the assumption of control by Colonel Qadhafi. The new regime demanded both higher prices and a 58 percent share of company profits. This was followed by a series of "leapfrog" maneuvers among the various companies, resulting in price increases on the order of 20 percent. More dramatic price increases occurred in association with the Fourth Arab–Israeli conflict and with the Arab embargo of 1973–1974. The net result was a quadrupling of prices to the $11–$12 per barrel range. After that, nominal contract prices remained fairly stable until late 1978, when an Iranian coup d'état appeared imminent. Then, in 1979, prices more than doubled, and, in absolute terms, the increases exceeded those in 1973–1974. Domestic crude oil prices in the United States lagged behind world oil prices because the U.S. Congress passed legislation to control prices and the Nixon administration imposed price controls in August, 1971. Controls on oil remained in effect until President Reagan ordered immediate decontrol in January, 1981.

Clearly, a complex process of price determination has been operative since about 1960. Does this new process stem from the fact that oil is a depletable resource? that OPEC now functions as a viable cartel? or do political considerations predominate? In truth, it is a combination of these, plus problems associated with inventory speculation. These issues are addressed at length in Chapter 7.

Plan of Study

An understanding of the policy options available to the importing and exporting countries requires knowledge of the theory of depletable resources, cartel theory, market institutions, and the modern structure of petroleum markets. These topics are covered in detail in subsequent chapters.

Good theory has something to tell us, but it may be inadequate or even misleading if not tempered with institutional knowledge and with good judgment in the use of valid principles. The *theory of depletable resources* teaches that, under purely competitive conditions, the net price—that is, the market price minus the costs of the resource—will initially be relatively low, will rise gradually at about the real rate of interest, and the resource will be depleted at an early date. Under monopoly, the net price of that same resource will be relatively high, rise gradually at less than the real rate of interest, and the resource will be depleted later than under competition. A cartel—or group of producers who have combined to substitute cooperation for competition—will set prices between the purely competitive and the monopoly prices, and the resource will be depleted later than under competition but sooner than under monopoly. The theory of depletable resources is developed in Chapter 2.

Traditional cartel theory teaches that cartels are inherently unstable because parties to cooperative agreements have an incentive to expand output; in addition, competition from outsiders can erode cooperative agreements. Although these forces are always operative, it is also true that cooperation has been successful for extended periods in petroleum markets. The theories of cartel formation and breakdown are presented in Chapter 3. The stability of OPEC viewed in light of these theories is assessed in Chapters 7 and 9.

Sandwiched between Chapters 3 and 7 are three historical chapters on the structure of world petroleum markets. These show how OPEC evolved through a complex process to reach a preeminent position in world oil markets. They explain that pure competition has never existed in world oil markets and that there has never been a master plan or overall conspiracy. They show that, instead, the principal actors have always operated with limited information and in their own self-interest; that they have both cooperated and competed in gaining control of oil reserves, production, refining, and marketing operations; and that early competition among the oil companies led to the development of integrated company operations from the well to the wick, and later from the well to the gasoline pump. The integrated companies are simply the survivors in markets which have periodically swung between the extremes of cooperation and competition.

OPEC is now the dominant influence in world petroleum markets; but it does not literally control prices. Choices on the part of non-OPEC oil producers, businessmen who select energy resources on the basis of relative prices, and consumers of final products also play a role. Government policies designed to affect relative prices also are important.

Understanding why oil prices were low and declining throughout the 1960s and why they increased sharply in the 1970s is important because policies designed to cope with price increases caused by resource depletion may be inadequate or even inappropriate in dealing with OPEC as a viable cartel. Similarly, pricing and output decisions by OPEC depend on both short- and long-run considerations. If oil prices increase too rapidly, the oil importing countries may experience slow growth and prematurely switch to alternative fuels, thus leaving the oil exporting countries a much smaller share of world energy markets.

The policy options available to the consuming countries and OPEC range from uncoordinated bilateral agreements to various degrees of economic integration. The more viable options are discussed in Chapters 8 and 9. The concluding chapter discusses the outlook for the future. Two preliminary conclusions are that OPEC will remain an important institution well into the twenty-first century, but that energy prices are *not* likely to increase very much from present levels *in real terms* because of actions undertaken by OPEC. The basis for these conclusions forms the subject matter of the book.

Further Readings

American Petroleum Institute. *Petroleum Facts and Figures.* Washington, D.C.: 1971.

Central Intelligence Agency. *Handbook of Economic Statistics.* Washington, D.C.: 1980.

International Petroleum Encyclopedia. Tulsa: The PennWell Publishing Co., 1980.

OPEC. *OPEC Member Country Profiles.* Vienna: OPEC Secretariat, 1980.

_____ *OPEC At A Glance.* Vienna: OPEC Secretariat, 1981.

Tiratsoo, E. N. *Oilfields of the World.* Houston: Gulf Publishing Company, 1976.

Depletable Resource Theory

Introduction:
Problem; Genesis of Depletable Resource Theory.

Fundamental Concepts:
Present Value; Economic Profit and Opportunity Cost; Other Depletable Resource Concepts.

Basic Theory:
Overview; Initial Price Determination in a Static Framework; Price Paths in a Dynamic Framework; Monopoly; Cartel with Competitive Fringe.

Application to the World Oil Market:
Usefulness of the Theory; Complications of the Real World; An Aid to Straight Thinking; Effects on Income Distribution.

Conclusion.

READER'S GUIDE TO CHAPTER 2

This chapter provides an overview of the theory of depletable resources, which is based on the work of Harold Hotelling. The first section explains Hotelling's primary role in the development of the depletable resource theory, and the following section provides a discussion of some of the fundamental concepts found in the literature. Specifically, this section explains the difference between *net prices* and *market prices*, and defines what is meant by *backstop technology*. The theory itself is outlined in the next section, where the primary focus is on the price paths followed under pure competition, pure monopoly, and intermediate market arrangements. The final part of the chapter is devoted to a discussion of the relevance of depletable resource theory to world petroleum markets. In general, the material may be viewed as helpful, but not sufficient, toward a proper assessment of trends in oil prices and output.

Introduction

Problem

Technically, it is conceivable that all resources could be depleted; but in fact, most resources are so abundant that they are not classified as *depletable*. Total exhaustion of salt, for example, is almost inconceivable. Similarly, lead, tin, zinc, and many other minerals will, for all practical purposes, be available into perpetuity. Even coal will be available for more than 500 years at present utilization rates. Other resources, however, are used so rapidly that they cannot be replenished. These are classified as *depletable resources,* and for some, such as oil and natural gas, the time frame of exhaustion is thought to be only two or three generations.

Genesis of Depletable Resource Theory

The *theory of depletable resources* is unique in that it arose almost in full bloom from the writing of a single article. This influential work was published in 1931 by the young American mathematician and economist Harold Hotelling. Hotelling's article, titled "The Economics of Exhaustible Resources," contained arguments so cogent that the work became nearly an instant classic.

Prior to Hotelling's article, the expectation underlying nearly all economic theory was that a firm will continue to operate indefinitely and that it will produce from a renewable resource base. It was thought that when these conditions cease to exist, the basic principles regarding the behavior of the firm must be modified. Depletable resource theory was designed to analyze just this case; that is, a situation in which the firm will eventually lose its base of operations. More specifically, the theory was developed to analyze such issues as the value of a resource to its owners, the relation between costs and prices, and the time frame in which extraction of the resource may be expected to take place.

Hotelling's interest in depletable resources was stimulated by the conservationist movement of the 1920s. The conservationists, concerned that resources were being used up too fast, had pointed to the depletion of such resources as the cypress groves in the great Okefenokee Swamp and proclaimed that the same principle applied to underground mineral deposits, only more so. Hotelling sympathized with the conservationist point of view, but perceived that resources could be extracted too slowly as well as too fast. In essence, he suggested that there is an optimal rate of resource extraction. His great contribution lay in specifying a methodology suitable for analyzing optimal prices and levels of output over time.

Hotelling's thesis underwent a number of refinements and extensions, but for the most part his basic ideas remain intact. In essence, they are that (1) depletion causes a resource to become more scarce; (2) scarce resources command higher prices than abundant ones; and (3) therefore the value of a depletable resource will tend to rise over time. Hotelling further contended that a depletable resource would command a lower current price under a competitive market structure than under a monopolistic structure. However, he also recognized that since low prices stimulate consumption, the resource would be depleted more rapidly under competition. Thus, the extraction period and price path followed under a monopolistic system would be fundamentally different than they would be under competition.

Hotelling's theory of depletable resources contains great insights. However, since it was developed through the use of a sophisticated mathematical technique known as the *calculus of variations,* and since extensions to the theory have employed similarly esoteric methods, dissemination of these fundamental truths has been greatly retarded. Perhaps it was necessary for Hotelling to formulate his theory in mathematical terms; but such knowledge is not essential in order to comprehend his main ideas. About all that is required is an understanding of such fundamental concepts as the *present value* of an asset, *opportunity cost, economic profit, economic rent,* and *monopoly profit.* These basic principles of economics are reviewed in the following section and precede further consideration of Hotelling's classic theory.

Fundamental Concepts

Present Value

The value of a depletable resource is determined by the same method that is used to determine the value of any other asset. In essence, private property rights entitle the owner of an asset to receive its market value when sold in the *capital market* (the flow of income generated from the sale of marketable commodities). If capital and product markets operated perfectly, an asset would be worth the same on both capital and product markets. But since markets are seldom perfect, economists speak of the *present value* (PV) of an asset, meaning the *discounted* value of expected income net of the costs associated with generating that income. More specifically,

(2.1)   PV = expected future income (R) minus costs (C),
               discounted to the present by a discount rate (r),
               or, using symbols,

$$PV = \frac{R_1 - C_1}{(1 + r)^1} + \frac{R_1 - C_2}{(1 + r)^2} + \dots \frac{R_n - C_n}{(1 + r)^n}$$

where PV, R_1, R_2, C_1, C_2, and so forth represent *expected income*, or *gross revenue*, and costs; r is the *rate of time preference*, or *discount rate*; and n is the number of years over which income will be received. Thus, the present value of an asset depends on when revenues will be received, when costs will be incurred, and what the rate of time preference for money is.

The general formula used to calculate present values is an extension of equation 2.1:

(2.2) $$PV = \sum_{t=1}^{n} \frac{R_t - C_t}{(1 + r)^t}$$

where the Greek symbol Σ denotes the summation from the initial period ($t = 1$) to the terminal period ($t = n$). The time period usually considered is a year, month, or day; but continuous discounting is also possible. The discount rate (r) must be expressed in comparable terms—that is, a rate per year, month, or day, as the case may be.

Compounding.   The reason that time affects the present value of an asset is that money can be invested at a positive interest rate to yield an even greater amount in the future. For example, a *principal* (original sum) of $1,000, invested at 10 percent *simple* (not compounded) interest, will yield $1,100 after one year—the $1,000 principal plus $100 in interest. If interest is compounded at an r' percent annually, the value of the principal (V_0) after t years is given by the formula

(2.3) $$V_t = V_0(1 + r')^t$$

where V_t is the value of the asset after t years. Compounding means that interest is received on both the principal and any accumulated interest earned during a previous time period. If the initial value of V_0 is $1,000, the interest rate (expressed in decimal form) is 0.10, and t equals two years, then V_2 is $1,210. If t were ten years, V_{10} would be $2,594. If t were twenty years, V_{20} would be $6,727. The basic idea is obvious: A given amount of money is worth more at present than it is at some date in the future, because money in hand can be invested to generate more income.

Discounting.   *Discounting* to obtain the present value of an asset is the reverse of compounding, and may be derived from equation 2.3. Thus,

$$(2.4) \qquad PV = V_0 = \frac{V_t}{(1 + r')^t}$$

From the above example, if V_2 is \$1,210 and r' equals 0.10, then V_0 is \$1,000. Simply stated, the present value of \$1,210 to be received two years hence, and discounted at 10 percent, is \$1,000. If V_t were \$1,000 and t were ten years, V_0 would be \$424. If t were twenty years, V_0 would be \$164. Again, the principle is clear: Money to be received at some future date is worth less than money in hand because the latter can be used to generate income.

Asset Valuation under Uncertainty.   The examples outlined above illustrate the power of *compound interest* and the importance of *discounting*. However, most analyses of asset values are much more complex than described here, for the simple reasons that the future is uncertain and each individual has a unique appraisal of the expected revenues and costs associated with a given project. In addition, the rate of time preference for money—the discount rate—differs among indi-viduals. A little reflection will show that the numerical value of the discount rate is a critical variable in a decision to buy, sell, or hold an asset.

Consider, for example, two oil companies, A and B, bidding for an offshore lease. Both companies are assumed to have the same appraisal of the field's characteristics and of the expected future income from the petroleum. Both believe that development drilling will reveal the exis-tence of a field containing 100 million barrels of recoverable reserves, that these reserves can be recovered at a uniform rate of 10 million barrels per year at a cost of \$20 per barrel, and that the assumed selling price is \$30 per barrel. The present value of the field then, can be explicitly defined as

$$(2.5) \qquad PV = \sum_{t=1}^{n} \frac{q_t(p_t - c_t)}{(1 + r)^t}$$

where q represents quantity expressed in barrels, and p and c represent price and cost per barrel, respectively. Assuming an annual time period,

q = 10 million barrels, p and c equal $30 and $20, respectively, and n is 10 years. *Net revenue*, which is defined as the difference between price and cost, is $10 per barrel, and the annual net revenue is $100 million. The present value of the field can therefore be calculated from equation 2.5 as:

$$(2.6) \qquad PV = \frac{\$100}{(1+r)^1} + \frac{\$100}{(1+r)^2} + \dots + \frac{\$100}{(1+r)^{10}}$$

Suppose Company A has a relatively low rate of time preference (r_A), whereas Company B "discounts" the future at a relatively high rate (r_B). Table 2–1 shows the present value calculations assuming an r_A of 0.10 and an r_B of 0.20. Thus, Company A would assess the present value of the field at $614 million, whereas for Company B, the present value would only be $419 million. Company A would therefore be willing to pay up to $614 million for a lease to exploit the field and would probably be the successful bidder.

But the reader should keep in mind that this is a highly simplified example. Assessment of recoverable reserves, extraction costs, future prices, and other factors related to project appraisal differ considerably among potential bidders, which is why asset valuation seldom turns solely on the discount rate. In addition, discount rates do not generally differ as much as was assumed in the above example; net revenue

TABLE 2–1
Present Value of an Oil Field Yielding Net Revenue of $100 Million Each Year, Discounted at 10 and 20 Percent

Year	"Undiscounted" Annual Net Revenue (*millions of dollars*)	"Discounted" Present Value (*millions of dollars*) $r_A = 0.10$	$r_B = 0.20$
1	$ 100	$ 90.0	$ 83.3
2	100	82.6	69.4
3	100	75.1	57.9
4	100	68.3	48.2
5	100	62.1	40.2
6	100	56.4	33.5
7	100	51.3	27.9
8	100	46.7	23.3
9	100	42.4	19.4
10	100	38.6	16.2
TOTAL	$1,000	$614.4	$419.3

streams are not constant over time; and many companies bid for drilling rights. Also, the risk associated with drilling a dry hole must be factored into the analysis.

There are other complications which involve managerial strategy. Say, for example, that the management of Company A miscalculates the amount that Company B is willing to pay. Company A might bid only $400 million for the lease if it thinks that Company B will bid even less. It may then find it has lost a profitable opportunity when B outbids it by $19 million. This would never happen in "open outcry" auctioning, but it is quite possible in "sealed bid" auctions, where bidders submit a single offer. In any case, the present value concept is the basis for asset valuation.

Economic Profit and Opportunity Cost

The concept of *opportunity cost* factors into the cost of any item the amount which inputs required to produce that item could have earned had they been employed in their next best use. Thus, the true cost of a firm's inputs is the amount management pays for labor, plant, equipment, and so forth, *plus* the forgone income that could have been earned had the firm invested its money in some other way. In competitive markets, the amount a firm pays for its inputs closely approximates the opportunity costs of those inputs; and the revenue it earns from its outputs approximates the total costs, including all opportunity costs of its inputs. Any difference between the firm's net earnings and the opportunity cost of its inputs is referred to as *economic profit*. This is distinguished from ordinary accounting profit which, in addition to economic profit, includes an ordinary return to capital and entrepreneurship.

Economic profit may be subdivided into three categories, based on the source from which it arises: (1) *monopoly profit,* (2) *economic rent* (sometimes referred to as Ricardian rent, after economist David Ricardo), and (3) *disequilibrium economic profit*. The latter may be negative as well as positive, but in either case will tend to be eroded as firms enter or leave the industry or otherwise adjust to market conditions. Economic rent refers to that return to a factor of production which is greater than the minimum amount required to keep it supplied in its present employment. Factors that earn economic rent generally are highly specialized, of superior quality, and/or extraordinarily scarce. Economic rent is usually assumed to be zero for ongoing concerns operating under normally competitive market conditions. This is a relatively harmless convention, since economic rent does not influence prices. Monopoly profit is the result of cooperation, as opposed to competition, among producers and, as such, it is always positive. Although monopoly profit may endure for a long time, there are always incentives in a market environment that tend to erode cooperative agreements.

Disequilibrium Economic Profits.   Economic profits arise in the normal course of business operations, even in highly competitive industries. In general, demand-increasing or cost-reducing technological changes generate *disequilibrium economic profits*. These profits provide an incentive for firms already in the industry to expand and for newcomers to enter the industry. Both these responses mitigate price increases and eventually erode the disequilibrium profit margins. Nevertheless, even when such profits prevail in a specific industry for a prolonged period, the industry may still be considered competitive.

Important innovations, such as the development of drilling technology, pipeline construction, and new refining and marketing techniques, provided disequilibrium economic profits in the oil industry sufficient to ensure its expansion for quite some time. Similarly, the internal combustion and diesel engines—revolutionary in effectively converting oil from an illuminant and lubricant to an energy resource—earned their inventors and early imitators a great deal of economic profit as a reward for their efforts. Eventually, however, competition among producers reduced the prices of these commodities, or mitigated increases in their prices, and thus transferred much of the net gain to consumers. This is typical. In general, as disequilibrium economic profits are eroded away, they become translated into consumers' surplus. Economists usually emphasize that disequilibrium economic profits are normal market phenomena which lead to a more efficient use of resources.

Economic Rent.   The concept of economic rent is basic to depletable resource theory. It originated in the theory of land rent developed by David Ricardo during the early 1800s. Ricardo's theory of land rent is based on the fact that available land varies considerably in potential usefulness—some is more fertile, some more accessible to other resources, and so on. Ricardo hypothesized that when superior land is abundant, even the best of it cannot command rent so long as comparable land is available for nothing. Eventually, however, as the best land gets used up, it becomes profitable to utilize land of the next best quality, then the next best after that, and so on. Any land that is just on the border between being used and not being used can earn no rent, since it is so abundant that some lies idle. Land rent, then, is the difference between the cost of producing output on the poorest parcel of land actually utilized—no-rent land—and the value of output on any other given parcel of land.

For example, if wheat can be produced for $1.50 per bushel on one piece of land, and the land yields 100 bushels per acre, then the nonland cost of producing the crop (labor, fertilizer, machinery, etc.) is $150 per acre. If at the same time it costs $350 per acre to produce an identical crop on the no-rent land, then economic rent on the first piece of land must be $200, the cost difference between the two pieces of acreage.

In regard to the oil industry, most of the oil produced and consumed today contains an element of economic rent because it is found in giant and supergiant fields where production costs are low. Seventy-five percent of all proved and probable petroleum reserves are thought to be in giant and supergiant fields, most of which are located in the Middle East. Giant fields contain more than 500 million barrels of reserves, and supergiants contain more than five billion barrels. Extraction costs in these fields are generally less than $1 per barrel, so high economic rents are at least possible, given present market prices.

Economic rent also arises as a result of variability in the quality of oil. Quality in this case refers both to the characteristics of the oil itself and to the costs associated with refining and bringing it to market. African crudes, for example, bring premium prices as compared with Middle Eastern crudes, because the former yield relatively large fractions of gasoline upon refining and because they are located closer to the European and American markets. These factors generate *economic rents* for the African producers.

Economic profits derived from reserves of superior quality, or from those whose costs of extraction, refinement, and distribution are relatively low, may persist as long as the resource continues to be exploited. Firms or countries in possession of such reserves have a competitive advantage over those whose reserves are on the margin between remaining profitable and becoming unprofitable. An important principle to remember in the analysis of oil markets is that competitive prices do not tend toward the costs of the inordinately efficient producers. Instead, prices are based on the costs of the marginally efficient producers, or those who, in the long run, are just able to survive and to remain in the industry. Thus, there are high economic rents available to those who have control of the low-cost resource deposits.

Monopoly Profit.   Another principal source of economic profits earned from oil comes from its sale in less than purely competitive markets. The law of demand emphasizes that consumers will pay more for scarce commodities than for abundant ones. Scarcity may result from natural phenomena (that is, finite stores of resources) or from human institutions designed to limit output. In the former case, production

costs determine prices, and economic profits are limited to the disequilibrium and Ricardian variety. In the latter case, economic profits also
include an element of *monopoly profit.*[1]

A *cartel* is a group of producers who agree to cooperate in limiting
output and raising prices. Because of its extraordinary market power, a
cartel or a monopoly is able to earn profits well above the normal return
to capital investment. As a result of continued cooperation, the cartel is
able to retain its market power by erecting barriers which keep other
firms out of the industry—thus prohibiting competition. Monopoly profits and the various barriers to entry in the oil industry are discussed in
a general, theoretical way in Chapter 3. Specific examples of cartel and
quasi-cartel arrangements are discussed in Chapters 4 through 7.

Other Depletable Resource Concepts

Every scientific discipline evolves its own concepts and terminology.
This specialized terminology, or "jargon," while often causing people
outside the field to shake their heads in confusion, is necessary to the
professionals. Their purpose is not to confuse the neophyte but to find
a way to express themselves precisely. Common English is sometimes
just too vague for the exacting needs of science. Three specialized terms
relevant to the depletable resource theory are in this category, (1) net
price, (2) real rate of interest, and (3) backstop technology.

Net Price.   Economists define the term *net price* as the difference
between a good's market price and its marginal cost.[2] It is comparable
to economic profit, and it is the variable which is of primary concern to
the owner of a depletable resource. Whereas the consumer is primarily
interested in market price, quite independent of costs, the producer
cares little about the market price except in its relation to costs. Thus,
consumers are motivated by market prices, but producers respond to
net prices. For this reason, net price is a useful concept in discussing
the decisions involved in the exploitation of a depletable resource.

Real Rate of Interest.   The difference between *real* and *nominal*
interest rates is an essential economic concept. The *nominal* rate of
interest is the percentage by which the number of dollars received back
exceeds the number of dollars invested, making no allowance for infla-

---

[1] Since a cartel, such as OPEC, may exhibit some characteristics similar to those of a monopoly,
the terms *monopoly profit* and *cartel profit* will be used interchangeably.

[2] The *marginal cost* of a good is equal to the amount necessary to produce one additional
unit of that good.

tion. The *real* rate of interest is the percentage of increased (or decreased) purchasing power earned as a result of the investment. For example, if the nominal interest rate (the price of simply borrowing money) is 15 percent per year, and the general price level rises at an annual rate of only 12 percent, then the real rate of interest (the earned increase in purchasing power) is 3 percent. There are knotty problems in deciding which nominal interest rate and which price index to use in making actual adjustments for inflation. But investors are naturally interested in the real rate of interest, not the nominal rate, so it is important to make some adjustment. The long-term historical real rate of interest is thought to be on the order of 3 percent per year. However, inflation-adjusted real rates of return may vary from negative rates to positive rates as high as 10 or 12 percent, or more.

Backstop Technology.   Except for air and water, which have until recently been classified as "free goods," no good is absolutely indispensable. All economic goods have substitutes. The reason a particular good is used, and the reason for the extent to which it is used, depends on its cost relative to that of more and less viable alternatives. This is the essential idea behind the concept of *backstop technology*.

Conventional energy resources, such as oil, natural gas, and coal, will be exhausted at some distant point in the future. As depletion proceeds apace, these conventional energy resources will become scarcer almost by definition. Since scarce resources command higher prices than abundant ones, the price of energy will tend to rise. Eventually, the price of energy derived from a renewable source, such as the sun, will become relatively cheap, and solar energy will then displace conventional energy resources. At that point it will become "uneconomic" to exploit fossil fuels.

Backstop technology, therefore, refers to technology developed for resources that are available in superabundance. Solar, wind, and tidal power are good examples of renewable resources which may provide a basis for the backstop to pertroleum. Nuclear fusion could also provide a source of energy that would last as far into the future as is possible to foresee today—although, strictly speaking, uranium (essential to the fusion process) is also a depletable resource. The price of energy derived from a superabundant source depends only on the capital and labor costs of producing the energy. Since the resource itself is superabundant, it is "free," meaning that it cannot command economic rent.

There can be little doubt that the value of depletable resources which are utilized today is related to the anticipated cost of producing energy from alternative sources, including possible backstop technologies. However, the present and future costs of energy derived from a backstop technology are shrouded in uncertainty. For the present, it is sufficient to note that the value of a depletable resource is related to the next best alternative resources that are currently available at comparable costs and to those that are likely to be available in the near future. The time of exhaustion should be thought of as the point in the future when conventional energy resources become "uneconomic" to exploit.

Basic Theory

Overview

The theory of depletable resources provides insight into probable price trends, rates of resource depletion, and the time frame in which extraction may be expected to take place. These can be predicted under idealized conditions, which assume the resource base and extraction costs are known and that owners of the resource operate under either purely competitive or purely monopolistic conditions. Another requirement is that the real rate of interest be known. The reason price paths and depletion rates can be predicted under these ideal conditions is that the opportunity costs to resource owners are fully specified.

Unfortunately, at least from the standpoint of developing a model capable of accurately forecasting the future, petroleum markets are neither purely competitive nor fully monopolized; nor can the resource base and the real rate of interest be known with absolute certainty. One might therefore ask whether such an idealized theory is of any value in the analysis of OPEC. Despite its limitations, the theory of depletable resources is clearly useful, just as it is useful to specify the idealized conditions of pure competition and pure monopoly. If the theory does nothing else, it at least enables us to focus on the key variables which leading authorities in the field have deemed important.

The theory will be presented in the same order as it was originally developed by Hotelling. The initial price, price trajectory, and time of exhaustion will be specified under purely competitive and then fully monopolistic conditions. The intermediate cases are more complex, since there is an infinitely large number of examples which could be considered. For the sake of simplicity, only one of these cases will be developed—that of a cooperative group of large producers, a "cartel," with a "competitive fringe" of smaller producers who operate under the umbrella of the cartel price. This case is one which has been considered extensively in the recent literature. OPEC, naturally, is the cartel, and all other free world petroleum resource owners are the "competitive fringe." This model, although a far cry from reality, is nevertheless important, because it more closely approximates reality than do either purely competitive or purely monopolistic models.

Initial Price Determination in a Static Framework

For producers of crude oil, the relevant returns are economic profits, whether earned as a result of disequilibrium in competitive markets, economic rent, or monopoly power. And these producers, as with all producers or owners of depletable resources, are assumed to be interested in maximizing the present value of their economic profits.

In purely competitive markets which have reached a supply–demand equilibrium, resource owners or producers receive only economic rent—disequilibrium and monopoly profits are zero. But in less than purely competitive markets, producers will earn some monopoly profit as well. The variables which influence economic profits include quantity, price, costs, and the real rate of interest, as given by the present value formula of equation 2.5. Abstracting from quality and transport-cost differentials, all producers receive the same price (p_t) for their oil and the same real rate of interest (r) on money derived from the sale of their oil. If these variables are assumed given, then costs (c_t) and quantities (q_t) from a specific field determine the present value of the resources that are extracted.

Using a comparative static framework, it can be shown that marginal costs will be slightly higher under pure competition than under monopoly. Figure 2-1 shows that production costs are very low in the giant and

---

FIGURE 2-1

Comparative Static Equilibrium under Pure Competition and Pure Monopoly

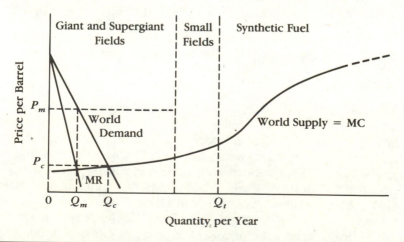

supergiant fields; so extraction will naturally occur there first. As these fields are depleted, smaller fields—where costs are somewhat higher—will begin to be utilized. Oil from shale, and synthetic fuels from coal will become viable alternatives at even higher prices. The general cost relations result in a positively sloped "world supply" curve, meaning that prices must increase if greater quantities are to be supplied.

World supply is determined by the marginal cost of extracting the oil and bringing it to market. The curve is drawn with the assumption that technology is a given. It may be noted that marginal costs will rise as the better resources are used up. So when conventional reserves are gone, at Q_t, oil derived from shale and coal will be available, but it will cost more (although there is always the possibility that technological innovations will reduce marginal costs and thus shift the world supply curve downward).

If the market is purely competitive, the initial price will be determined by the relation between world demand and marginal costs. In Figure 2-1, this competitive price–quantity relation is shown by P_c and Q_c. There is no economic rent on the last unit produced, but all of the "inframarginal" units, from zero to Q_c, generate economic rent. Economic rents are equal to P_c minus the marginal cost as specified by the world supply schedule.

The monopoly price, P_m, and quantity, Q_m, are determined by the intersection of the marginal revenue (MR) and marginal cost (MC) curves. The difference between monopoly price and competitive price $(P_m - P_c)$ on Q_m units is the monopoly profit. The monopolist will extract from the lowest-cost fields first—just as do purely competitive firms—because he receives economic rent equal to P_c minus marginal costs on all Q_m units. Of course these economic profits can then be invested at the market rate of interest to generate additional future income, or they can be used to enjoy increased current consumption.

Price Paths in a Dynamic Framework

Hotelling developed the depletable resource theory by assuming conditions of both pure competition and pure monopoly. He found that initial prices would be higher under monopoly and that less would be consumed; thus, depletion would take place at a later date than under competition. Recent contributions to the theory which relate more specifically to the world oil market have focused on an intermediate case, that of OPEC considered as a cartel with all other free world producers treated as a "competitive fringe." According to this framework, the competitive fringe erodes the price-setting power of OPEC by producing more than they would under purely competitive conditions. In this case, the expected initial price and time of depletion falls between the competitive and monopolistic extremes.

Pure Competition.   Where market prices are initially determined by competitive forces, they may be expected to rise over time. There are two reasons why this is so. First, extraction costs will rise as the giant and supergiant fields are depleted; second, resource owners must be paid a rate of return on money invested in oil reserves which is comparable to the real rate of interest. Among the offsetting considerations is innovative technology that lowers marginal costs and thereby mitigates price increases. Hotelling's classic theory dealt with only one of these determinants of market prices. He was concerned with the net price, and thus abstracted from extraction costs and technology. According to Hotelling, the net price would rise at the market rate of interest, thus

$$\text{Net price}^* = \text{Initial net price}^* \times (1 + r)^t$$

$$p^*(\text{net})_t = p^*(\text{net})_0 (1 + r)^t$$

where [*] denotes equilibrium values. This has become known in depletable resource literature as the *r percent rule*. Thus, if the real rate of interest is 3 percent per year, then net prices may be expected to rise at 3 percent annually. Why? Because there is a direct relationship between the expected rate of return on oil held in the ground and financial assets which can be bought from revenues derived from the sale of oil. The argument is subtle, and goes like this: If the market is not in competitive equilibrium, such that the *initial* net price, $p(\text{net})_0$, exceeds the *equilibrium* net price, $p^*(\text{net})_0$, then resource owners will have an incentive to expand output, buy financial assets, and thus earn more than they could by holding oil in the ground. However, as producers expand output, the net price is driven down toward the equilibrium level. And when markets are in equilibrium, oil in the ground earns the same rate of return as do financial assets. The same process works when $p(\text{net})_0$ is less than $p^*(\text{net})_0$; producers will simply withhold oil from the market and drive the net price *up* to the equilibrium.

But since the equilibrium net price is just one component of the market price, market prices may rise at a faster or slower rate than net prices. However, both marginal costs and net prices tend to rise only gradually over time, so market prices under purely competitive conditions may be expected to rise slowly (though technological changes may offset these tendencies).

In Figure 2-2, the price path depicted by curve $P_c T_c$ reflects the general tendency for prices to rise. The initial market price is low, but

FIGURE 2-2
Cartel with Competitive Fringe

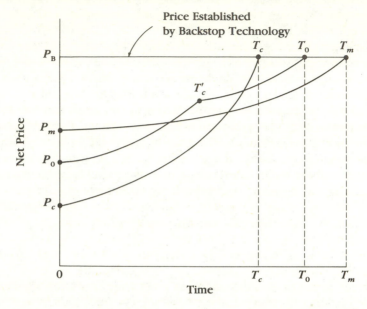

it rises at a relatively rapid rate compared with the prices depicted by the other curves. The price path is smooth and the resource is depleted fairly early, at T_c. These price paths are drawn under the assumption that there are no major cost-reducing or demand-stimulating technological changes, and no deviations from the market structure initially posited. A cost-reducing technological change which increases demand for a substitute will tend to lower the optimal price path. An example is a coal-slurry pipeline which would lower costs of utilizing coal, reduce oil demand, and thereby lower oil prices. Similarly, a technological change which increases the demand for oil may shift the price path upward. The internal combustion engine, for example, greatly increased the demand for gasoline and raised oil prices. In the absence of such technological changes, the optimal price trajectory will be smooth and stable as long as markets remain competitive.

Monopoly

The price path that one might expect under pure monopoly is characterized by an initial price which is substantially higher than under pure competition, because the monopolist can withhold oil from the market.

This price covers production costs, generates economic rent on each barrel produced, and includes a monopoly profit. Consumers respond to the monopoly price by consuming less, so depletion will occur later than under pure competition. Thus, the monopoly price path depicted in Figure 2-2 by curve $P_m T_m$ is drawn to reflect a high initial price, a relatively slow rate of increase, and depletion occurring later than under the competitive situation.

The monopolist is willing to accept lower resource utilization rates and slower price increases because his returns are realized sooner. Since monopoly profits can be invested at the market rate of interest, it is better to withhold oil from the market and earn a monopoly profit than to produce more and drive prices to a competitive level. As in the case of pure competition, the monopoly price path is drawn under the assumption that technology is given. In addition, it is assumed that there is no erosion of monopoly control over output or prices.

It may be noted in Figure 2–2 that the monopoly price falls below the purely competitive price at some distant point in the future. How could this be true? Wouldn't the monopolist always charge more than a group of competitive producers? The answer would clearly be "yes" if all other things were equal. But, inherently, other things are not equal. Since competitive producers deplete their reserves at a relatively rapid rate, the resource base becomes smaller more rapidly under competition than it does under monopoly. Thus, the monopolist of the distant future will operate with a much larger resource base than would a group of competitive producers. This is what led distinguished economist Robert Solow, in his presidential address to the American Economic Association in 1974, to quip, "The monopolist is the conservationist's friend, although both of them would be surprised to know it."

Cartel with Competitive Fringe

The monopoly price trajectory of Figure 2-2 may be considered the upper limit which could be achieved by a group of cooperative producers. The competitive path may be seen as the lower limit obtained by producers who do not cooperate at all. Between these extremes is a vast range of degrees of competition and cooperation. Of particular interest is the case of OPEC, considered as a perfectly cohesive cartel, in conjunction with a group of competitive "outside" producers. This model is shown by the intermediate price path curve labeled $P_0 T'_c T_0$ in Figure 2-2. The trajectory represents the price path followed by the cooperative group faced with a "competitive fringe" of producers who are attracted by the high cartel price.

The competitive fringe will extract resources at a rapid rate relative to their reserves because their economic profits include some monopoly profit which can be invested at the market rate of interest. This large volume of output will hold the initial cartel price below a monopoly price. Eventually, however, as the competitive fringe's reserves become depleted (as they surely will with a relatively low reserve-to-production ratio), the cartel price will rise toward a monopoly level. The monopoly price will then increase more slowly until the cartel's reserves also become depleted, at T_0 in the figure.

Since the initial cartel price depends on the degree of cohesion among its members and on the size and number of competitive fringe producers, the actual price cannot be determined without full information on these variables. But in any case, the price trajectory will increase smoothly assuming the cartel remains stable and in control of prices. (Again, however, technological changes will cause shifts in the price path.) Some analysts believe that this model provides a reasonable approximation of conditions in today's world oil market.

Application to the World Oil Market

Usefulness of the Theory

The models outlined thus far provide insight into the variables which should be considered in assessing probable price trends and levels of output in the world oil market. Naturally, world oil production does not take place under purely competitive conditions; the sovereignty of Middle Eastern governments ensures that entry into the most prolific fields will be severely limited. On the other hand, the oil industry is so large and geographically dispersed that it cannot be characterized as monopolistic. Even the model of OPEC as a perfectly cohesive unit with a competitive fringe is a great oversimplification. In fact, much of the material in the latter half of this book chronicles the ways in which OPEC is a far cry from the ideal that was projected in the model.

The models simply serve to alert us to the fact that if market conditions are altered from more or less competitive to highly cooperative, as indeed they were during the 1970s, then the price path may become very unstable. Such a path is shown in Figure 2-3 by curve $P_c BA$, which is drawn with the assumption that the market structure is vacillating between the competitive and monopolistic extremes. Under these conditions, practically anything is possible; so the model alerts us to the danger of simple extrapolation. For example, the view that prices will follow a purely competitive or cartel path will almost surely prove false, yet one frequently encounters the view that market prices may be expected to rise at the real rate of interest. This view is based on a

FIGURE 2-3
Effects of Uncertainty, Imperfect Knowledge, and Conflicts of Interest on the World Oil Market

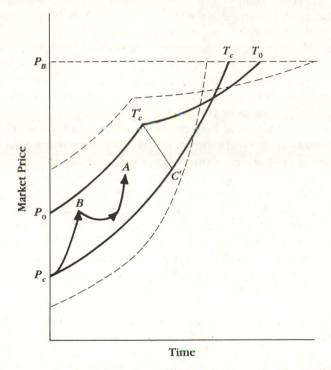

simple—and false—application of the *r* percent rule. Knowledge of depletable resource theory will help avoid this pitfall.

Complications of the Real World

The lack of cohesion that in fact characterizes OPEC introduces an element of competition within the cartel itself and further complicates the problem of selecting its most probable price path. It alters the problem from that of selecting the best price path for the group considered as a whole to that of selecting the best price path from the standpoint of a dominant member, or group of members, who have similar views about prices and output.

Divergence of opinion regarding the proper or optimal pricing strategy will generally be resolved in favor of the larger countries—those who prefer relatively low initial prices, and those who prefer slow rates of price increases. In general, a country with its own large reserves will prefer a price greater than that which would prevail under pure competition but less than would prevail if there were a monopoly. The reason the large producer will oppose a monopoly price is that it would cause him to lose a share of the oil market; also, a monopoly price will promote the use of alternative resources, which would also cause him to lose a share of the energy market. These issues will be pursued at length in Chapter 3. A country with large reserves can influence prices by developing reserves slowly (or rapidly) and producing below (or temporarily above) capacity. A country with few reserves can exert little influence on output or prices.

The determination of dynamic price and output paths is difficult if not impossible in the real world. No single country or group of countries can fully determine either one. The price paths depend on the total reserves held by each country; on the producer's knowledge of ultimately recoverable reserves; on the investments required to bring oil to market; and on operating costs, lag relations, and the rate of time preference for money by individual OPEC leaders. It also depends upon the response by consumers and producers outside OPEC as they reach decisions to utilize alternative energy resources, to substitute capital and labor in production and consumption processes, and to alter long-established standards of comfort and convenience in order to conserve energy.

Imperfect information about the quantity and quality of reserves, uncertainty about probable technological changes, political unrest, and revolutions within and wars between important producing countries all exert an influence on price and output trends. It is also impossible to predict price and output trajectories without knowing the extent to which cooperative arrangements dominate the market, whether cooperative producers will follow policies which best serve their long-term interests, and how compeitive fringe producers will react to changes. In addition, policies of the consuming countries designed to reduce consumption, such as mandatory fuel-efficiency standards, reduced speed limits, prohibitions on the use of oil in generating electricity, and so on, will influence price paths and the time of exhaustion.

Finally, the need to explore for oil introduces yet another element of uncertainty. The quality and quantity of resources is not known precisely, and when additional resources will be proven cannot be predicted with accuracy. Simple probabilities suggest that giant and supergiant fields will be found early in the exploration process, and this has generally been borne out by historical experience. Naturally, there will be "surprises," such as the Alaskan North Slope Sea, the North Sea, and the Mexican oil finds; but it is reasonable to assume that most of the more prolific fields have already been found.

An Aid to Straight Thinking

A popular slogan which has been used in a variety of contexts states that "Oil in the ground is worth more than money in the bank." But this proposition is based neither on sound financial theory nor on empirical evidence. If it were literally true, the expected return on oil held in the ground would exceed the expected return on money held in banks or other financial institutions. And the fact remains that oil is currently being produced at the hardly inconsequential rate of 60 million barrels each day. It may thus be presumed that producers who sell this oil are covering the opportunity costs of their imputs, including capital. Otherwise, they would prefer to hold all their oil in the ground and wait for prices to rise still higher.

Undoubtedly, some sellers are on the razor's edge between selling now and holding for future delivery; but others sell willingly and feel quite content doing so. There are naturally many *potential* sellers whose resources are more costly to extract than can be adequately covered by current prices. These people will prefer to hold their oil in the ground until current sellers deplete their resources or until technological changes or other developments reduce their extraction costs or until prices rise sufficiently to provide them at least a normal return on their investments.

Thus, rather than assert that the slogan is true or false, it is best to think of it as meaningless. High-cost oil deposits are best left in the ground, whereas low-cost reserves are ripe for exploitation right now. The rate of exploitation will naturally differ under competitive, monopolistic, and intermediate market conditions.

Effects on Income Distribution

Although it is not generally acknowledged by industry spokesmen, it is nevertheless true that the formation of OPEC has increased the present value of reserves held by non-OPEC producers. In fact, the formation of OPEC has increased the present value of a barrel held by these producers far more than a barrel held by a member of OPEC. The reason is that non-OPEC producers can extract their reserves early and invest their economic profits at the real rate of interest. OPEC producers, on the other hand, must wait in order to realize their monopoly returns. This basic phenomenon has caused dissension within non-OPEC countries as government and private forces fight over who should have the lion's share of the economic profits generated by OPEC. The outward manifestations of these conflicts are written for all to see in the tax laws and related legislation which have been designed to maintain the status quo with respect to oil prices and/or to redistribute income from producers to consumers or to government.

Conclusion

The theory of depletable resources provides some guidance in examining price and output trajectories. Assuming other things equal, future prices will be different under pure competition, monopoly, and intermediate market structures. Under pure competition, the market price will start out low and rise at a rapid rate compared with other market forms, and the resource will be depleted early. Under monopoly, the market price will be higher than under pure competition, rise more slowly than under other market conditions, and the resource will be depleted late. Market arrangements between these extremes will yield intermediate price paths and depletion dates.

If the market structure abruptly changes from competitive to more cooperative arrangements, then prices may rise sharply over a short time period. Similarly, if the market structure changes from cooperative to more competitive, then prices may fall sharply. A central conclusion, however, is that it is impossible to predict either the magnitude or direction of price changes without an intimate knowledge of market structures and how they are evolving. These topics constitute the subject matter of Chapters 3 through 9.

Further Readings

Hnylicza, E., and R. S. Pindyck. "Pricing Policies for a Two-Part Exhaustible Resource Cartel: The Case of OPEC." *European Economic Review*, 8 (1976), 130–154.

Hotelling, Harold. "The Economics of Exhaustible Resources." *Journal of Political Economy,* 39 (April 1931), 137–175.

Nordhaus, William D. *The Efficient Use of Energy Resources.* New Haven and London: Yale University Press, 1979.

Pindyck, Robert S. "Gains to Producers from the Cartelization of Exhaustible Resources." *Review of Economics and Statistics,* 45 (May 1978), 238–251.

Salant, Stephen W. "Exhaustible Resources and Industrial Structure: A Nash-Cournot Approach to the World Oil Market." *Journal of Political Economy,* 84 (October 1976), 1079–1093.

Solow, Robert M. "The Economics of Resources or the Resources of Economics." *Proceedings of American Economic Assoc.,* 64 (May 1974), 1–14.

Sweeney, James L. "Economics of Depletable Resources: Market Forces and Intertemporal Bias." *The Review of Economic Studies,* 44 (February 1977).

Cartel Theory

The Status of Cartel Theory.

Cartel Arrangements:
Monopoly; Profit Sharing Cartel; Market Sharing Cartel; Price Fixing Cartel and Price Leadership.

Conditions Favorable to Cooperation:
Demand Conditions; Supply Conditions; Cost Conditions; Time.

The Spatial Pricing Problem:
F.A.S. Pricing; C.I.F. Pricing.

Cartelization and Oil Markets:
Supply; Demand.

Short- and Long-Run Problems of OPEC:
Short-Run Problems; Long-Term Problems.

Conclusion.

READER'S GUIDE TO CHAPTER 3
This chapter presents the basic concepts of oligopoly and cartel theory. The first section contains a discussion of cartel problems and the status of cartel theory. The theory of cartel formation, which is outlined in the following section, is especially helpful for the analysis of many problems which will be discussed in Chapters 4 through 6. The next section offers an outline of the categories and degrees of cooperation observed in oligopolistic markets. Spatial pricing and cartel theory as applied to oil markets are presented in the fourth and fifth sections, respectively. These theories are designed to explain the conditions which promote cartel stability or breakdown. The final section contains an application of the tools developed in Chapters 2 and 3, with emphasis on the problems faced by OPEC.

The Status of Cartel Theory

The traditional theory of cartel behavior stresses the incentives among firms to compete with one another or "chisel" on cartel agreements. More recently it has been formally acknowledged that firms or countries in a competitive industry have an equally strong incentive to cooperate. Professor Gary Becker has explained the traditional focus of economists succinctly:

> For most practical purposes, economists usually have assumed either the fully competitive equilibrium ... or the fully monopolistic one ... even though both may have shortcomings, because *they have lacked a reliable general theory that also covers intermediate positions.*[1]

A reasonable first approximation to a more comprehensive theory of cartel behavior is the *cost-benefit* proposition that a cartel will form whenever the expected benefits accruing to cartel participants exceed the anticipated costs of forming and maintaining the cooperative arrangement. Although general and apparently simple, this represents an important advance over previous formulations because it admits the possibility of a solution between the competitive and monopolistic extremes. The focus of this chapter is on cooperative arrangements, modern cartel theory, and cooperative institutions which are peculiar to world petroleum markets.

Cartel Arrangements

A *cartel* is a confederation of independent business firms or countries which have reached an accord with respect to prices, market shares, and other matters of importance to them. The purpose of a cartel is to enhance the wealth of the participants. The means employed involve fixing prices and/or limiting output.

The degree to which cooperation can be substituted for competition ranges from merger to simple price fixing agreements. A comprehensive agreement involving the integration of ownership and control is a *merger*. When all the participants in an industry merge they form a *monopoly*. A monopoly is the most extreme form of a cartel arrangement, but it is difficult to construct and maintain because agreement must be unanimous on all aspects of property rights.

A *profit sharing* cartel does not entail the surrender of individual property rights, but it is also difficult to organize and maintain because agreement must be reached on price levels, the geographic location

---

[1]Gary Becker, "Crime and Punishment: An Economic Approach," *Jnl. of Political Economy*, April 1968, p. 164.

where production will take place, and how much profit each participant will receive. Even less comprehensive cartel arrangements are difficult to form and maintain because quotas and price fixing arrangements always provide incentives to produce incremental quantities.

Monopoly

A pure monopolist produces a product which has no close substitutes and barriers are sufficient to prevent entry into the industry by potential rivals. However, a monopolist is constrained from charging an infinite price both by consumer demand and potential rivals. The nature of the latter may be illustrated by J. B. Clark's idea of a *limit price*. According to Clark, if a combination of producers raises prices beyond a certain limit, new mills will spring into existence; even the fear that the new mills will spring up is often enough to keep prices down. Thus, the potential mill, though it may never be built, is already a power in the market.[2] The nature of the consumer demand constraint is embodied in the concept of *own price elasticity*. These concepts will be briefly reviewed.

Consumer Demand Constraint.   Demand for a monopolist's product is the same as industry demand, since the monopolist *is* the industry. Assuming the market cannot be segmented to promote price discrimination, the monopolist is faced with marginal and average revenue scheduled (MR and AR) such as those shown in Figure 3-1. A harmless convention which simplifies the analysis is to assume the monopolist's marginal cost (MC_m) is zero at all levels of output. In order to maximize profits, the monopolist produces at the level where MR = MC_m, or Q_m, units, and charges a price P_m. The monopolist would not operate on an inelastic portion of the industry demand schedule even under the extreme assumption that marginal costs are zero. Profit maximization in this case dictates that he should operate where the elasticity of demand is unitary. If marginal costs were positive he would operate on an elastic portion of the demand schedule. However, a price such as P_m is not generally attainable because of the limit price constraint imposed by potential rivals.

Limit Price Constraint.   If in addition to the monopolist with zero marginal costs there are potential rivals with marginal costs less than P_m, the "monopolist" is necessarily constrained to charge a price below P_m. In Figure 3-2, any price above the marginal costs of potential

[2]John B. Clark, *Essentials of Economic Theory* (New York: Macmillan, 1915), p. 381.

FIGURE 3-1
Monopolist with Zero MC

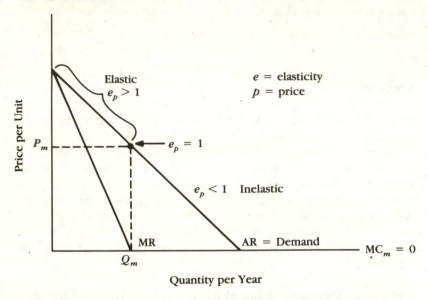

FIGURE 3-2
Monopolist with Potential Rivals

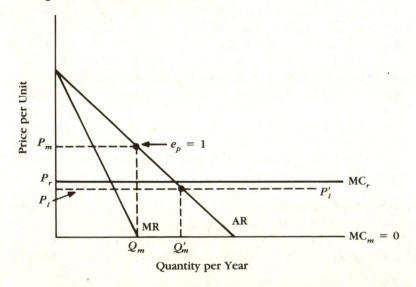

entrants, denoted by MC_r, will encourage expansion by rivals. Thus, the monopolist must charge a price lower than P_r or lose some share of the market to potential rivals. A price low enough to completely discourage entry, such as P_l, is a *limit price,* and the *constrained* profit maximizing quantity is Q'_m. Thus, potential entry leads to a lower price and higher level of output than would prevail if the monopolist were constrained only by consumer demand.

If marginal costs are positive for both the monopolist and for potential rivals, the analysis is in principle the same and only slightly more complicated. Producers who have low marginal costs are constrained from raising prices by their potential rivals. However, if time is taken into account, the optimal strategy may be to charge a price higher than a static limit price, such as P_l, and witness the erosion of market share. In fact, *dynamic limit price* theory stresses that there is an *optimal rate of market share erosion* for a dominant group of sellers in any industry; this applies in spades for a depletable resource cartel, since high levels of output cause reserves of the resource to be used up. In the remaining analysis the term *dynamic limit price* is used to denote an *optimal price* from the standpoint of a cartel with a competitive fringe of rivals. The dynamic limit price may involve the erosion of market share for cartel participants.

Profit Sharing Cartel

Any group of producers which has combined for the purpose of substituting cooperation for competition may be viewed as a cartel. Merger which results in a monopoly is the most extreme form of a cartel arrangement, but a *profit sharing* cartel ranks as a close second. A profit sharing cartel falls short of merger since ownership of capital equipment and resources remains in the hands of the individual participants. The best strategy for a profit sharing cartel is to produce from resource deposits where costs are lowest, and to charge the dynamic limit price.

Constructing an agreement to pool profits and produce from the lowest cost fields is by no means easy. High-cost producers are reluctant to close down facilities, fearing their bargaining power will be impaired and that low-cost producers will ultimately refuse to share profits. Similarly, low-cost producers are hesitant to produce only from their resource base and to share profits without guarantees that the next generation of producers will include them in any profit sharing scheme. These and similar disagreements on how to slice up the pie are so severe that forming and maintaining a *profit sharing cartel* is extremely difficult. There are only two major examples of such institutions in the entire history of world petroleum markets, and these were very imperfect profit sharing agreements. Monopolies and profit sharing cartels illustrate the limit cases of cartel arrangements but real-world institutions rarely approximate these extremes.

Market Sharing Cartel

A group of producers who band together to limit output and distribute market shares among the individual participants is classified as a *market sharing cartel*. A market sharing cartel has the same problems with respect to consumer demand and potential rivals as a monopolist, and the decision-making process is complicated by the necessity of maintaining the sharing agreements among cartel participants. Each market sharing cartel member is a potential rival to other members since each may choose to produce more than its allotted share of the market. The two central problems of a market sharing cartel are to determine the optimum level of output for cartel members as a whole and to prorate the limited total to individual participants. The optimal level of output depends on consumer demand, rival costs, and cost differentials among cartel members. Prorating the limited total to individual participants is a matter of bargaining. A market sharing cartel is one of the more common cartel arrangements found in practice.

The assumption of zero and constant marginal costs used to analyze the monopoly case may be modified to allow for low but rising marginal costs for cartel members. In Figure 3-3, marginal costs are MC_0 for cartel members and MC_r for the potential rivals. The constrained profit-maximizing price imposed by consumer demand is given by the intersection of MR and MC_0, at quantity Q_0. The constrained level of output imposed by potential rivals is given by the limit price of P_l at Q_0'. If the cartel adopts a quota of Q_0', the market price will be P_l. Cartel members must be allocated shares of Q_0', perhaps on the basis of reserves, capacity, historical market shares, or some other criteria mutually agreed on.

There are two inherent problems in maintaining this cartel price. The *internal cartel problem* arises because marginal costs for cartel members (MC_0) are less than the market price (P_l). Since profit maximization calls for expanding output as long as marginal revenue exceeds marginal costs, each cartel member has an incentive to increase production. However, if individual cartel members produce more than their prorated share, output will increase toward the competitive level at Q_c, with consequent downward pressure on prices. The traditional theory of cartel behavior stresses this problem and provides the basis for the prediction that cartel members will expand output and drive prices toward a competitive level, such as P_c.

FIGURE 3-3
Market Sharing Cartel and/or Price Fixing Cartel

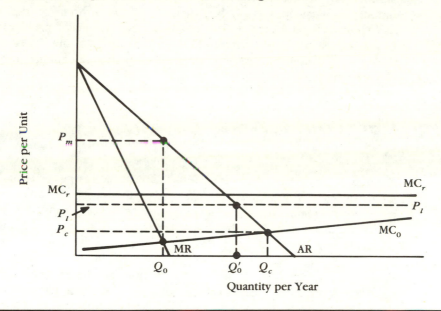

The second problem in maintaining the cartel price is termed the *external cartel problem*. If the price is set above the marginal costs of potential rivals, there naturally will be incentives for them to initiate and/or expand production. In reality, potential rivals do not have universally high and constant marginal costs. Rather, some have relatively low costs and will produce even when prices are low. But the higher the price, the greater will be the number of rivals who can cover their costs and make an economic profit. Thus, when the cartel sets prices too high, there will be additional pressures brought to bear on the price level by rivalry from those who are not parties to the cartel agreement.

Market Demand Prorationing.   Market sharing cartels have emerged so frequently in oil markets that the arrangement has acquired a generic name peculiar to the industry. *Market demand prorationing* is a quota system whereby a decision is reached regarding what total demand will be at a specified price. This is called the *market demand*. As practiced in the United States for many years, *market demand* was determined at the beginning of each month and shares of the fixed total were allocated, or *prorated*, to individual producers.

Market demand prorationing is a reasonably efficient way of maintaining prices because quantities are relatively easy to monitor. The system is so effective that the more knowledgeable producers in the oil industry have usually come to the conclusion that *prorationing* is desirable, at least from the producer's point of view. The major problems include devising a system which will keep participants from exceeding their prorated quotas and setting prices low enough to discourage entry by potential rivals.

Price Fixing Cartel and Price Leadership

A group of producers who combine to establish the market price and sell to all buyers is a *price fixing cartel*. This is the most common of all cartel arrangements. It has the same consumer demand constraint as any other cartel as well as the internal and external cartel problems which are inherent in all cartels. In fact, a price fixing cartel is the *dual* of a market sharing cartel, focusing on price rather than quantity. A market sharing cartel establishes a quota and final consumers determine the price. A price fixing cartel establishes a price and final consumers determine the quantity. The effect can be identical if the cartel is successful in selecting a profit maximizing level of output or a profit maximizing price.

Unlike the market sharing cartel, a price fixing arrangement does not solve the problem of sharing the limited market. Its participants must therefore devise a system for allocating market shares or for fixing price differentials in such a way as to ensure that all participants are reasonably content. Allocating market shares on the basis of geographic location and establishing price differentials to reflect transportation costs are common arrangements. The intent is to eliminate competition and nullify the incentive to produce when marginal revenue exceeds marginal cost.

Empirical evidence indicates that cartels almost always use a form of price leadership, with one participant initiating price changes and others following suit. Quotas, side payments, and legally enforceable agreements are found less frequently. The price leader is generally the firm or country with the largest share of the market and/or the lowest production costs. OPEC is a price fixing cartel with Saudi Arabia generally acting as the price leader. When Saudi Arabia fails in its role as the price leader, there is said to be *price disunity*. This was the situation during the period 1979 through 1981. However, Saudi Arabia still qualifies as the price leader by virtue of both its size and its low costs.

Conditions Favorable to Cooperation

The hallmark of a cartel is the substitution of cooperation for competition. Cooperation is a goal constantly sought but seldom achieved. The conditions favorable to cooperation include (1) an inelastic and stable demand, (2) relatively few and large resource owners, (3) high costs for producers outside the cartel, (4) unorganized buyers, (5) similar costs for producers within the cartel, (6) similar perceptions of future price levels, and (7) similar rates of discounting future earnings. Of these, the first three listed are the most important: (a) an inelastic demand, (b) number and size of resource owners, or, *concentration,* and (c) high costs for firms outside the cartel. Rather than consider these factors in the order given, they will be discussed under the headings demand, supply, cost, and time.

Demand Conditions

An inelastic industry demand is a necessary condition to the formation of a cartel. But every product has an inelastic industry demand over some price range. In general, prices tend to be inelastic at low prices and more elastic as prices rise. Oil is the principal energy resource at present because it is cheap relative to alternative fuels, and world demand is inelastic even at current prices. However, OPEC is concerned with the elasticity of demand for its own oil rather than with the elasticity of total world demand. In a very real sense, OPEC functions as a *residual supplier*, with an elasticity of demand much greater than for non-OPEC suppliers.

Residual Demand.   The idea that OPEC serves as a residual supplier can be illustrated using a simple supply-and-demand framework. Figure 3-4(a) shows non-OPEC supply and the total free world demand for oil. Imports are the difference between supply and demand; P_0 is the equilibrium price assuming self-sufficiency or zero imports from OPEC. Prices such as P_1 or P_2 will result in oil imports into free world countries and exports of b or a by OPEC.

Figure 3-4(b) shows the free world *demand for imports*, or the *residual demand* for oil from OPEC. Oil consumed by OPEC is assumed to be $0Q_0$ regardless of the price. The *residual demand on OPEC* in Figure 3-4(b) is Q_1Q_0 at price P_1 and Q_2Q_0 at P_2, or the difference between free world demand and non-OPEC supply as shown in Figure 3-4(a). The residual demand for oil from OPEC is clearly more *elastic* than total free world demand, since it shows the combined effect of consumer demand and non-OPEC supply.

FIGURE 3-4
OPEC Residual Demand Model

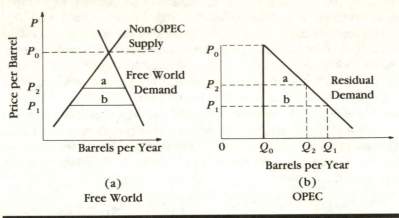

(a)
Free World

(b)
OPEC

The residual demand idea may be extended to illustrate potential conflicts of interest within OPEC over who shall play the greatest role as residual supplier. The idea has been extended to a variety of subgroups, such as "price hawks" and "doves," and to particular countries, such as Saudi Arabia. If Saudi Arabia is regarded as the residual supplier within OPEC, the elasticity of demand for Saudi oil is naturally greater than the elasticity of demand for oil from OPEC. Thus, a highly inelastic world demand may be translated into a relatively elastic demand for oil from the country or countries called upon to serve as residual suppliers. The possible conflicts of interest within a cartel regarding who shall serve as a residual supplier are patently obvious.

Unorganized Buyers.   Buyers influence oil prices by substituting alternative energy resources for oil and changing patterns of consumption to truly conserve energy. This is the case whether or not buyers are organized. But cooperation among buyers has a potential payoff similar to cooperation among sellers. The extreme form of organization on the buyers' side is a single buyer, or *monopsony*. Under this arrangement a single buyer faces one or more sellers. Cooperation is desirable from the consumers' point of view for essentially the same reason as for producers. For the latter, the marginal revenue derived from selling additional quantities falls more rapidly than the price. On the buyers' side, the marginal cost of buying additional quantities *rises more rapidly than the price*.

A simple monopsony model may be used to illustrate the point. Suppose the price of oil is $30 per barrel and demand for OPEC oil is

30 million barrels per day. If the monopsonist demands 33 million barrels per day, the price will be bid up to $33 per barrel on all units.[3] Initial expenditures are $900 million per day and the subsequent outlay is $1,089 million. Thus, an additional three million barrels per day are purchased for $189 million. Marginal acquisition costs are therefore $63 per barrel. A single buyer would utilize the incremental three million barrels only if the marginal benefit were at least $63 per barrel, but unorganized buyers would use oil if the marginal benefit were only $33 per barrel. Thus, a single buyer would buy less and be able to hold prices down much more effectively than unorganized buyers.

With such a handsome potential payoff, why is it true that buyers are generally unorganized? The reason is essentially the same as why producers are not usually monopolists or members of a cartel. Cartels are difficult to organize and maintain for both buyers and sellers. But cooperation is potentially beneficial for either group.

Supply Conditions

Number of Producing Countries and Size of Reserves. The *number of resource owners* is important because of the need to communicate and coordinate policies. Without a central organization to determine prices or levels of output, each country would have to communicate with each potential collaborator on an individual basis. If N is the number of countries and C the number of two-way communication channels, then

$$C = N(N - 1)/2$$

Since OPEC has 13 members, $C = 13(12)/2 = 78$. For the nine large OPEC members, each with more than ten billion barrels of reserves, $C = 36$; and for the five founding members, $C = 10$. Without a central organization such as OPEC, agreement among the 13 member countries would be virtually impossible. Even with such an organization the probability of disagreement increases with the number of countries involved.

The *volume of reserves* held by each country is also important because large resource owners can exert a substantial influence on volume and prices, whereas small resource owners have relatively little impact. Owners of large reserves are relatively wealthy and are presumed to have less urgent needs for revenue. If true, they would be more likely to play the role of residual supplier. There is evidence that

---

[3]Assuming a unitary supply elasticity.

Saudi Arabia, Kuwait, and other wealthy members of OPEC have cut production when required to maintain prices. On the other hand, large reserves are a valuable asset to be protected by military preparedness or alliances. These forces increase revenue requirements and thus encourage greater production and consequent moderate prices.

Similarity of size and a limited number of potential collaborators are conducive to cartel cohesion. If substantial monopoly profits can be received in the present, but such profits hasten the day when a backstop technology is developed, it is obviously important who produces at low levels in the present time frame. For this reason, owners of large reserves tend to prefer low prices to ensure a market far into the future. These are frequently referred to as the price moderates or *doves*. Owners of only a few reserves, or the *hawks*, prefer high prices. They are less concerned with the effect of high prices on future demand because they will no longer produce in the distant future anyway. Thus, differences in size of reserves promote conflicts of interests among cartel members.

Cost Conditions

Internal Cost Conditions.   Cartel prices generate monopoly profits and make the exploitation of relatively high-cost resources feasible at an early date. However, low-cost resources must be withheld from the market to maintain cartel prices. Incentives to expand output are inherently greater for owners of relatively low-cost reserves because they sacrifice more economic profit than owners of high-cost reserves. Therefore, *similarity of costs* promotes cooperation because the sacrifice each owner must make in withholding a barrel of oil from the market is approximately equal.

Low costs per se are the great enemy of cooperation. Professor Morris Adelman, a leading expert on production costs, provides insight into this important issue:

> The real cost or incremental supply price of Persian Gulf crude oil (including a 20 percent return on all needed investment) is about 10 cents per barrel. If new discoveries were zero, growing pressure on the reserves in these fields would put costs up to about 20 cents ($1.50 per metric ton) by 1985. The difference is about 10 cents. That is the extreme upper limit, since there will be new discoveries and new technology. The aggressive policies of new competitors or old ones, or the misguided actions of companies or governments, etc., are only the "limbs and outward flourishes"; the central fact of world oil supply is the cost condition, which will persist for at least 15 years.[4]

---

[4]Morris Adelman, *The World Petroleum Market* (Baltimore: Resources for the Future, Inc., Johns Hopkins Univ. Press, 1972), p. 6.

Although written around 1970, this analysis still applies with equal force. Even with the substantial inflation since 1970, production costs remain extraordinarily low in the Middle East. Thus, there are great incentives for member countries of OPEC to break ranks, increase production, and gain a larger share of the market. But the success of OPEC is evidence that internal cost conditions are not absolutely decisive. The central fact of world oil supply is not the cost condition; it is political and economical in the broad sense that cooperation to withhold supply is in the interests of producers.

External Cost Conditions.   Costs of production by potential competitors places an upper limit on the price a cartel can charge. This was covered earlier using the concept of a *limit price*. Many of the oil, natural gas, coal, nuclear and solar alternatives controlled by non-OPEC sources represent very high-cost alternatives indeed compared to oil from the Middle East. However, it is appropriate and accurate to think of external costs as gently rising schedule similar to that shown in Figure 2-1 on page 33, with possible discontinuities at points where fuel switching is warranted by conditions in the market.

Estimates made with a view to assessing the cost of alternative resources have turned out to be gross underestimates. For example, an article published in *Technology Review* in January, 1974, stated:

> However, all estimates agree that to construct a plant to produce about 100,000 bbl./day of shale oil (about 0.6 percent of our present petroleum demand) will involve a capital investment of several hundred million dollars; and the oil will have to sell in the range of $4/bbl. to yield a reasonable return on investment.[5]

Cost estimates for alternatives have escalated almost in step with oil prices. In addition, unit costs at the margin vary depending upon how much of the 60 million barrels per day of oil the alternatives are presumed to displace. Decisions are always made at the margin, and external cost conditions are so high relative to the cost of oil from the Middle East that OPEC can relinquish or recapture energy market shares within fairly broad limits. Nevertheless, costs of energy from sources outside OPEC are probably the single most important constraint on how high oil prices can be pushed up.

Time

Future Prices and Discount Rates.   Future price levels are uncertain because of the possibility of technological change in both the demand and supply of alternative energy resources. In addition, differ-

---

[5]Gerald U. Dinneen and Glenn L. Cook, "Oil Shale and the Energy Crisis," *Technology Review*, Jan. 1974, p. 33.

ences of opinion among cartel participants regarding future prices affect their desired rates of exploitation. These differences are usually expressed as differences in the time preference for money, or the *discount rate*. Countries with urgent wants due to population pressures, political instability, and/or pressing military needs are generally presumed to have high discount rates. Thus, they tend to prefer current to future income. Such countries are likely to prefer a rapid rate of resource exploitation even though it means early depletion and somewhat lower present prices. Homogeneity with respect to wealth, political stability, and military requirements thus promote cartel cohesion. Again, such conditions are neither necessary nor sufficient for a viable cartel arrangement.

The Spatial Pricing Problem

The theories discussed thus far have implicitly assumed that producers and consumers are all located in one place. In reality, geographic characteristics are important enough to warrant separate consideration. This is particularly true for petroleum markets, where fixed costs typically represent a high proportion of total costs, demand fluctuates cyclically, and, until the remarkable price increases of the 1970s, shipping costs represented a large fraction of the delivered price. All of these factors influence the degree of competition or cooperation in petroleum markets.

The various forms of spatial pricing include "free on board" at shipping point and "cost, insurance, and freight" at destination. These are commonly abbreviated as F.O.B. and C.I.F., respectively. An alternative of particular relevance to oil markets, comparable to F.O.B., is "free alongside ship" at loading port, or F.A.S. pricing. Contracts related to the purchase/sale of oil always specify who shall bear the shipping costs. The pricing practices which have been used most often in the petroleum trade are F.A.S. and a particular form of C.I.F. pricing called the "basepoint system."

F.A.S. Pricing

Two types of F.A.S. pricing can be used in quoting petroleum prices: (1) uniform and (2) nonuniform, or discriminatory prices. Under uniform F.A.S. pricing, a seller quotes the same price to each buyer and the buyer pays shipping costs to a selected destination. With discriminatory F.A.S. pricing, a seller quotes different prices to buyers, depending on their geographic location. Discrimination by a single seller on the basis of the geographic location of the buyer is so difficult to implement that it is relatively unimportant in the petroleum trade. Uniform F.A.S. pricing is the system generally used at present.

The general properties of uniform F.A.S. pricing are illustrated in Figure 3-5. The horizontal line running East and West represents the distance between the major producing and consuming regions. Delivered prices are measured vertically. Oil at the Gulf of Mexico (called the U.S. Gulf) sells for the posted price of *GA*. Shipping costs from the U.S. Gulf to all points east are added to *GA*, so the delivered price is denoted by *AD*. If oil loaded at Ras Tanura sells for a posted price of *RB*, the addition of shipping costs results in delivered prices of *BC* to the west of Ras Tanura and *BE* to the east. (Ignore *RB'*, *B'C'*, and *B'E'* for now.) No buyer east of New York will purchase U.S. Gulf oil, because it can be obtained cheaper from Ras Tanura. No buyer west of New York will purchase oil from Ras Tanura, because it can be obtained cheaper from the U.S. Gulf. Buyers in New York are indifferent between the two supply sources.

Uniform F.A.S. pricing involves no geographic price discrimination. Each seller receives an identical price per barrel from each buyer. The markets are segmented on the basis of posted prices and shipping costs. Each buyer can obtain oil at the lowest price possible, given the pattern of posted prices.

FIGURE 3-5
Delivered Price per Barrel under Uniform F.A.S. Pricing

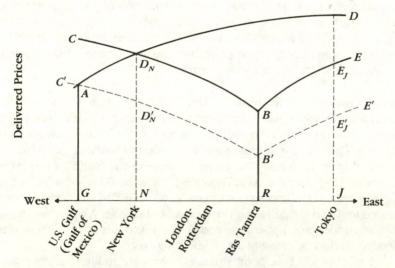

Sellers in either Ras Tanura or the U.S. Gulf (but not both) could expand their market territory by lowering posted prices, thus shifting the delivered price schedule down. For example, sellers at Ras Tanura could expand their market to the U.S. Gulf by posting *RB'* rather than *RB*. Delivered prices would then be given by *B'C'*, and sellers in Ras Tanura would capture all points to the east of the U.S. Gulf. This assumes the U.S. Gulf price remains at *GA*.

C.I.F. Pricing

When a seller quotes a delivered, or C.I.F., price, he is obligated to pay the freight; naturally, the price quotation will be high enough to cover variable costs including freight, and it will generally provide a contribution to fixed costs and profit. The C.I.F. quotation may be a competitive price or contain an element of monopoly profit. In a competitive market, the price paid by the consumer at each destination equals the competitive cost from the lowest-cost source of supply plus shipping charges from that supply source. In less competitive markets, the delivered price may be only remotely related to costs.

There are two C.I.F. systems of particular importance in analyzing the petroleum market: (1) the single and (2) the multiple base-point price systems. Both are less than purely competitive by nature. Under a single base-point system, one geographic location is accepted by all sellers and buyers as the point at which the base price should be calculated. Delivered prices are determined by taking the posted price at the base point and adding shipping costs from that point to the destination. Under a multiple base-point system, two or more geographic locations are used as reference points for purposes of quoting delivered prices. Base-point systems are discriminatory from the standpoint of all sellers located outside a base point because they receive a higher price, or *netback*, from buyers located nearby.

Single Base-Point System. Until the early 1950s prices in world petroleum markets were often established using a single base-point system called the Gulf-Plus system. Under the Gulf-Plus system, posted U.S. Gulf prices plus shipping costs provide the basis for price quotations all over the world. The general nature of the Gulf-Plus system is illustrated in Figure 3-6. As in Figure 3-5, oil at the U.S. Gulf sells for the posted price *GA*. Shipping costs from the U.S. Gulf to all points east are added to *GA* so the delivered price is *AD*. Oil sells for ND_N in New York, LD_L in London and Rotterdam, and JD_J in Tokyo, regardless where it is loaded, and irrespective of actual shipping costs.

Under single base-point pricing, buyers are indifferent regarding

FIGURE 3-6
The Gulf-Plus Base-Point Pricing System

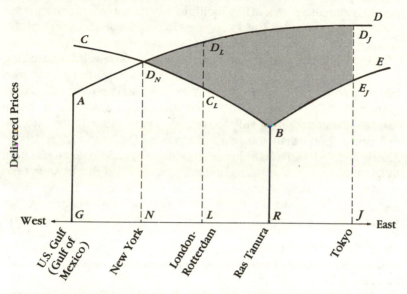

from whom they buy because all sellers quote identical delivered prices. Posted prices at the U.S. Gulf may be determined by competition or by a cartel arrangement, but at least tacit cooperation is required for a base-point system to remain operative. The reason is that sellers in Ras Tanura, for example, receive "phantom freight" of $C_L D_L$ and $E_J D_J$ on shipments to London–Rotterdam and Tokyo, respectively. The shaded area in Figure 3-6 indicates the phantom freight obtainable from sales east of New York. If sellers in Ras Tanura want to increase their market share, it is easily within their power to do so by lowering prices or "absorbing the phantom freight." A single base-point pricing system is difficult to sustain where there are many low-cost and potentially large rivals.

Multiple Base-Point System.   The Gulf-Plus system was established prior to World War II because the U.S. Gulf was the principal oil exporting region. It began to break down after the war as the Persian Gulf became more important. When a single base-point system breaks down it may be replaced by a multiple base-point system. The latter arises because marginal revenue exceeds marginal costs for many of the sellers receiving phantom freight. By lowering prices they can sell additional quantities, increase their market share, and receive larger monopoly profits. Competition among sellers therefore leads to the breakdown of a single base-point system. If competition is severe enough it will lead to the erosion of all monopoly profit (that is, to a purely competitive system). A multiple base-point system is an intermediate solution which checks competition before all monopoly profits become transformed into consumers' surplus.

Figure 3-7 illustrates the multiple base-point system. Prices from the U.S. Gulf to New York are determined by the posted price *GA* plus shipping costs. Prices east of New York are based on the Ras Tanura posting of *RB* plus freight. The price structure is described by curve AD_NBE. Phantom freight still accrues to sellers located closer to the destination ports than the two base points. For example, sellers in Algeria and Indonesia have lower shipping costs and receive phantom freight indicated by the shaded areas to the west and east of Arzew and Langkat, respectively. Multiple base-point pricing causes buyers within a particular region to be indifferent regarding from whom they buy within their own region.

FIGURE 3-7
Delivered Prices Under a Multiple Base-Point Pricing System

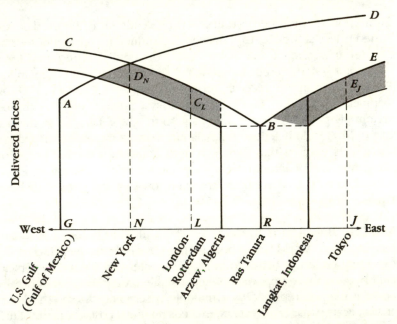

Cartelization and Oil Markets

The success of OPEC during the 1970s provides a classic example of cartel formation. Since producers of many other commodities believe the "value" of their products is greater than the prices they receive, the question of emulation naturally arises. On May 1, 1974, the United Nations General Assembly adopted a Declaration and Programme of Action on the Establishment of a *New Economic Order*. The Lomé conference, held in December, 1974, was designed to promote this "New Economic Order." The central question regarding mineral and agricultural commodities was the possibility of emulating OPEC. Initial enthusiasm for a New Economic Order has waned as its advocates have come to realize the difficulty of gaining agreement on the distribution of income and other matters essential to a cartel arrangement.

Since OPEC epitomizes a successful cartel, it is informative to inquire how oil and OPEC differ from other commodities and other attempts to restrict output in order to elevate prices above competitive levels. It can be shown that the formation of a cartel depends on objective considerations of resource availability and institutional features which influence the utilization of known resources. The rhetoric of officials in the producing and consuming countries matters relatively little. An essential message of this book is that basic considerations of supply, demand, and inventory management make oil almost unique among depletable resources. A simple enumeration of conditions favorable to the formation of a cartel cannot explain the success of OPEC. However, the combined characteristics of oil and OPEC go a long way in explaining why OPEC is the most successful cartel in history.

Supply

Nature of the Resource.   Certain physical and technical characteristics of oil distinguish it from other commodities. Oil produced from giant and supergiant fields flows freely from beneath the earth under natural pressure. These conditions make extraction costs extraordinarily low. In addition, the quantity lifted from already developed fields can be varied within wide limits. The technical considerations of pressure maintenance, water injection, and equipment upkeep constrain operators within certain broad limits, but supply can be increased *rather easily* to meet inordinate demands or it can be reduced to prevent surpluses.

The possibility of varying production with minimal cost penalties reduces the need to carry large inventories. This may be contrasted with an agricultural commodity which must be planted, fertilized, dusted, harvested, stored, and brought to market. Once the agricultural production cycle is underway, the costs of abandonment are severe and storage costs are high. The degree of flexibility is much greater in the production and distribution of oil and natural gas.

The concentration of low-cost reserves in the Middle East is another distinguishing characteristic of oil. Only a few other minerals exhibit similar levels of concentration. Uranium is found mostly in the United States, Canada, and the USSR; oil shale or tar sands are also found in these countries and Venezuela; and gold, bauxite, and tungsten are found in large commercial quantities in only a few countries. Most minerals are widely distributed, and nearly all agricultural commodities can be grown in many different countries. Only commodities which can be controlled by a few countries have much potential for worldwide cartelization.

Demand

The main substitutes for oil used in space heating, raising steam for industrial processes, and the generation of electricity are natural gas, coal, and nuclear fission. In transportation industries, where diesel or gasoline engines are used to power railroad locomotives, trucks, buses, and automobiles, there are virtually no viable substitutes for oil except "conservation." Conservation is not a panacea. In the short run, it is inefficient to leave expensive capital assets idle simply because fuel costs have increased. In the long run, substitution possibilities are greater, but high capital and labor costs act as constraints. The upshot is that the demand for oil is highly inelastic at present prices and will remain so in transportation industries at even substantially higher prices. In fact, fuel costs are already equivalent to $120 per barrel in many European countries due to very high taxes on gasoline. The main effect of high gasoline prices appears to be on the size of automobiles and driving habits, but not on the choice between using oil or an alternative fuel. Oil predominates in the transportation sector and will continue to do so at prices several times present levels.

In contrast, foodstuffs do not require much capital equipment in consumption, and consumer demand for a particular agricultural commodity is generally not very urgent. Metals are more likely to have close substitutes than oil, and scrap overhangs the market to compete with new ores. The higher the price of new ore, the larger the volume reprocessed as scrap. The recovery of scrap iron, copper, and lead accounts for 30 to 45 percent of total consumption in the United States and Western Europe. When a metal becomes as valuable as gold or silver, the term "scrap" is even inappropriate. Stocks of these metals always overhang the market and compete with current production. In contrast, once oil is burned, it never again competes with current production. The absence of a scrap market represents a highly favorable characteristic of oil and thus promotes cartelization. Coal is similar, but it is comparatively abundant, widely dispersed among countries, and it costs a great deal to produce and transport. Thus, oil is not unique, but among all the candidates for cartelization, it possesses some of the more favorable characteristics. Diamonds, gold, and uranium are other prime candidates for cartelization, and there is ample evidence of producer cooperation or cartelization in these industries.

Inventory Considerations.   Oil from giant and supergiant fields is inexpensive to produce, but it has great bulk relative to its value, and it is expensive to store above the ground. Physical storage costs in steel tanks are two or three cents per barrel per month, or about 30 cents per barrel per year. In all but the most recent years this was a fraction ranging from 10 to 20 percent of its wellhead price. Since 1973, storage costs have been dwarfed by the financial investments required to carry inventories. The financial carrying costs of oil at $32 per barrel and a 10 percent interest rate are $3.20 per barrel each year. Since inventory carrying costs are high and production from developed fields can be varied within broad limits, there has always been an incentive for industry executives to fashion a delivery system with relatively low inventory requirements. This narrow, or lean, delivery system has had a profound effect on oil prices in recent years.

The delivery system for oil consists of pipelines, tankers, barges, and tanks containing working inventories as well as a managerial system which decides when and at what level of capacity to utilize available facilities. On a worldwide basis, combined crude oil and refined product inventories currently vary between five and six billion barrels or between 80 and 100 days of supply. On the average, oil lifted in April will be utilized during July. Refined product inventories are typically on the order of 50–70 days of supply. Thus, there is very little slack in the delivery system. There is sufficient excess capacity at all levels to meet seasonal variations in demand and to allow modest levels of inventory accumulation. However, scheduling between production and final utilization is so tight that even a slight disruption in supply is sufficient to provoke a *supply crisis.*

Short- and Long-Run Problems of OPEC

The member countries of OPEC have entered into a cooperative arrangement to hold oil prices far above a competitive level. Every successful cartel faces the short-run problem of maintaining the established cartel price and of allocating shares of total output to its members so that each participant is reasonably content. In the long run the cartel faces the same set of problems, but they are complicated by the fact that additional capacity can be brought on stream.

Short-Run Problems

To remain successful, OPEC must limit total output and distribute market shares among its members. Since about 1970 this has been accomplished by setting the Saudi Arabian marker crude price; each of the other countries then sets its price to reflect quality differentials and transportation costs. Buyers determine how much of each crude they will take at the established price. Therefore, OPEC determines prices but buyers determine the level of total output and its distribution among the member countries. The arrangement is a classic example of a *price fixing cartel.*

The Differentials Problem.   The announced goal of OPEC is to maintain stable prices at a level near the value of oil to the end user, but this is difficult to accomplish in practice. The major difficulty is that of maintaining price differentials such that market shares of individual members do not fluctuate too widely. OPEC is not a profit sharing cartel, so market shares determine who benefits most from the set of cartel prices. The main determinant of market shares is the price differential among the various crude oils. The differentials problem will be discussed at length in Chapter 7, but it needs to be emphasized here because it lies at the heart of the cartel problem from OPEC's point of view.

Prices are discussed at the OPEC ministerial meetings held in June and December each year, but it is Saudi Arabia, and not OPEC, who specifies the Saudi "marker crude price." Each member of OPEC calibrates its price schedules around the "marker" price to reflect differences in quality (that is, gravity and sulfur content) and transportation costs. Refiners who buy crude oil are willing to pay more for what the American Petroleum Institute (API) has classified as *high gravity* crudes, because more gasoline and other more highly valued products can be produced from such crudes. Refiners will also pay a premium for crudes with low sulfur content because this characteristic lowers refining costs. Finally, refiners are interested in the delivered, or C.I.F., price and will pay a higher F.A.S. shipping-point price if transport costs are low.

These differentials vary from day to day depending on market conditions, but they tend to remain near the same order of magnitude among the various crudes. The "sulfur differential" amounts to about 4 cents per barrel per percentage point of sulfur content, and is seldom more than 10 cents per barrel. The "gravity" differential is about 10 cents per barrel per degree of API gravity. The "transport cost differential" is rarely more than $1.25 per barrel. Some illustrative examples are shown in Table 3-1. The February, 1978, date was selected because it reflects more normal deviations from the Saudi marker price than figures since 1979. Many of the differentials since 1979 reflect a degree

TABLE 3-1
Price Differentials Attributable to Variations in Gravity, Sulfur Content, and Transportation Costs, February, 1978

VARIATION DUE LARGELY TO GRAVITY AND SULFUR CONTENT		
Crude Type	Official Sales Price (*dollars per barrel*)	Price Differential vs. Arabian Light (*dollars per barrel*)
ARABIAN		
Berri 39°	13.22	0.52
Hout 35°	12.69	−0.01
Light 34° (marker crude)	12.70	0
Medium 31°	12.32	−0.38
Khafii 28°	12.03	−0.67
Heavy 27°	12.02	−0.68
VARIATION DUE LARGELY TO GEOGRAPHIC LOCATION		
ARABIAN		
Light 34° (marker crude)	12.70	0
IRANIAN		
Light 34°	12.81	0.11
VENEZUELAN		
Oficina 35°	13.99	1.29

of "disunity" in pricing within OPEC due to the Iranian crises and other events to be discussed in Chapter 7.

Under the arrangements just described, a country can increase its share of the market by reducing its price differentials. Stable market shares require that the pricing authorities accurately assess market conditions and set their differentials accordingly. It is a difficult and ongoing balancing act, but a necessary one, because the distribution of output depends upon the relative price differentials selected by each member country in relation to what buyers are willing to pay.

The Relative Value Problem.   The problem of selecting price differentials has become known within OPEC as the *relative value problem*. It is inherent in all markets where prices are pegged. If the pegged differentials do not exactly correspond with the market appraisal of crude values, then market shares will change. The overvalued crudes cannot be sold and the undervalued crudes fetch advantageous prices downstream. Officials charged with selling the overvalued crudes may eventually lower their prices in an attempt to recoup lost markets, or those selling undervalued crudes may raise prices to gain additional revenues or restore unity in pricing. There is no way to predict which will happen.

The relative value problem is an ongoing one because weather conditions, recessions, acts of terrorism, and so forth, affect the market appraisal of relative values. A few pennies can tip the scales in favor of one crude over another; in short, the price elasticity of demand for a particular crude, given the Saudi marker crude price, is *highly elastic*. Thus, even if the OPEC ministers were omniscient in selecting price schedules, these fixed prices would soon become obsolete because of changing market conditions.

Long-Term Problems

The Optimal Price.   Decisions regarding the Saudi marker crude price and the relative value problem are also the source of OPEC's long-term problems. A marker price which is "too high" will result in high levels of production outside OPEC, greater incentives to expand output by member countries of OPEC, more capital investments requiring the use of fuels other than oil, and intensive research and development efforts to find alternatives to fossil fuels. A marker crude price which is "too low" will result in more intensive use of oil from OPEC and early depletion. The depletion issue is the more readily apparent, but it is not necessarily more important. There is an *optimal* price trajectory from the standpoint of OPEC considered as a whole, but there are inherent conflicts regarding what is optimal for individual member countries.

The Cartel Problem.   Traditional cartel theory stresses that shaving prices to gain market share, or "chiseling," is the central cartel problem. Chiseling is relatively easy within OPEC because of the manner in which prices are selected. In effect, each country, except Saudi Arabia, is free to establish its own differentials. Thus, it is possible for a country to *underprice* its crude, produce at capacity, and expand production facilities at a rapid rate, all at the expense of Saudi Arabia and other countries who reduce production rather than compete on the basis of price. However, the theoretical possibility of chiseling does not prove its existence. And it is by no means certain that the inherent tendency to chisel will dominate rational decisions to cooperate. The proof of the pudding is in the eating, and thus far OPEC has managed to maintain prices far above competitive levels.

Conclusion

Based on the theory of depletable resources one might expect the price of oil to rise gently over time. However, cartel theory stresses the instability of prices and their tendency to decline. There is an obvious inconsistency between a model which predicts declining prices and one which predicts price increases. However, theoretical possibilities do not constitute empirical events. The characteristics of oil and the distribution of reserves are favorable to the cartelization of the oil industry, and OPEC has exhibited a degree of cohesiveness few thought possible even a decade ago. In order to understand why OPEC has been relatively successful requires knowledge of the institutional history of the world petroleum industry, which is the subject of Part Two of this book.

Further Readings

Bobrow, Davis B., and Robert T. Kudrle. "Theory, Policy, and Resource Cartels: The Case of OPEC." *Journal of Conflict Resolution,* March 1976, 3–56.

Danielsen, Albert L. "Cartel Rivalry and the World Price of Oil." *Southern Economic Journal,* 1976, 407–415.

Frank, Helmut J. *Crude Oil Prices in the Middle East.* New York: Praeger, 1966.

Kuenne, Robert E. "A Short-Run Demand Analysis of the OPEC Cartel." *Journal of Business Administration,* 10, Nos. 1–2, (1978/1979), 129–164.

Osborne, Dale K. "Cartel Problems." *American Economic Review,* Dec. 1976, 835–845.

Sherer, Frederick. "Conditions Limiting Oligopolistic Coordination." In *Industrial Market Structure and Oligopolistic Performance,* Chap. 7. Chicago: Rand McNally, 1979.

Stigler, George J. "A Theory of Oligopoly." *Journal of Political Economy.* Feb. 1964, 44–61.

Telser, Lester. *Competition, Collusion, and Game Theory.* Chicago and New York: Aldine Atherton, 1972.

Part Two

Early Institutions

Part One's explanation of the geographic distribution of petroleum reserves and of the theoretical principles of depletable resources and cartel behavior provides a good basis for understanding the evolution of OPEC. But applying these principles to the analysis of petroleum markets also requires knowledge of specific institutions. The term "institution" as used in this book refers to a significant practice or set of relationships which prevail in the conduct of economic, social, and political activities. Private property, freedom of contract, self-interest, and competition are all "institutions" found in free-market societies. In some countries, petroleum markets are governed by these institutions, whereas other countries have nationalized their energy producing industries. In either case there are additional institutional arrangements peculiar to each country.

Part Two contains a description of the specific institutional arrangements in the United States and in the world during the period 1860–1970. A recurrent theme is that competition leads to the rapid exploitation of petroleum reserves, physical waste of the resource, and low prices. The response to low prices by producers is to devise new institutional arrangements which substitute cooperation for competition. Chapter 4 is devoted to an explanation of how cooperation was substituted for competition in the United States, first by the Standard Oil refining

69

monopoly and later by a quota allocation system called *market demand prorationing*. Chapter 5 contains a discussion of similar developments on the world scene. It will be shown that cooperation was substituted for competition on a worldwide scale during roughly the same period of time as in the United States. The main difference between the development of U.S. and world petroleum markets is that they evolved in slightly different institutional frameworks. The principal actors involved on the world scene also differed: they were the leaders of the international oil companies and of the countries which eventually formed OPEC.

Chapter 6 integrates the material covered in Chapters 4 and 5 and explains how OPEC evolved during the period 1945 to 1970. The institution of *profit sharing*, which was inaugurated in Venezuela and then adopted in the Middle East, was the major institutional change leading to the formal organization of OPEC. Ironically, it was also one of the main contributors to the decline in petroleum prices during the 1950s and 1960s. The decline in prices during the period 1950–1970 and the subsequent price increases of the 1970s cannot be explained solely in terms of the theories of depletable resources and cartel behavior. Nor can these trends be explained without a knowledge of theory. The specific institutions which evolved from the beginning of the petroleum industry are also important. The subtle interactions among the principal actors in world petroleum markets, the institutional changes they devised to enhance their own wealth, and the recurrent effects of competition provide fascinating and essential material for an understanding of the modern structure of world petroleum markets and of the policy options available to oil exporting countries—subjects that occupy Part Three of the book.

READER'S GUIDE TO PART TWO
In this part we explain the early evolution of OPEC through the 1960s. Chapters 4 and 5 contain an analytical history of U.S. and world petroleum markets, respectively. They can be profitably read by the reader who has had relatively little exposure to the economic history of petroleum markets. Chapter 6 outlines the evolution of OPEC during the period 1945–1970, and is essential background for an understanding of the modern structure and policy options discussed in Part Three.

United States States Dominance (1860–1945)

4

Overview.

Early U.S. Oil History:
Discovery; The Rule of Capture.

The Standard Oil Refining Monopoly:
Background and Beginning; Modus Operandi; Decline of the Standard Monopoly.

State Regulation of Crude Oil Production:
Crude Price and Production Trends; Regulatory Authorities; Regulatory Issues.

Origin and Impact of Market Demand Prorationing:
Origin; Early Results of Market Demand Prorationing.

World War II.

Pause.

READER'S GUIDE TO CHAPTER 4
This is the first of three chapters dealing with the *analytical history* of world petroleum markets. Many of the concepts peculiar to petroleum markets which will be used throughout the remainder of the book are introduced and defined in this chapter. In particular, the reader should become familiar with the institution called *market demand prorationing* as developed and practiced in the United States. This is essential for an understanding of world petroleum markets and of the evolution of OPEC as discussed in Chapters 5 and 6.

Overview

Known recoverable reserves, private property, freedom of contract, a highly literate population conditioned to seek its own self-interest through competitive markets, and a stable political environment combined to make the United States almost unique in the development of the petroleum industry from about 1860 until the 1870s. Russia enjoyed a similar position after oil wells were drilled in 1871 until the Bolshevik revolution in 1917, and several European countries exploited reserves in their respective colonial empires during the 1890s. The United States was clearly the early leader in the exploitation of its petroleum reserves. Except for a few years around the turn of the century, the United States until 1951 produced more oil than all other countries combined.

Competition is a beneficial process from the standpoint of consumers because it keeps prices low while ensuring that oil is extracted at an optimum rate over time. But competition is not always considered desirable from the standpoint of producers. The history of the U.S. petroleum industry illustrates the remarkable degree to which independent businessmen have periodically combined to raise prices, lower costs, and/or expand markets. Since competition generally leads to low prices, it stimulates producers to cooperate in order to raise prices. Cooperation, then, leads to high prices and encourages entry as well as additional production by those already in the industry. The fact that cooperative behavior has been tried repeatedly is evidence in itself that forces have been at work tending to erode cooperative agreements.

The principal cooperative arrangements within the United States that can be judged more or less successful include: (1) the Standard Oil refining monopoly and (2) market demand prorationing. The Standard Oil monopoly was formed by merger and acquisition largely without the assistance of the government. It lasted from about 1880 to at least 1911. *Market demand prorationing* is a quota and allocation institution. Although organized through state governments, it was sanctioned and strengthened by the federal government in 1935 when the interstate shipment of oil produced in violation of state laws was declared a federal offense. The institution of market demand prorationing was most influential during the period 1935–1970. However, it remains in force in the United States and is a latent power capable of influencing petroleum prices.

Early U.S. Oil History

Discovery

Rock Oil.   The age of illumination by oil began in 1859 when Colonel Drake successfully drilled for oil in Titusville, Pennsylvania (see Figure 4–1 on page 76). Oil was soaked from ponds and streams using

PRICE 25 CENTS

The Wonder of the Nineteenth Century!

ROCK OIL,

IN

PENNSYLVANIA AND ELSEWHERE.

BY THOMAS A. GALE.

(A RESIDENT ON OIL CREEK.)

"The Rock poured me out rivers of oil."----Job, 29--5.

ERIE:
SLOAN & GRIFFETH, PUBLISHERS.
1860.

woolen blankets long before drilling technology was developed. Its uses were many and varied, but principally it was bottled and sold as a medicine for man and beast. The humble beginnings of the oil industry are illustrated by a quaint book written by Thomas Gale in 1860 called *Rock Oil*. Gale prefaces the book by saying:

> Many all over the country are desirous of information in relation to *Rock Oil*—they would know whether it is a humbug or not. That reasonable desire, this book is designed to gratify.
> The writer having his *habitat* in *oildom*, desired to make public his observations. We hasten to communicate to friends any small event which falls under our notice. Why then to one of amazing magnitude, occurring before our eyes, should we not seek to lend a publicity correspondingly great? The discovery of this vast liquid deposit has been termed the wonder of the age. Certainly, it is a wonder to which the world cannot often furnish a parallel.

Gale goes on to define what constitutes rock oil, to indicate where it is found, and to discuss the geological structure of the oil region. He also outlines the history of the rock oil enterprise—its costs, uses, and prospects. The superiority of rock oil relative to whale oil for illumination is recounted:

> Sperm of the first quality burns well; but this new burner ranks above it in light-giving capacity, while at the same time, it can be afforded at $\frac{1}{4}$ the price of the best sperm, which cannot be less than $2.50 per gallon.

Dozens of other examples of the illuminating and lubricating qualities of rock oil are given. Testimonials from merchants, master mechanics, and a variety of end-users are duly recorded. All in all, Gale's *Rock Oil* is a delightful book showing the qualitative and cost advantages of oil over lard and sperm whale oil for illumination and lubrication. He predicted a bright future for rock oil.

The Rule of Capture

The discovery of oil in large quantities through drilling resulted in a predictable scramble for oil comparable to a gold rush. Indeed, there were "black gold" rushes every time oil was discovered in new fields, from Pennsylvania (1859) to Oklahoma (1903) to Texas (1920s) and beyond. The famous oil rushes were attributable to private property and the *rule of capture*. According to the rule of capture, petroleum belongs to the landowner who extracts it from beneath his land, regardless of its original location. The owner can protect his title by taking possession of the oil in place before it is drained away by his neighbor. Consequently, the rule of capture promotes a race for the possession of oil by competitive owners. According to Stephen McDonald:

> **The results are dense drilling, especially along property lines; capacity production of both oil and associated gas; rapid dissipation of reservoir pressure; irregular advance of displacing fluids through the reservoir oil zone; and, therefore, loss of ultimate recovery.**

The rule of capture ensured that the early production of crude oil in the United States would take place under very highly competitive conditions. Furthermore, the evolving transportation, refining, and distribution networks were also highly competitive during the first 12 years after "Drake's Folly" (as many considered the drilling project). Oil flowed from wells at rates of 3,000 to 4,000 barrels per day as early as 1861. Thus, two years after Drake's Folly, oil which had sold for $20/barrel had fallen to as low as 10 cents per barrel. Producers considered such severe competition "ruinous," and sought ways to maintain prices. Similar experiences were to become typical as new producing areas were discovered. But competition at the wellhead was not to be effectively constrained until compulsory prorationing was adopted in 1935. A point to be emphasized is that a highly competitive producing sector ensured that oil would be available to refiners at highly competitive prices.

The Standard Oil Refining Monopoly

Background and Beginning

Competition and Cooperation.   Between 1870 and 1899 the Standard Oil Company, under the leadership of John D. Rockefeller, Sr., first attained and then maintained an 85 to 90 percent share of the refining market in the United States. Like the other great monopolists of the day, Rockefeller and his associates used a combination of cost-cutting efficiencies, railroad and pipeline rebates, predatory pricing, and merger to gain their preeminent position. The Standard Oil Company was simply the most successful oil corporation in the battle for a larger share of the petroleum market. In fact, Standard Oil was the largest corporation in America until 1901, when J. P. Morgan merged a number of steel companies to form the United States Steel Corporation.

Rockefeller was the central figure in the development of the Standard Oil Company, but men such as Samuel Andrews, H. M. Flagler,

FIGURE 4–1
The Pennsylvania Basin

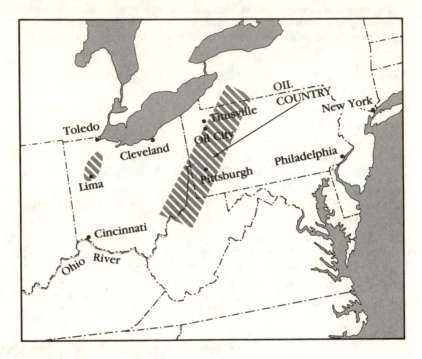

William A. Rockefeller, and others contributed almost equally. Rocke-feller was a man mindful of costs and ever alert to the opportunity to turn a dollar in profit. Even Ida Tarbell, the famous muckraker–historian of the Standard Oil Company, extolled the efficiency of the Standard. But efficiency alone cannot explain its success. The Standard Oil monop-oly provides one of the first major illustrations of how competition leads to cooperation among individuals and groups in the industry.

Rise of the Standard Oil Company.   John D. Rockefeller was born on a farm in central New York on July 8, 1839. In 1852 his family moved to Cleveland where he went to school until 1855. Then it became nec-essary for him to work. According to Ida Tarbell, "He proved to be an admirable accountant—one of the early-and-late sort, who saw every-thing, forgot nothing and never talked." He always saved a little out of his $25 per month salary, and in 1858 he pooled his savings with another young man, M. B. Clark, to open a produce commission business on the Cleveland docks along Lake Erie. In its first year the business grossed $450,000.

In 1862, Rockefeller and Clark provided financial backing of $4,000 for an Englishman of great promise and ability, one Samuel Andrews, in starting an oil refinery. The business of refining oil was a gamble, but Andrews proved to be a mechanical genius. He devised new processes, made a better quality oil, and got larger percentages of refined products from his crudes. By 1865 the $4,000 investment had grown to $100,000. Other ambitious men with business acumen were earning similarly spectacular rates of return. Refining thus became one of the most promising industries in Cleveland by the end of the Civil War. Rockefeller, believing this was only the beginning, sold his share of the produce commission business and formed the oil firm of Rockefeller and Andrews.

Andrews attended to processing and Rockefeller to finances, crude oil acquisition, and marketing. Both men were extraordinarily adept at their part in the business. Rockefeller was a shrewd bargainer and a financial wizard at raising capital. Their business ventures expanded and new blood was brought into the operation. John D. started a second refinery with William A. Rockefeller and opened a distribution house in New York with H. M. Flagler. These were all young, able, and ambitious men: Rockefeller was not yet 30 years old and the others were of comparable age. In June, 1870, the firms were combined into the Standard Oil Company with refining capacity of about 1,500 barrels of crude per day and a book value of $1 million.

Modus Operandi

Rebates, Merger, and Growth.   In 1870 Standard held about 10 percent of the refining interests in Cleveland, but there were 26 other refineries and some were nearly as large as the Standard. The refining industry in the early 1870s provides a classic example of a competitive industry. The product was homogeneous and entry was fairly easy. A new refinery could be started with a $50,000 investment and there were plenty of refiners with the technical knowledge to strike out on their own. With rates of return on equity of 50 percent and more, there were ample incentives for men of wealth to back ventures financially. In addition, enterprising men could always raise capital by selling stock to the public. But entry had the predictable effects of driving down refined product prices. Kerosene, which Rockefeller sold for 59 cents a gallon in 1865, had dropped to 26 cents in 1870.

Rockefeller recognized that high rates of return could be maintained if costs could be held down and/or prices could be raised. He had little control over prices but he could influence costs. In those early days transport costs were an important part of total costs. Oil transport was mostly via railroads, which were experiencing rapid growth and relatively high rates of return on equity. But they were also faced with greater competition from pipelines and new entrants to the railroading industry. This added competition was resulting in declining freight rates. Thus, it is not too surprising that the refining and railroad industries might form a close alliance.

The alliance between the railroads and refiners was brought about by John D. Rockefeller and a group of associates who controlled about 10 percent of U.S. refining capacity. In 1872 they organized a corporation called the South Improvement Company and soon reached an agreement with the railroads to implement an ingenious system of rebates and railroad rate fixing. The complex rate structure involving "Oil Country," Cleveland, and New York is illustrated in Figure 4–2.

The rebate and rate-fixing scheme allowed the railroads to net about $1.50/barrel on all eastbound refined product shipments and 40 cents/barrel on all westbound shipments of crude oil from Oil Country to Cleveland. Crude acquisition costs for refiners in Oil Country were lower than for refiners in Cleveland. The base freight rate on products to New York paid by Oil Country refiners was set at $2.80/barrel. Refiners in Cleveland, including members of the South Improvement Company, were charged only $2 per barrel for a longer haul. This ostensibly equalized the cost of delivering products to New York for both Oil Country and Cleveland refiners. But the South Improvement Company received a rebate on all its own eastbound shipments as well as a rebate on shipments made by its competitors in Cleveland and in Oil Country. This provided a distinct competitive advantage for members of the South Improvement Company. Similar rate structures and rebate schemes were devised for all major points of origin and destination.

This transport cost advantage allowed Rockefeller and his associates to engage in *predatory pricing* and to press other refiners to merge with Standard. Predatory pricing refers to the practice of selectively cutting prices below competitors' costs, thus inflicting heavy losses upon them and providing the opportunity to buy them out or to merge on favorable terms. Because of its efficiency and the railroad rebates, Standard could compete with any refiner, engage in selective price cutting when the opportunity presented itself (that is, predatory pricing), and otherwise bring pressure to merge upon the refiners. As a result, within three months after formation of the South Improvement Company, 21 of the 26 independent Cleveland refiners had joined the combination. It marked the beginning of the Standard Oil monopoly.

FIGURE 4–2
Railroad Rate Structure, 1872

SHARE OF WEST AND EAST BOUND TRAFFIC		
WEST	**CARRIER**	**EAST**
33%	New York Central Railroad W. H. Vanderbilt	27½%
33%	Pennsylvania Railroad Tom Scott	45%
33%	Erie Railroad Jay Gould	27½%

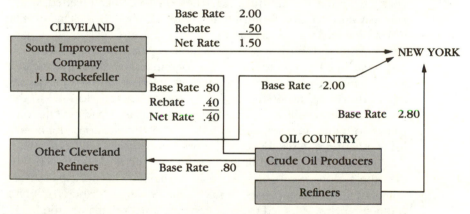

NOTE: All rates are expressed in dollars per barrel. Rebates were paid only to members of the South Improvement Company.

Limit Pricing.   There is little question that Standard gained its monopoly position by rebates; purchase of pipelines, which enabled it to withhold crude supplies from competitors; predatory pricing when the occasion warranted; business espionage; and merger with rivals. But Standard *maintained* control by the use of *limit pricing*. Standard generally held prices low enough to discourage entry. And the operating and transport cost advantages were the principal source of its economic rent. The refinery that was never built was therefore a power in the market.

Decline of the Standard Monopoly

At its peak in the 1880s and 1890s Standard controlled from 80 to 90 percent of the refining business in the country. Its decline may be attributed to passage of the Interstate Commerce Act (1887), various state laws which made the pipelines *common carriers*, the Sherman Antitrust Act (1890), expansion of crude oil production westward to Oklahoma and Texas, and the development of the motor transport industry. Considered together, these were sufficient to cause the *relative* decline of the Standard Oil Company.

Standard had originally been incorporated in Ohio, but attempts by the state of Ohio to restrain the corporation's discriminatory and monopolistic practices resulted in a change in corporate headquarters to New Jersey (1899). The Standard Oil Company of New Jersey was a Trust or "holding company", consisting of 33 individual subsidiaries dispersed throughout the various states. The decisive suit against Jersey Standard was filed by the U.S. government in Missouri in 1906, alleging violations under the Sherman Act. These proceedings resulted in the famous Court decision requiring divestiture. In the U.S. *v.* Standard Oil Co. of New Jersey *et al.* decision in 1911, the Court declared that Standard's intent and purpose was to exclude others from doing business and, as such, it represented an illegal combination in restraint of trade. Jersey Standard was ordered to divest its interests in the subsidiaries and to distribute ownership of the 33 companies thus formed to the owners of the parent company. Today's numerous Standard Oil companies (of Ohio, Indiana, and so forth), as well as Exxon, Mobil, and many others, are descendants of the original Standard Oil Company.

The Standard case did little in itself to negate Rockefeller's control over the various companies, since he remained the principal shareholder in the new companies. But as his shares were distributed to heirs and new stock was issued to meet new investment demands, the Rockefeller influence gradually diminished. Perhaps equally important in explaining the decline of the Standard monopoly is that the individual states enacted utility statutes forbidding discrimination by *common carriers* such as railroads and pipelines. Laws forbidding common carriers to discriminate among shippers were passed because discrimination was rampant and those harmed were politically influential. In addition, the oil market was in its infancy when Standard was at its peak. Standard was built during the age of illumination, before oil was widely used as a source of power or as an energy resource. The automobile and the demand for gasoline greatly altered the demand for refined products. Thus, while it is accurate to say that the decline of Standard Oil was due to government antitrust and common carrier laws, it is also true that the expansion of markets, population increases, new sources of crude supply, and foreign competition were contributing factors.

State Regulation of Crude Oil Production

Crude Price and Production Trends

Prices. U.S. institutions prior to 1935 ensured that oil production would increase rapidly and that crude prices would be close to production costs. Oil which sold for $20/barrel in 1859 declined erratically for almost 20 years before settling around the $1/barrel level. During the period 1880 to 1916, the *average* price per barrel never exceeded $1.20 and dropped to as low as 60 cents (see Table 4–1). Field prices for oil located in unfavorable geographic regions and not connected to a main distribution network sometimes sold for 10 cents per barrel.

Production. After its humble beginnings in Pennsylvania, the trend in production was steadily upward; but the regional distribution gradually shifted—first to Ohio and Illinois and then to Oklahoma, Texas, and California. During the period 1900 to 1930 the three western states produced comparable amounts of oil and were the principal U.S. producers. After 1930, production declined in Oklahoma, tapered off considerably in California, and continued to rise sharply in Texas (see Table 4–2). These trends in production and the regional distribution had a profound effect on the institutions developed to limit output and maintain crude oil prices.

Regulatory Authorities

All oil producing states have a regulatory authority that monitors oil producing activities. These agencies are usually called the Corporation Commission prefaced by the state name (for example, the Oklahoma Corporation Commission). But by far the most influential of these regulatory authorities is the Texas Railroad Commission. The Railroad Commission was created in 1891 to regulate the railroads, but legislation has been enacted from time to time expanding its activities to include pipelines and field regulation of oil and gas production. The main intent and effect of regulation was to *prevent damage* to the producing fields and environment and to *maintain prices* above competitive levels.

The Interstate Oil Compact Commission (IOCC) is an institution designed to promote a dialogue among producers and to advance their interests. The IOCC was created in 1935 under authority granted by Congress. It is purely an advisory body which fosters a dialogue among officials in the producing states, collects information, and drafts *pro*

TABLE 4–1
Crude Oil Prices and Production, 1859–1920

Date	Nominal Price (dollars per barrel)	Percent Change in Price	Production (1000 barrels)	Percent Change in Production
1859	20.00		2	
1860	9.60	−48	500	24,900
1861	.52	−94	2114	323
1862	1.05	102	3057	45
1863	3.15	200	2611	−14
1864	8.15	159	2116	−18
1865	6.59	−19	2498	18
1866	3.75	−43	3598	44
1867	2.40	−36	3347	7
1868	3.62	51	3646	9
1869	5.60	54	4215	15
1870	3.90	−30	5261	25
1871	4.40	12	5205	−1
1872	3.75	−14	6293	21
1873	1.80	−52	9894	57
1874	1.15	−36	10,927	10
1875	.97	−15	11,963	9
1876	2.52	159	9,133	−23
1877	2.38	−5	13,350	46
1878	1.17	−50	15,397	15
1879	.86	−26	19,914	29
1880	.94	9	26,286	32
1881	.92	−2	27,661	5
1882	.78	−15	30,511	10
1883	1.10	57	23,450	−23
1884	.85	−22	24,218	3
1885	.88	4	21,859	−10
1886	.71	−19	28,065	28
1887	.67	−6	28,283	1
1888	.65	−3	27,612	−2
1889	.77	18	35,164	27
1890	.77	0	45,824	30

forma rules, regulations, and legislation to prevent waste. The IOCC has no regulatory authority. Such authority resides with the individual states. But on a domestic scale the IOCC is similar to what OPEC is on the international scene. It provides a forum through which its members can discuss common problems and seek mutually beneficial solutions.

TABLE 4–1
(Continued)

Date	Nominal Price (dollars per barrel)	Percent Change in Price	Production (1000 barrels)	Percent Change in Production
1891	.56	−27	54,293	18
1892	.51	−9	50,515	−7
1893	.60	18	48,431	−4
1894	.72	20	49,344	2
1895	1.09	51	52,892	77
1896	.96	−1	60,960	15
1897	.68	29	60,476	−1
1898	.80	17	55,364	−8
1899	.94	18	57,071	3
1900	.80	−15	63,621	11
1901	.96	20	69,389	9
1902	1.19	24	88,767	28
1903	1.13	5	100,461	13
1904	.86	−24	117,081	17
1905	.62	−28	113,717	−3
1906	.73	18	126,494	11
1907	.72	−1	166,095	34
1908	.72	0	178,527	7
1909	.70	−3	183,171	3
1910	.61	−13	209,557	14
1911	.61	0	220,449	5
1912	.74	21	222,935	1
1913	.95	28	248,446	11
1914	.81	−15	265,763	7
1915	.64	−21	281,104	6
1916	1.10	72	300,767	7
1917	1.56	42	335,316	11
1918	1.98	27	355,928	6
1919	2.01	2	378,367	6
1920	3.07	53	442,929	17

SOURCE: American Petroleum Institute, *Petroleum Facts and Figures, 1971 ed.*, Washington, D. C., 1971, pp. 70–71.

Regulatory Issues

Preventing Waste.   The low and sometimes volatile price trends shown in Figure 4–3 are attributable to the rule of capture, to competition, and to the periodic discovery and subsequent depletion of

TABLE 4–2
Annual Oil Production, Principal States and Total United States, 1860–1980
(thousands of barrels)

Year	Eastern United States[1]	Oklahoma	Texas	Louisiana	California	Alaska	Total United States	Other (Mostly Western) States[2]
1860	500						500	
1870	5,261						5,261	
1880	26,246				40		26,286	
1890	45,147				307		45,824	370
1900	56,753	6	836		4,325		63,621	400
1910	66,239	52,029	8,899	6,841	73,011		209,557	1,487
1920	43,558	106,206	96,868	35,714	103,377		442,929	56,419
1930	38,500	216,486	290,457	23,272	227,329		898,011	54,985
1940	181,793	156,164	493,209	103,584	223,889		1,353,214	150,455
1950	102,413	164,599	829,874	208,965	327,607		1,973,574	288,631
1960	133,969	192,913	927,479	400,832	305,352	559	2,574,933	614,009
1970	91,980	223,745	1,249,760	807,025	372,300	83,605	3,537,505	589,110
*1980	118,089	151,960	975,239	466,964	356,644	591,684	3,146,519	541,225

[1]Includes Pennsylvania, Ohio, West Virginia, Illinois, Indiana, Kentucky, Alabama, Florida, Tennessee, New York and Virginia.

[2]Arizona, Arkansas, Colorado, Kansas, Michigan, Mississippi, Missouri, Montana, Nebraska, Nevada, New Mexico, North Dakota, South Dakota, Utah, Washington, Wyoming, and all others.

SOURCE: American Petroleum Institute, *Annual Statistical Review,* Washington, D.C., 1974, p. 9; *Petroleum Facts and Figures, 1971 ed.,* pp. 68–71.

*U.S. Department of Energy, Energy Information Administration, *Energy Data Reports,* "Crude Petroleum, Petroleum Products, and Natural Gas Liquids," Washington, D.C.: Energy Information Administration, December 1980, p. 8.

1970—Daily Averages × 365 (Virginia, Missouri, and Washington not listed).
1980—Washington not included.

reserves. Rapid development of reserves occasioned by the rule of cap-ture resulted in low prices and caused waste. But there are two kinds of waste from a regulatory point of view, *physical waste* and *economic waste*. Economic waste refers to selling oil below its "true value." Pro-ducers and their spokesmen have always assumed that oil has an *intrinsic value* not related to its *market value*. Thus, state regulatory author-ities have long been concerned about preventing economic waste. The question of whether it is desirable to prevent economic waste was debated extensively from about 1900 onward. During the period 1915–1935 the regulatory authorities generally adopted the view that preventing economic waste was in the public interest. Actually, pre-

FIGURE 4–3
U.S. Crude Oil Prices and Percentage Changes in Prices, 1859 to 1920
(nominal prices)

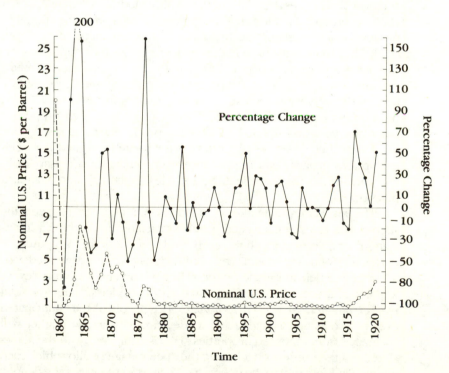

SOURCE: API, *Petroleum Facts and Figures, 1971*, pp. 46–71.

venting economic waste is a euphemism for *price fixing*. The prevention of physical waste has never been controversial and has been actively pursued by the regulatory authorities since before 1900.

Unitization.   Since the natural producing unit is the reservoir and not the well or lease, the reservoir must be *operated as a unit* to avoid physical waste. *Unitization* facilitates the extraction of oil at the maximum efficient rate (MER) and thus increases recovery, reduces drilling and operating costs, and ensures equal returns for owners with equal above-the-ground property rights. Unitization has also been standard operating practice in the United States since the early 1900s. In most states unitization is compulsory.

Market Demand Prorationing.   *Market demand prorationing* is a quota and allocation system which allows the states to limit output and maintain prices (that is, prevent economic waste). Each state regulatory authority determines the total amount of oil, called the *allowable*, which could be produced in the state each month. For most wells the allowable production for regulatory purposes is also the maximum efficient rate (MER), but some wells have higher or lower allowables depending on such arbitrary factors as depth of well, age, capacity, and recovery methods employed. In general, deep, new, low-capacity, and secondary or tertiary recovery wells are exempt from production restrictions based on *market demand*. The rationale is that owners of such properties incur high costs and should be allowed to produce without restrictions to recover their investments. Critics have repeatedly argued that such exemptions penalize efficient producers, encourage unnecessary drilling, and reward the inefficient. Nevertheless, such rules are standard practice.

The mechanics of market demand prorationing are conceptually simple. The state regulatory authority asks each buyer to submit a "nomination" or an estimate of how much crude oil they expect to purchase during the following month. The nominations are then compared with a forecast of demand made by the U.S. government. Inventory levels, imports, and economic conditions are also considered. After the total *market demand at a predetermined price* is calculated, anticipated exempt production is subtracted to determine what the market will "demand" from regulated properties. This is compared with the allowables, and then orders establishing the "percentage of allowable" each may produce are sent to the operators. The terminology is, for example, "wells may produce at 58 percent of allowable," or "100 percent of allowable." This is the mechanism by which oil production has been limited to "market demand" in the United States since 1935.

Origin and Impact of Market Demand Prorationing

Origin

The Problem.   State regulation of oil and gas production is yet another example of how competition among producers leads to cooperation. In this case, the police power of the state and federal governments was used to enforce cooperation. The price and output trends discussed earlier indicate the general nature of the problem as it might be viewed by producers. Prices were low and highly volatile. In fact, the average figures discussed thus far conceal the magnitude of the problem encountered by the most marginal of producers.

Under the rule of capture, without unitization, oil was often produced at such a frantic pace that it was stored above ground or in makeshift tanks. In remote areas where transport costs were relatively high, oil was sometimes sold for as little as 10 cents per barrel. Producers were naturally appalled by these low prices and sought to limit output and thereby maintain prices through cooperative action. The early history of U.S. crude oil production can be written largely in terms of how producers tried to voluntarily limit output in order to maintain prices, how these voluntary agreements broke down, and how compulsory, state and federally enforced market demand prorationing became established. Experience repeatedly demonstrated that voluntary agreements break down when the number of producers is very large. Finally, producers sought to limit output through their own state governments.

Oklahoma Takes the Lead.   The problems of overproduction and physical and economic waste were particularly acute in Oklahoma during the early 1900s when oil was found in unprecedented quantities. In 1905 the Oklahoma legislature responded to producer pressures by passing the most comprehensive conservation measures to that date, including a law which established a price floor, or minimum price, for which oil might be sold. But the price floor was ineffective since there was no mechanism for buying up surplus oil or for preventing its production. The law illustrates a recurrent theme among oil producers: they frequently want minimum prices but few, if any, restrictions on output. Producers accept output restrictions reluctantly and only after years of experience which convinces even the more recalcitrant that prices can be maintained by no other means than limiting production.

In 1915 the rich Cushing field discovery created a severe supply glut. Shortly thereafter, Oklahoma became the first state to enact prorationing. The law provided for the state to restrict private production under three circumstances: (1) when waste was evident in a particular field, (2) when "market demand" was insufficient, and (3) when prices fell below production costs.

The second provision is the most relevant from the standpoint of the history of world petroleum markets. The law was subsequently upheld by the U.S. Supreme Court in Champlin Refining Company *v.* Oklahoma Corporation Commission (1932). The Court ruled that market demand prorationing was a reasonable method of preventing physical waste, and that any effect on price was incidental. The Champlin ruling was made during an era of extraordinarily low prices brought about by the large new fields discovered in Texas during the late 1920s.

Other states were slow to follow the Oklahoma lead on the prorationing issue. The Texas legislature even enacted a law in 1931 which specifically prohibited the Texas Railroad Commission from limiting production *on the basis of insufficient market demand*. The issue had been debated for more than a decade and overproduction and low prices were important problems of the day. In late 1932 the Texas legislature reversed itself on the prorationing issue. The new law did not specifically authorize market demand prorationing, but neither did it restrict the Commission merely to preventing physical waste. Given the persuasions of the regulatory authorities on the Texas Railroad Commission, it effectively brought Texas into the prorationing camp. Kansas adopted the language of the Oklahoma law in 1933 and events were underway which would soon make prorationing nearly universal.

Federal Role.   In late 1933 the Petroleum Code of the National Recovery Administration was written. This code called for market demand prorationing as well as a host of other restrictions on oil production. These included minimum prices and allocation of production among the various states. Section 9(c) of the National Recovery Act (NRA) prohibited interstate shipment of oil produced in violation of state laws. The code even provided for controls on oil imports. Although the NRA was declared unconstitutional in 1935, it strengthened established market demand prorationing programs where they existed while promulgating the practice in important new areas such as California, Louisiana, and New Mexico.

In early 1935 it appeared the NRA would be declared unconstitutional, and Congress moved swiftly to replace its more important features. The Connally "Hot Oil" Act (1935) largely replaced Section 9(c) of the NRA; the Connally Act made the shipment of oil produced in violation of state laws a federal offense. Congress also authorized the states to enter into a "compact" to conserve oil and gas, thus leading to the establishment of the Interstate Oil Compact Commission. The IOCC had no power to determine total demand or distribute production quotas among the states, but it did facilitate communication and promote uniform laws. Each state was free to determine its share of total demand and allocate quotas among its own producers to ensure that production did not exceed self-imposed limits. Subsequent events demonstrate there was tacit cooperation in limiting total output to market demand, especially in the larger producing states such as Texas, Oklahoma, and Louisiana. These states accounted for over 70 percent of U.S. crude oil output during most of the years after 1935. In terms of size and influence on the domestic scene, these states are comparable to Saudi Arabia, Iran, and Kuwait within OPEC. Tacit cooperation among them was sufficient to bring about the relative price stability during the period 1935–1970 as shown by the price trends in Figure 1–3 (page 17).

Early Results of Market Demand Prorationing

The result of market demand prorationing and the Connally Hot Oil Act was to grant the state regulatory authorities control over the level of output and prices. But the price in 1937 was only $1.18/barrel. It contained very little pure economic rent for most producers. Control over the domestic price was at first sufficient to prevent prices from falling but insufficient to bring about a price increase. A notable achievement, and an indicator of the degree of market control, was the reduction in domestic output and the maintenance of prices of over $1 per barrel during the so-called "unrestrained" Illinois oil boom during the period 1937–1940. Production in Illinois was inordinately large for a few years around the late 1930s, averaging 382,000 barrels/day. But Oklahoma reduced production by 200,000 barrels/day and Texas reduced production by another 50,000 barrels/day. Thus, the deleterious effects on prices threatened by the Illinois "Oil Bubble" were largely avoided. Illinois production was effectively "accommodated" by cooperative prorationing. This was the first real test of cooperation among the regulatory authorities in the major producing states. Subsequent events in the 1950s were to show even greater cooperation among them.

World War II

World War II resulted in a more active role for the federal government in oil industry operations and policy. The Office of Price Administration (OPA) was charged with the regulation of oil prices. The problem from the OPA point of view was how to hold prices down to minimize the cost of conducting war. The solutions adopted were price ceilings, direct allocation, and rationing. Petroleum allocation and the coordination of transportation required to deliver oil and petroleum products to strategic locations were vested in the Petroleum Administration for War (PAW). And control over the allocation of materials required to produce and deliver more oil was vested in the War Production Board.

There were obvious jurisdiction problems and inherent conflicts among the federal regulatory authorities. The OPA staunchly favored a crude oil price ceiling comparable to the pre-War level of $1.20/barrel. The PAW was equally adamant that higher prices were needed to stimulate production. In the final analysis, the OPA prevailed and a lid was kept on oil prices for the duration of World War II.

There are many interesting war stories and issues which are important from the standpoint of the history of the U.S. oil industry. But they are mostly incidental to the evolution of OPEC. Perhaps the most germane issue was the close working relationship between U.S. government authorities and oil industry executives. In both World War I and World War II industry executives were brought into government to coordinate and regulate the activities of the industry itself. This often resulted in charges of the "fox in the hen house." Recruiting oil industry executives was a common practice in other consuming countries as well, primarily because the production and distribution of oil requires a high degree of technical skill and few persons outside the industry have the requisite knowledge to operate and/or regulate the industry. The issue of government–industry relations will be discussed at greater length in the following chapter.

Pause

This section is designated "pause," rather than "summary" or "conclusion," because an understanding of the institutions which were in the process of development in the rest of the world prior to 1945 is necessary to comprehend what transpired after World War II. The most important institutional relation which had evolved in the United States was market demand prorationing. The other major institution to be considered in the next chapter is market demand prorationing in the remainder of the world as conducted by the international oil companies. Prorationing in the United States and voluntary prorationing by the companies in the rest of the world played a major role in shaping the events of the 1950s. These events led to the formation of OPEC and will be considered in Chapter 6.

Further Readings

Gale, Thomas A. *The Wonder of the Nineteenth Century, Rock Oil*. Erie: Sloan & Griffeth, Publishers, 1860.

Getty, J. Paul. *My Life and Fortunes*. New York: Duell, Sloan and Pearce, 1963.

McDonald, Stephen. *Petroleum Conservation in the United States: An Economic Analysis*. Baltimore and London: Resources for the Future, Inc., The Johns Hopkins University Press, 1971.

Nash, Gerald. *United States Oil Policy, 1890–1964*. Pittsburgh: University of Pittsburgh Press, 1968.

Nordhauser, Norman E. *The Quest for Stability*. New York and London: Garland Publishing Company, 1979.

Tarbell, Ida. *The History of the Standard Oil Company*. Briefer Version, Ed. David M. Chalmers. New York: W. W. Norton & Company, Inc., 1966.

Williamson, Harold F., and Arnold R. Daum. *The American Petroleum Industry*. 2 vols. Evanston, Ill.: Northwestern University Press, 1959.

World Oil Markets (1870–1945)

Overview.

The Cast of Characters.

United States and Russian Dominance, 1861–1895:
Production and Export Trends; Russia; The United States.

The Eastern Market:
Role of the Dutch; Market Structure; The Asiatic Petroleum Company.

World Oil Markets Prior to 1900:
New York-Plus Base-Point Pricing System; Competition and Cooperation.

World Oil Markets After 1900:
Early Developments in the Middle East; Role of the British; The Turkish Petroleum Company (TPC); The Red-Line Agreement; The As-Is Agreement; Saudi-Arabia and Aramco; Kuwaiti Concessions.

Pause.

READER'S GUIDE TO CHAPTER 5

This chapter presents an analytical history of petroleum markets outside the United States from 1870 to 1945. It explores the institutions peculiar to world oil markets, concession agreements, royalties, renegotiation, expropriation, and cartel arrangements. Emphasis is placed on the geographic distribution of petroleum reserves, the evolving state of knowledge about the value of those reserves, and the resulting interactions among corporate and government officials. The origins of the major international petroleum companies, joint ventures, and major cooperative agreements are traced in detail. These relations, combined with events in the United States during the same period, set the stage for the evolution of OPEC, which will be discussed in Chapter 6.

Overview

The distinguishing characteristic of world as opposed to domestic oil markets is the sheer magnitude of reserves. Non-Western cultural and political institutions are also important, for the interaction among corporate officials, government bureaucrats, and politicians is largely what shapes world oil markets. The historical constant seems to be recurrent competition which leads to cooperation among the principal producers. However, cooperation leads to above-normal returns for those already in the industry and promotes new entry. Entry sooner or later alters established cooperative relations and erodes profits. This results in new efforts to cooperate and maintain prices. The ebb and flow of competition and cooperation is nowhere more evident than in the world petroleum markets prior to 1945.

The principal international cooperative agreements which can be judged successful and enduring include (1) the Red-Line Agreement (1914) and (2) the As-Is Agreement (1928). The former provided the basis for cooperation among the major European and American companies producing in the Middle East, whereas the latter provided for "orderly" marketing of products in the consuming countries. Even before these major alliances were established, there were numerous cooperative arrangements between Standard Oil Company and various Russian, Dutch, and British companies. This chapter outlines these major alliances and explains how they evolved. Since there has never been an international agency to enforce agreements, the cooperative arrangements were voluntary. Government officials and bureaucrats were involved in the process, however, and they often played a decisive role.

The original Red-Line Agreement was made among the leading international oil corporations of British, Dutch, and German national origin, with active encouragement from government authorities in their respective countries. It was designed to ensure that oil from the Middle East would be developed in an "orderly" manner and that the participating corporations would share in the development of all available reserves. The original Red-Line Agreement did not include American interests, but upon the insistence of the State Department the agreement was altered in 1928 to include American companies. An earlier realignment, growing out of hostilities in World War I, had transferred the German interest to the French.

The As-Is Agreement in 1928 involved the three largest companies in a market-sharing pool. The increasing level of known reserves in the United States, Venezuela, and especially the Middle East, made the orderly marketing of products seem imperative to the leading oil companies. During the 1930s three more American companies discovered major fields and grew large enough to warrant tacit inclusion in the As-Is Agreement. The As-Is proved adequate to accommodate new entrants and provided the basis for cooperation for about 25 years. In the 1940s and 1950s OPEC began to emerge and usurp control from the companies; but these developments are the subject of Chapter 6. This chapter deals with the principal countries, companies, and economic events that shaped international oil markets prior to 1945.

The Cast of Characters

The world oil market prior to World War I may be viewed as an extension of oil interests in the major consuming regions, mainly the United States, Russia, Great Britain, Germany, the Netherlands, and France. Western institutions and innovations simultaneously generated a demand for refined petroleum products and rewarded businessmen who could find oil and deliver it to industrial markets.

The principal countries, companies, and individuals involved in the development of world petroleum markets prior to 1920 are shown in Table 5–1. Companies from the United States—mainly Standard Oil Company (New Jersey), which sold kerosene in virtually all countries—were the first to operate on a world scale. Russian producers led by the Swedish Nobel family and the French Rothschild family were the first to provide competition to the Standard. Russian oil wells were more highly productive and the production costs were lower than in the United States, so the Russian producers were able to compete effectively. Had it not been for the labor unrest of 1907 and the Bolshevik revolution of 1917, both of which destroyed much of the Russian refinery capacity, it is probable that Russian companies would have played a more prominent role in the development of world petroleum markets. Names of Russian companies such as Bnito and Branobel might have become as familiar as Exxon, Shell, and British Petroleum.

The British and Dutch proved more enduring competitors by gaining a foothold through commercial shipping interests and by discovering oil in their colonial empires. The British and French first became involved in the oil industry as shippers and traders. Cooperation among several of the leading shippers in a "Tank Syndicate" led to incorporation of the Shell Transport and Trading Company (1897). Operating on a different front, the British-Australian explorer and developer William D'Arcy obtained concessions for the development of oil in Persia (Iran) and Mesopotamia (Iraq) as early as 1902. Dutch efforts to find oil began in the early 1870s but were largely unsuccessful until the 1880s and 1890s. The Royal Dutch Company was established to exploit deposits

TABLE 5–1

Principal Countries, Companies, and Individuals Involved in the Development of the World Petroleum Market Prior to 1945

1860	1870	1880	1890	1900	1910	1920	…	1980[1]

UNITED STATES (1859)

Standard Oil Co. (1872) ----------Standard Oil (New Jersey) (1899) ----------Exxon (1972)
John D. Rockefeller   Walter Teagle

Vacuum USS Oil (1866) ----------Standard Oil (New York) (1882) ----------Socony-Vacuum (1931) ----------Mobil (1966)

SAUDI ARABIA (1933)
Abdul ibn Saud

Standard Oil (California) (1913) ----------SOCAL
Aramco (1944) -Aramco

RUSSIA (1871)
Branobel (1879
Ludwig (influential 1890–1910) and Emanuel Nobel
Caspian and Black Sea Petroleum Company (1883)
French Rothschilds (1892)

GREAT BRITAIN
Tank Syndicate (1870s) ----------Shell Transport and Trading Company (1897)
Frederick Lane   Marcus Samuel
Marcus Samuel

DUTCH in INDONESIA (1884)
Royal Dutch (1890) ----------Royal Dutch-Shell (1911) ----------Shell
William Kessler   Henri Deterding
Henri Deterding

1860	1870	1880	1890	1900	1910	1920	...	1980[1]

GREAT BRITAIN in IRAN and IRAQ
de Reuter Concession (1872)
Baron Julius de Reuter

D'Arcy Concession (1901)
Anglo-Persian (1906)
Anglo-Iranian (1935) ------------- BP (1954)
Sir John Cadman

GERMANY (1900–1910) and FRANCE (1910–1920) in IRAQ
Deutsche Bank (1903)----Compagnie Française des Petroles------CPE (1923)

Anglo-Persian (1906)
Turkish Petroleum Co. (1914)
Iraq Petroleum Co. (1938)
Calouste Gulbenkian (1904)

DUTCH (1915) and UNITED STATES (1920)
in VENEZUELA
Royal Dutch Shell
Creole Oil Co. (1920)

NOTES: The dates included in this chart may be interpreted as follows:
Date after country name: Indicates year oil was first discovered by drilling.
Date after company name: Indicates year company was chartered or incorporated.
Date after concession name: Indicates year concession was granted.
Dashed Line: Indicates acquisition or merger.
[1] Name of company as known in the 1980s.

found in the Dutch East Indies, now Indonesia. The Germans first held interests in Rumania and later in the Middle East. The interplay of companies of these various national origins shaped world petroleum markets prior to 1945 and provided the basis, as well as the model, for the formation of OPEC.

United States and Russian Dominance, 1861–1895

Production and Export Trends

A central factor in understanding the ebb and flow of competition and cooperation in world petroleum markets is the basic availability of crude oil and refined products. The United States dominated production and exports during the period 1861–1895 and Standard Oil held a virtual monopoly in the export of refined products until 1884. The United States accounted for over 90 percent of world oil production until 1875 and for nearly 60 percent until 1890. The only other country with substantial production during this period was Russia (see Table 5–2).

U.S. and Russian producers supplied their respective home markets but also exported substantial quantitites to Western Europe and the Far East. "Case oil," or kerosene, packed in ten-gallon tins, two tins to the case, began to appear on the docks in London, Rotterdam, and Bremen in early 1861. Consumption and importation of case oil increased

TABLE 5–2

Crude Oil Production by Major Countries and Regions, 1860–1895
(million barrels)

Year	United States	Russia	All Other	Total World	Percent Produced by U.S.
1860	0.5	—	—	0.5	98.4
1865	2.5	0.1	0.1	2.7	92.0
1870	5.3	0.2	0.3	5.8	90.7
1875	12.0	0.7	0.5	13.2	91.0
1880	26.3	3.0	0.7	30.0	87.6
1885	21.9	13.9	1.0	36.8	59.5
1890	45.8	28.7	2.2	76.7	59.8
1895	52.9	46.1	4.7	103.7	51.0

SOURCE: American Petroleum Institute. *Petroleum Facts and Figures, 1971 ed.,* Washington, D.C., 1971, pp. 548–553.

throughout Europe by way of established commercial channels and newly established trading companies specializing in oil transport. By 1882 the United States was exporting 51 percent of its output of petroleum products. Most exports were via New York and Philadelphia and under the control of the Standard Oil Company. A similar pattern was beginning to emerge in Russia, where oil was finding its way from the Caspian Sea, up the Volga River, to Baltic ports. When rail connections between Baku and Batum were completed in 1883, the competitive position of Russian producers was greatly enhanced vis-à-vis Standard. The virtual monopoly enjoyed by Standard until 1884 was thus transformed into a duopoly in the late 1880s.

Russia

Discovery.   Oil and natural gas had long been known to exist in Russia along the western coast of the Caspian Sea near Baku (see Figure 5–1). The Caspian region was distinctly Asiatic in character, essentially Persian, and a crossroads of civilizations. Before 1800 control of the region vacillated between the Persians, Turks, and Russians, thus accounting for the polyglot nature of the population. The area came under Russian control in 1801 but remained a problem for the authorities until the Russo-Turkish War of 1877.

The Persians had long used oil for lubrication, illumination, and as a medicine. An active trade with Baku developed early on. Oil was first extracted from man-made pits, packed in small casks, and transported to the consuming regions by camel. In 1735 there were more than 50 oil pits in the region around Baku. By 1849 there were 136, with annual production of about 37,000 barrels; by 1870 there were 415 pits and an annual production of 140,000 barrels. Thus, although oil had been discovered and developed into a commercial activity for quite some time, output remained comparatively small until drilling began in 1871.

The Contract System and Rule of Capture.   The contract system in Baku was similar in its effects to the rule of capture in the United States. Ownership of land and mineral rights resided in the hands of the czar. Under the contract system the government granted a monopoly for exploitation of a specific plot for a period of four years. The contract could be revoked without notice by the czarist administration and there were no options for renewal. Under these circumstances, those working the oil pits were primarily interested in maximizing current production.

In 1872 the Baku administration convinced the czar that the contract system should be replaced by long-term lease arrangements. On January 1, 1873, regulations were released calling for public auction of slightly

FIGURE 5–1
Caspian and Mediterranean Routes to World Oil Markets, 1900

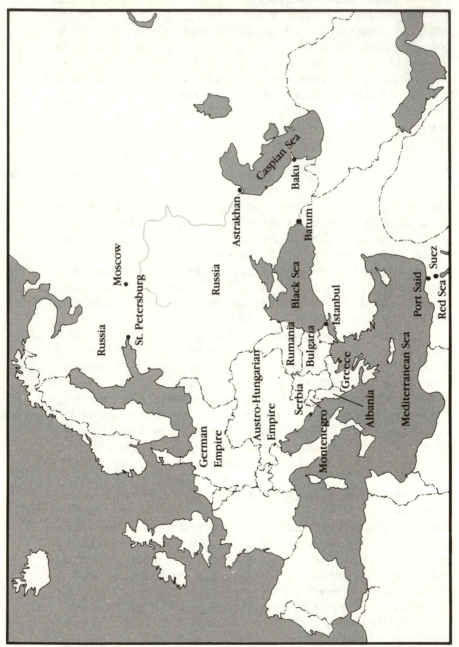

more than two square miles of land around the oil pit regions of Baku. The size of each tract was 1 hectare (2.7 acres), or slightly larger than two football fields. Lease holders were to pay the bid price plus a small rental of 10 rubles per year. In 1897 this royalty fee was increased to 100 rubles per hectare. Within the Baku region the rule of capture prevailed, which, as in the United States, ensured a rapid rate of exploitation and physical waste of the resource. It also meant fluctuations in crude oil prices as new "gushers," or "fountains" as they were called by the Russians, were struck.

The Age of Nobel.   The Nobel name is associated with the famous peace prize made possible by an endowment from Alfred Nobel (1908). But the Nobel family was also an early leader in the Russian petroleum industry, dominating it there almost as completely as the Rockefellers did in the United States. The patriarch, Immanuel Nobel, was a brilliant Swedish inventor, builder, and engineer. Born in Sweden in 1801, his early endeavors were ambitious but doomed to failure. In the late 1820s he obtained contracts to build several bridges and renovate a number of houses. However, when three barges of building materials were lost at sea in 1832 he was forced into bankruptcy. Undaunted, he developed elaborate defense plans based on the tactical principle that mining of harbors with explosives could prevent entry by enemy navies. These plans were rejected by the Swedish government and Immanuel moved to St. Petersburg to seek support for his ideas. About his only successes during the formative stages of his life were his marriage and siring of three offspring, Robert (1829), Ludwig (1831), and Alfred (1833).

Immanuel eventually gained fame in the early 1850s under Czar Nicholas I. During the Crimean War his underwater mines were used to defend key Russian harbors against the British and French. Government contracts for his munitions and machine tools earned him a small fortune as well as the prospect for much more. Immanuel expanded his enterprises at a rapid rate only to find that the new czar, Alexander II, preferred to use government revenues for nonmilitary purposes. Once again he was bankrupt, and he returned to Sweden.

Ludwig Nobel succeeded where his father had failed. He insisted on signed contracts *before* work would be undertaken, refused to become exclusively dependent on government contracts, included an adequate profit on each contract, with an allowance for risk, and otherwise followed prudent business practices. Alfred Nobel was equally successful in his chosen profession. A chemical industrialist, he made his fortune mostly in explosives. Alfred was also a financial expert and served the family in raising money for the numerous projects Ludwig was destined to undertake.

Robert Nobel, the eldest but least successful of the Nobel brothers, led Ludwig into the oil industry. In 1872 Robert was sent by Ludwig to study the manufacture of rifle stocks and to learn the type, source, and handling of wood for that purpose. Robert went to Europe and then to Baku, carrying 25,000 rubles which Ludwig had given him to purchase walnut lumber. What he found in Baku was a bustling Asiatic trading port in the middle of an oil boom. The first oil well had been drilled sometime between 1871 and 1872, and on January 1, 1873, government auctions of oil lands were held. This meant that an abundant amount of oil would be forthcoming from the wellhead and that crude oil acquisition costs would be low.

Robert studied the primitive methods of oil extraction, transport, and refining and made an impulsive decision to buy an oil refinery, using the 25,000 rubles to accomplish that end. Ludwig and Alfred thought it was another of Robert's ill-advised schemes, for he had failed in nearly all previous endeavors. However, they were resigned to the decision. Robert was a good chemist and soon brought his talents to bear on improving the refining process. Within a year he was turning out the best quality kerosene in Baku. In 1875 Ludwig provided him enough money to build the most advanced refinery in Baku. In April, 1876, Ludwig and his 16-year-old son Emanuel took a steamship down the Volga to Baku for a first-hand appraisal of the operation.

After a brief inspection of the region, Ludwig became an enthusiastic and optimistic participant in the oil industry. As an industrialist, he critically examined every phase of the oil industry, and like Rockefeller in the United States, he found that substantial savings could be made in the transport sector. Ludwig methodically began to rationalize the transportation of Russian oil. At the time, oil was carried by "arbas," or hand-driven Persian carts, a distance of eight miles from field to refinery. Ludwig built a five-inch pipeline. But as in Pennsylvania, this endeavor was considered foolish and/or a threat to the producers' livelihood, so Ludwig hired Cossack guards to protect the pipeline. It proved to be a spectacular success. The $50,000 investment required to build the pipeline was repaid in just one year; transport costs were reduced to one-twentieth of their previous level, and other producers soon followed Nobel's lead.

Ludwig pressed on to resolve ever more challenging transport and storage problems. In order to carry oil up the Volga to Russian towns and cities, he commissioned the construction of a "cistern ship." This was the first real oil tanker. It was christened the *Zoroaster* after the ancient fire worshippers in the Baku region. *Zoroaster* went into service in 1879 and was truly revolutionary, resulting in a quantum reduction in transport costs as compared with case oil carried by ordinary ships.

Standard Oil had failed to develop a ship capable of carrying oil in bulk, and many thought Ludwig foolish. They argued that if it were practical, Standard would already be doing it. But Ludwig succeeded again and continued his innovations downstream by constructing railroad tank cars and storage tanks at major terminals.

The work of Ludwig Nobel and of his close associates was as significant for the oil industry as that of Rockefeller and the Standard. Ludwig was responsible for much of the early technical progress which allowed Baku oil to flow up the Volga to Moscow, thence by rail to St. Petersburg, and thus to compete with Standard for world markets. The corporate framework through which these activities took place was the Nobel Brothers Petroleum Production Company, or "Branobel." The distribution network utilizing tankers, rail tank cars, and bulk storage tanks was to serve as a model for the system introduced in other areas of the world, particularly in the Far East.

Russian Competition and Cooperation.   The high rates of return received on Russian petroleum investments naturally attracted competitors. There were many, but the French Rothschilds—Edmond and Alphonse—were the most formidable. The Rothschild name in Europe was synonymous with conglomerate banking, railroads, and large industrial enterprises. There were important contingents of the family in Austria, Paris, and London. The French Rothschilds were oil traders but had to buy kerosene and other refined products from Standard. They entered the Russian petroleum market in 1883 by financing a refinery at Fiume on the Adriatic, and a rail line from Baku to Batum. This rail line was particularly important for world petroleum trade because Baku was landlocked. The Caspian offered water access to Russia via the Volga; but the rest of the Eastern Hemisphere relied on access to oil via the Volga and then overland by rail to the Baltic. Completion of the rail line would permit Russian crude oil and refined products to compete against Standard much more directly via the Black Sea, the Mediterranean, and the Suez Canal.

The rail line was a prodigious undertaking, traversing more than 500 miles of mountainous country. But the effort was well rewarded. Output had increased so rapidly in Baku that oil prices in the early 1880s were substantially below those in the United States, and many Baku refiners were on the verge of bankruptcy. The Rothschilds provided them with financial capital and acquired properties through the Caspian and Black Sea Petroleum Company, or "Bnito," an abbreviation based on the firm's Russian initials. Upon completion of the railway, Bnito became a major competitor of both Branobel and Standard for the Russian and world markets, respectively.

The United States

Independents.   The Standard Oil Company held a virtual refining monopoly in the United States, but it was not without opposition. Attempts had been made as early as 1861 to organize the producers, and there were concerted efforts again in 1873, 1878, and 1884. In all cases the problem was "overproduction" and low prices. By 1883 production had begun to decline in Pennsylvania but was on the increase farther to the west in Ohio. Since the Standard monopoly was based on control of rail and pipeline transportation from fields in Pennsylvania, the westward shift of the center of production was a threat to its established position. As production in Ohio increased at a rapid rate, it had the predictable effect of lowering prices. The producers blamed Standard and again attempted to organize with the express purpose of denying Standard access to crude oil.

The independent oil producers first organized the Producers Oil Company, which bought crude oil at the wellhead for storage. However, their major long-term problem was transportation, or "access" to the coast and to foreign markets. So in 1888 they laid plans for a pipeline. Meanwhile, Standard was trying to buy a controlling interest in the various independent companies. The independents responded by forming a trust, or holding company, chartered in New Jersey and called the Pure Oil Company. Standard and Pure were essentially the only two exporters in the United States until the producers in Texas completed a pipeline to the Gulf of Mexico.

The New York Base-Point Pricing System.   When markets are in the process of becoming well organized, the general terms "competitive" and "monopolistic" lose some of their significance. For instance, a company may have a virtual monopoly in one market but be highly competitive in others. The model which most closely captures conditions in the world oil market prior to 1895 is the *base-point pricing model*, with New York as the base point. Export prices were at first determined by the Standard Oil Company, which had a near monopoly on the export market. The only other export center of any consequence was Batum, from which flowed an increasing volume of Russian oil. The United States and Russia each constituted separate markets. The Balkans were regarded as the local market for a small quantity of Rumanian oil, and the remainder of the world was divided into the Western and Eastern markets. The Western market comprised all the countries in Europe, North and West Africa, and those around the Mediterranean, except for Turkey. The Eastern market extended from Alexandria and Port Said on the Suez to Cape Town at the tip of Africa, east to New Zealand, north past Japan to Vladivostok in Russia, and along a straight line back to the Suez (see Figure 5–2). Turkey remained an area shared by Russian and Rumanian producers in competition with each other.

The Eastern Market
Role of the Dutch

The Netherlands came to play an important role in Eastern markets because of the oil found in the Dutch East Indies (Indonesia) and also because of the efforts of Henri Deterding, who began his career in the East Indies, and who was one of the men primarily responsible for promoting cooperation among producers during the period 1900–1930. A historian for the Royal Dutch Petroleum Company has succinctly stated Deterding's contribution: "Deterding has done for the petroleum industry in the old world what Rockefeller accomplished in the new. He has given to Eastern oil, distributed out of one hand, his own, the mastery over the Eastern market."[1] Cooperation among producers was first accomplished through the Asiatic Petroleum Company, a profit-pooling organization designed to limit output, raise prices, and distribute profits to its members.

Origin of the Royal Dutch.   As early as 1596 a Dutch explorer reported the discovery of a well in Sumatra " . . . from which pure balsam flows." The natives were already using the smelly substance to ignite torches for illumination. But it took another 300 years before a Dutch tobacco planter named Aeilko Zijlker rediscovered the oil and obtained a concession to promote its development. Zijlker was familiar with kerosene, and upon observing the oil seepages in Langkat, Sumatra, he quickly perceived the possibility of a petroleum industry. Like pioneers in other countries, his vision and tenacity were remarkable. In Zijlker's case, it required four years to drill the first well and eight more years before oil was produced in commercial quantities.

The Royal Dutch Company was chartered in 1890 with the express purpose of raising capital to finance construction of a refinery in Langkat. Owing to the isolated nature of the area and the easy sea access, distribution from this refinery was originally intended for the Orient. This put the Dutch in direct competition with both Standard and a British syndicate headed by Marcus Samuel. Langkat's geographic location proved a mixed blessing. On the one hand, drilling and refining equip-

FIGURE 5–2
The Eastern Market according to the Asiatic Contract

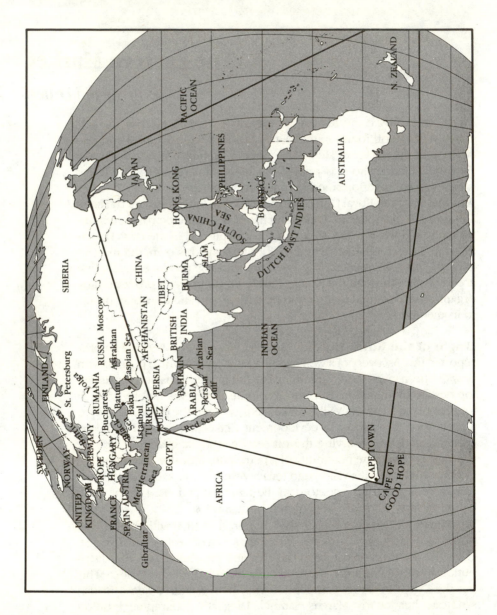

ment had to be transported halfway around the world from Europe and the United States. On the other hand, once the refinery was in place, the proximity to Eastern markets provided an important cost advantage, since Standard's prices were based on New York postings plus shipping costs.

The men primarily responsible for the success of the Royal Dutch Company were William Kessler and Henri Deterding. Kessler's perseverance and attention to costs when establishing the refinery at Langkat helped the Royal Dutch avoid bankruptcy during the critical years from 1892 until his death in 1900. Deterding assumed control upon Kessler's death. At the time he was only 30 years old and in many respects like John D. Rockefeller. He was an intelligent, industrious accountant, always alert for opportunities to cut costs, expand markets, and raise prices. Deterding was willing to compete, but he excelled in his ability to secure cooperation among producers.

Other East Indies Producers. Many independent producing companies were organized in the Dutch East Indies. Most of them were Dutch, but the British also had important interests. Adriaan Stoop founded the Dordrecht Company in heavily populated Java a year before Royal Dutch was founded. The Dordrecht produced for the local Java market. The Moeara Enim, founded in 1897 and headed by Jan IJzerman, was a producing company in Palembang, Sumatra. Like the Royal Dutch, the Moeara Enim produced for the export market. Marcus Samuel, a British subject and head of the Shell Transport and Trading Company, Ltd., held a producing interest in Borneo and sold oil produced by the Moeara Enim in the Eastern market. There were several other Dutch concerns, but these were the early and more important entrants. The reason so many companies were able to operate in the East Indies was that relatively small concessions were granted and also that the concessionaire was required to begin drilling within two years or lose his exclusive rights. Additionally, care was taken to ensure that one company did not obtain territory sufficient to exercise monopoly power.

Market Structure

Principal Actors. Structurally, the Eastern market during the 1890s can be characterized in terms of the important influence the oil-producing companies had over production, refining, transportation, and marketing. Oil for the Eastern market came from New York, Philadelphia, Baku via Batum, Sumatra, and Borneo. These were the only sources of oil at the time. Standard was by far the largest exporter and sold worldwide, but the Pure Company made significant inroads during the

1890s. Nobel and Rothschild sold products directly on the Western market, but Russian output was limited by a state monopoly of the Caucasian Railroad. Shell Transport and Trading, Royal Dutch, and several smaller transport concerns bought oil from Rothschild and Nobel at Batum for distribution on the Eastern market. These companies also operated in the East Indies as producers and transporters.

Product Characteristics.   The crude oils produced in the United States, Baku, Sumatra, and Borneo were not identical in quality. This had particularly important consequences around the turn of the century. Oil from Borneo and Baku yielded a large fraction of fuel oil, whereas oil from Sumatra and the United States was lighter and yielded illuminating oil and gasoline. Gasoline from the first refinery runs at Langkat was a waste product which was burned because of inadequate demand—a practice that was greatly altered with the introduction of the internal combustion engine. The use of fuel oil was pioneered in Russia by the Nobels using a revolutionary engine developed by a German, Rudolf Diesel. As Diesel's technology spread worldwide, fuel oil (or "diesel" fuel) became a substitute for coal. Increasingly, within a short span of time around the turn of the century, steamships, naval vessels, and industrial equipment were being powered by diesel engines. By the 1930s and 1940s the railroads were converted to run on diesel fuel, and, later, agricultural equipment was similarly converted.

A significant result of such changes in end usage was that the demand for crude oil was no longer based solely on the demand for lamp oil and lubricating oils. Oil was rapidly becoming a source of energy as well as of illumination. There was no longer a single market but many markets. Gasolines of various grades, light fuel oil, heavy fuel oil, and other oil derivatives each, in many respects, constituted a separate market. Oil was made even less a homogeneous product by the fact that different crude oils yielded different fractions of the various end products. This greatly complicated the market structure.

It was generally conceded that Standard produced the highest quality lamp oil and could obtain a premium price. Russian lamp oil varied considerably in quality and was sold at discount prices, mainly to the poor. Thus, there was slight product differentiation and segmentation of the market, which helps explain why Standard was able to compete worldwide even though transport costs greatly favored Russian and East Indian producers in Eastern markets.

Transport Costs.   Transport costs were typically as large as or larger than crude oil acquisition costs. The cheapest form of land transport was by pipeline. The East Coast of the United States was served by both pipeline and rail, but Batum was served only by rail, which greatly increased its costs. In addition, state ownership of the Trans-Caucasian Railroad resulted in very high freight rates. In effect, the Russians followed policies which resulted in their gaining most of the difference between product prices in the principal European markets and prices in Baku. However, Russian products were still priced lower than American products in Eastern markets.

A complicating factor was that the Trans-Caucasian Railroad was not always reliable, and storage facilities were inadequate to smooth fluctuations in delivery. Consequently, Batum would either be "awash in oil" with prices plunging downward or in extremely short supply with prices increasing sharply. The uncertainty created by uneven deliveries made the transport and distribution of oil a hazardous business. In these early days there were only a few people who had sufficient breadth of industry knowledge to grasp the situation and understand the problem. Fewer still had a solution.

The Asiatic Petroleum Company

The Problem.   The increased level of competition and price instability led producers, refiners, and those engaged in transportation to seek cooperation in the distribution of their products. Producers gradually learned the hazards associated with reliance on a single oil field, one transport company, or a single market. The companies which survived were those willing to expand production, develop their own transport network, and spread into many markets. They frequently accomplished their expansion plans by acquisition of smaller companies or by merger. One of the more interesting developments in the Eastern market was the formation of the Asiatic Petroleum Company. It is a classic example of a joint sales organization, or profit-pooling cartel.

The Asiatic was formed in response to the low and unstable pricing pattern which evolved after the spring of 1900. The low prices resulted from both supply and demand conditions. The Boer War and other military actions restricted demand in war-torn areas, and high levels of output in Russia, the United States, and the East Indies greatly aggravated the problem. It became increasingly evident to Deterding and other leaders in the Eastern market that cooperation would better serve their ends. Deterding outlined the basic problem to Frederick (Shady) Lane, an English oil broker and merchant. The problem was how to limit output to maintain prices. Deterding and Lane correctly perceived that control over production must reside in the hands of one man and that either tacit or explicit agreements had to be made with the American, Russian, and Dutch producers.

Cooperation in Eastern Markets.   More than three years were required to negotiate contracts to establish the Asiatic Petroleum Company; but it was finally organized on June 27, 1902. Deterding took the lead in organizing the Committee of Netherlands Indian Producers, whose function was to proration oil produced in the Dutch colonies. Rothschild worked out an agreement with three of the large Baku producers for the consignment of their oil to Bnito. These were the Dutch and Russian "producing" companies. As producers, Royal Dutch and Shell belonged to the Committee of Netherlands Indian Producers. They were also principal shareholders of the Asiatic Petroleum Company. Each agreed to lease their transport, tank, and distribution equipment to Asiatic for a yearly reimbursement of 10 percent of cost. Shell and Royal Dutch thereby relinquished their sales in the Eastern market to the Asiatic. Expansion of facilities was to take place on the same purchase–lease basis.

Exclusive territories were established: Asiatic agreed to sell only on the Eastern market and only oil supplied by Russian and East Indian producers. The Russian and East Indian producers agreed not to sell on the Eastern market in competition with Asiatic and to sell gasoline and kerosene on the Western market only through Asiatic.

The mechanism of control was a form of prorationing. Asiatic estimated consumption for the following year and assigned quotas to East Indian producers according to an agreed formula. The remainder was to be bought from Bnito. If other Russian producers sold on the Eastern market, the share of Bnito was to be reduced accordingly. Bnito was thereby responsible for organizing the Russian producers and bringing them into the fold and for keeping newcomers out or suffering the consequences in the form of reduced sales.

Asiatic's profits were distributed to the producers and shareholders also according to an agreed formula. Ownership of Asiatic was in the hands of Royal Dutch, Bnito, and Shell, each with a one-third share. Payment to the producers was made in two parts: A basic price approximately equal to the cost of the product was paid within three months of delivery, and the second payment, amounting to 75 percent of Asiatic's profits, was distributed annually. Distribution of profits among producers was based on the volume of product supplied—an amount which had been prorated in a prior agreement. Shell, Royal Dutch, and Bnito received the remaining 25 percent share of profits, which was distributed equally among them.

These agreements greatly enhanced the profits of all concerned and provided the basic framework for distribution within the Eastern market until World War I. Nevertheless, new production in both the United States and the Middle East resulted in a number of price wars as newcomers were successful in entering the market. The fields in Oklahoma,

Texas, and the Middle East were to prove far too productive for Asiatic to survive indefinitely. One of the more enduring results, however, was the merger of Royal Dutch and Shell in 1911.

World Oil Markets Prior to 1900

New York-Plus Base-Point Pricing System

Prior to 1880, the price of lamp oil all over the world was determined by its price in New York. This price was based on high crude oil acquisition costs in the United States (as compared with those in Russia), the low costs of refining and transportation, and an element of monopoly profit. It was a classic example of a base-point pricing system. The development of the New York-Plus system, illustrated in Figure 5–3, exemplifies how a base-point pricing system arises naturally in an emergent market.

The price in New York, P_N, consists of crude oil acquisition, refinery, and transport costs, as well as pure economic profit. Prices at all points

FIGURE 5–3
The New York-Plus Base-Point Pricing System

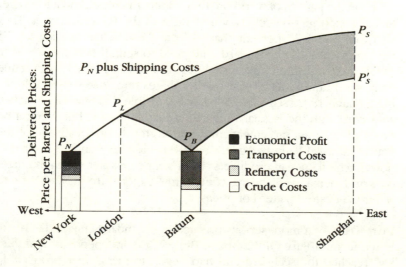

east of New York are shown by the price trajectory $P_N P_L P_S$. Crude acquisition costs were relatively low in Baku, whereas refinery costs were comparable to those in New York. However, the railway linking Baku and Batum was run as a state monopoly, and freight rates were set to capture most of the economic profit attributable to the low costs of crude acquisition.

If the world had been as depicted in Figure 5–3, and production outside the United States had been purely competitive, the relevant world prices would have been $P_N P_L P_B P'_S$. Standard would have driven out Russian companies from all points west of London and the Russians would have dominated to the east of London. This scenario assumes production and transport facilities from Baku as sufficient to supply all markets to the east formerly served by Standard—a situation that clearly was not the case. Relatively small suppliers confronting a giant such as Standard, and having a relatively favorable geographic position, were able to price their products equal to or just below those quoted by Standard. As long as the inroads made by small producers were not too great it paid Standard to maintain prices. Thus, the price pattern depicted by $P_N P_L P_S$ prevailed in the Eastern market prior to 1890, and economic rent as indicated by the shaded areas, accrued to producers in the United States, Russia, and the East Indies.

Competition and Cooperation

Russia.   The entry of Russian oil through Batum had a profound effect on the pattern of world oil trade. Bnito, Branobel, and a few other Russian exporters quickly captured most of the Eastern market. They also captured a 27 percent share of the Western market, leaving 73 percent for Standard. Standard continued to sell all over the world in more limited quantities because they produced a superior product and there was brand loyalty. These market shares remained remarkably stable through 1892 (see Table 5–3). It is possible that Standard reached an accord with the Russians regarding market shares, but there is no proof of such an agreement. In addition, the limited capacity of the Trans-Caucasian Railway made it relatively easy for Standard to predict how much oil Russian producers could bring to market. Given estimates of world demand, Standard could limit exports from New York to achieve a desired pattern of prices.

Pure Oil.   A more serious problem for Standard emerged at home in the form of Pure Oil Company. By 1892 the independents and Pure had reached the seaboard and had begun to bring their products to world markets. Standard's first reaction was to maintain its prices, which

TABLE 5–3
Oil Exports as a Percent of the Total Western Market
1888–1895

Year	United States	Russia
1888	73	27
1889	73	27
1890	73	27
1891	72	28
1892	73	27
1893	76	24
1894	78	22
1895	79	21

SOURCE: F. C. Gerretson, *History of the Royal Dutch*, Leiden, Neth.: Royal Dutch Petroleum, 1955, II, 34.

caused a loss of market share as it was everywhere undercut by Pure companies. Pure supplanted not only Standard but Russian producers as well. The increasing market share of the United States after 1892 is attributable to independents operating through the Pure Oil Trust.

In October, 1893, representatives of Rothschild, Nobel, and Rockefeller met in Paris to negotiate an agreement. The Russians stipulated that the American independents should be brought into an alliance, but the independents simply would not cooperate. Standard had no way to control the independents except by a price war. In the autumn of 1894 Standard started a price war by dramatically lowering prices in New York. The result was lower prices worldwide, which inflicted great harm on foreign as well as domestic producers. Nevertheless, by about 1895, largely because of entry by the American independents and the Russians, the Standard monopoly was badly crippled if not broken.

World Oil Markets After 1900

Early Developments in the Middle East

Institutions.   With few exceptions the institutions in Middle Eastern countries such as Iran and Iraq took exactly the opposite form from those in the United States, Russia, and the East Indies. The former were characterized by despotic rulers, ultimate ownership of land in the hands of a single individual, low levels of literacy, very little knowledge of the outside world, and archaic methods of production. These institutions effectively retarded the exploitation of hydrocarbon deposits until British, Dutch, German, French, and American adventurers arrived in their lands.

Iran, known as Persia until 1935, provides an illustration of despotic rule and Western influence. It is also important because it was the first Middle Eastern country to develop its oil reserves. The primary social and economic groups were the peasants, landlords, merchants, religious hierarchy, and nomadic tribes. The peasant farmers were legally free but practically bound to the soil. The landlords lived in the larger cities, leaving the management and collection of rents to their stewards. The shah derived his revenue from the landlords and was the ultimate owner of the land. When the needs of the treasury or maintenance of power demanded it, the shah confiscated lands and redistributed income according to his personal desires.

The bazaar, or merchant class, represented the group most nearly comparable to the Western middle class, but this group remained small and lacked political influence. The religious hierarchy consisted of two groups: the *mujtahids*, who were learned in philosophy, literature, and religious law and held in esteem by the upper classes; and the mullahs, who were less learned and cultured but esteemed by the masses. This religious schism is still evident in Iran, Iraq, and other Middle Eastern countries. The nomadic tribes constituted about one-fourth of the population but were isolated from the remaining inhabitants. They lived in the mountain ranges along the eastern and western borders and perceived themselves to be independent from the shah and, especially, under no obligation to pay taxes.

Role of the British

The de Reuter Concession.　　Rulers need money to expand, to protect, and to enjoy the fruits of their empire. The shah of Persia in the early 1870s, Nasir ed-Din Shah, was no exception, and he looked with increasing favor on concessions as a means to augment the royal treasury. In 1872, Baron Julius de Reuter, a naturalized British subject, approached the shah with a remarkable proposition. Baron de Reuter agreed to exploit all the mineral resources in Persia, construct and operate all railroads and telegraphs, exploit the government forests, and collect all customs duties. He was also to have an option to form enterprises connected with the construction of roads, mills, factories, and public works of all kinds.

The shah agreed to de Reuter's proposal but excluded gold, silver, and precious stones from the concession. In return, the shah was to receive £40,000 plus 20 percent of the profit on the railways and 15 percent of the profit from all other enterprises. Thus, history recorded the famous *de Reuter concession*. According to Lord Curzon, the concession represented "... the most complete and extraordinary surrender of the entire industrial resources of a kingdom into foreign hands that has probably ever been dreamt of, much less accomplished in history."[2]

The fate of the de Reuter concession was to become prophetic of most concessionary arrangements. News of the "amazing document" fell like a bombshell on Europe.

> According to Curzon, the British government, aware of the political complications likely to arise from the exercise of such an all-inclusive monopoly by one of its subjects, received the scheme coldly. Russian reaction was more positive and hostile, so menacing in fact that the Shah on his return to Persia cancelled the concession and confiscated de Reuter's £40,000 deposit.[3]

In a nutshell, efforts to discover oil in Persia began early but were unsuccessful until the 1900s.

Origin of British Petroleum (BP).   Although the British were latecomers to the production of crude oil, they played an important role during the twentieth century. In 1901, William D'Arcy, an Australian and British businessman, was granted a 60-year concession which covered the whole of Iran except for five provinces along the Russian border. The area was as large as France and Germany combined. It required seven years of exploration and drilling before oil was finally discovered near an ancient fire temple known as the "Mosque of Solomon." The well was located in what has become the prolific oil producing region in southwest Iran near Abadan.

The search for oil is an expensive proposition, and when, by 1905, D'Arcy's financial resources were almost depleted, the British Admiralty helped him gain additional financing through the Burmah Oil Company. After oil was discovered, the Anglo-Persian Oil Company was formed (April 14, 1909) to exploit the finds. The company started with a captial stock of £2,000,000. It was jointly owned by D'Arcy, the Burmah Oil Company, and the public. Almost from the beginning, military support was required to protect both the drilling crews and the facilities from local inhabitants. But by 1912 a refinery was constructed at Abadan on the Persian Gulf, complete with a pipeline connecting it to the producing field.

---

[2]George W. Stocking, *Middle East Oil* (Kingsport: Vanderbilt Univ. Press, 1970), p. 7.
[3]Ibid.

The British Admiralty, and particularly Winston Churchill, maintained an interest in Anglo-Persian because they viewed the Middle East as a reliable and inexpensive source of oil. In 1914 the British Admiralty was just completing the transition of its navy from coal to oil. Churchill advocated government purchase of a controlling interest in Anglo-Persian, and on June 17, 1914, the issue was debated in the House of Commons. The agreement to purchase Anglo-Persian placed the British government in the unique position of being the company's largest shareholder and (as purchaser of oil for the navy) its principal customer.

Anglo-Persian thus gained (1) financial resources to expand its operations, (2) greater certainty that the British government would defend its interests, and (3) an assured outlet for its production. The purchase price of Anglo-Persian was £2.2 million. By 1923 Churchill figured the government had already saved £40 million resulting from dividends and lower prices of oil purchased for the navy. In 1935, when Persia became Iran, the company's name was changed to the Anglo-Iranian Oil Company; and in 1954 its name was changed again to British Petroleum (BP), reflecting the fact that its Iranian concessions had been nationalized.

Renegotiation.   During World War I the Turks severed one of Anglo-Persian's pipelines. This set off a controversy concerning who should assume financial responsibility, the company or the Persian government. An agreement providing compensation for Anglo-Persian was reached in 1919, but Reza Shah Pahlavi repudiated the agreement when he assumed power in 1921. There were a string of controversies throughout the 1920s between the Pahlevi regime and the British, involving adequacy of payments, accounting procedures, and the pace of oil development. Finally, in 1932 the original D'Arcy concession was renegotiated.

The Persian government contended that the company had limited its exploitation to about 1 square mile, when the concession covered 500,000 square miles. In addition, the Persian government had no control or oversight over expenses charged against gross income, so the royalty of 16 percent on *net income* had little validity. The British defended their position but negotiated a new contract which became effective in 1933. The new concession was to run 60 years; the concession area was reduced from 500,000 to 100,000 square miles; the company was required to provide all technical information to the government; and a Persian representative would be allowed to participate in meetings of the board of directors. The last two provisions were important in that they enhanced Persians' knowledge about the conduct of oil affairs.

Fixed Royalties per Ton.   An important change was made in royalty payments, from a profit share of 16 percent of net revenue to a fixed royalty per ton. Anglo-Persian was obligated to pay four shillings per ton of oil produced in Persia. This seemingly innocuous provision was to become important because it divorced government receipts from the market price. Government revenues would henceforth depend only on quantity, whereas company profits, of course, would depend on market prices and costs as well as quantity. The fixed royalty per ton therefore created an inherent conflict of interest between the company and the host government. This was a factor instrumental in the nationalization of the Iranian oil industry in 1951.

The Turkish Petroleum Company (TPC)

Background.   The sacred fires and oil seepages in the Kirkuk area of northern Mesopotamia (Iraq) provided a hint of the rich reserves lying below, and there was intense interest in the area. Between 1900 and 1910, German, Dutch, British, and American groups each obtained oil concessions through negotiations with various Turkish authorities. The man most responsible for the particular course of petroleum development in Iraq, however, was an Armenian, Calouste Gulbenkian, known as "Mr. Five Percenter," a name derived from his share in the Turkish Petroleum Company (TPC). Gulbenkian and his father before him had studied the commercial possibilities for oil in the Turkish empire for many years, but it was Calouste who wrote up the comprehensive geological report in 1904.

Based on this report the Deutsche Bank secured mineral rights to a 40-kilometer strip traversing a proposed rail line between Baghdad and Mosul. After two years of exploration the German concession was cancelled and William D'Arcy began negotiations for the tract. Before these negotiations were completed, the Young Turk Rebellion brought a new group into power and the D'Arcy claims were taken over by Anglo-Persian. Meanwhile, the Royal Dutch-Shell group had formed the Anglo-Saxon Oil Company and enlisted the support of Gulbenkian in obtaining a concession. In 1910 an American rear admiral, Colby Chester, entered into agreements similar to those of the Deutsche Bank, but the Turco-Italian and Balkan wars prevented the Turkish parliament from acting upon them. Thus, there was intense competition and considerable vacillation in obtaining concessions.

Formation of TPC.   In 1912 a German-born English banker named
Ernest Cassel formed the Turkish Petroleum Company (TPC) to unite
European interests in obtaining the Mesopotamian concessions. After
two years of negotiations TPC was formed with Anglo-Persian (BP) in
control of 47½ percent of the stock, Anglo-Saxon (Royal Dutch-Shell)
with 22¼ percent, Deutsche Bank (German) with 25 percent, and Gulbenkian with 5 percent. Gulbenkian's voting rights were split evenly
between Anglo-Persian and Anglo-Saxon. This agreement was concluded
on March 19, 1914, at the British Foreign Office in London. On June 28,
1914, the Grand Vizier of Mesopotamia, Said Halim, communicated his
consent to lease a region between Baghdad and Mosul to TPC.

The Red-Line Agreement

One of the more important provisions of the agreement forming TPC
was the so-called *self-denying clause*. Paragraph 10 read:

> The three groups participating in the Turkish Petroleum Company
> . . . [agree] *not to be interested directly or indirectly in the production
> or manufacture of crude oil in the Ottoman Empire in Europe and
> Asia*, except in that part which is under the administration of the Egyp-
> tian Government or of the Sheikh of Koweit or in the "transferred ter-
> ritories" on the Turco-Persian frontier, *otherwise than through the
> Turkish Petroleum Company*. (*Foreign Relations*, II, 1927, 821–822)

According to Henri Deterding, the signers marked off the designated area on a map with a large red pencil, hence the name Red-Line
Agreement. The self-denying principle welded together the major European oil companies in the exploitation of those Middle Eastern oil
reserves known to exist in 1914. Because of its 50 percent voting rights,
control was effectively in the hands of one country—Great Britain—and
one company—Anglo-Persian. Anglo-Persian was also in sole control of
Persian oil reserves.

Effect of World War I.   World War I postponed development of oil
in the region but strengthened British control over TPC. In December,
1918, the Deutsche Bank's 25 percent interest in TPC was placed in the
hands of a British trustee, thus giving Great Britain voting rights over 75
percent of the stock. In addition, the head of Royal Dutch-Shell, Henri
Deterding, had become a naturalized citizen in 1915 and was knighted
for his services to the British government during the war. Deterding
would have posed no threat to cooperation and limitation of output
even if he had been in control. He favored cooperation over competition
and perceived the problem of oil markets as that of having too much
production rather than too little. After the war the German interest in

TPC was transferred to the French, but control remained in the hands of the British. However, the important consideration was that the French adopted the self-denying principle of the Red-Line Agreement.

Open-Door Policy.   The British and French had been allies during World War I, and they were extraordinarily influential in European and Middle Eastern affairs thereafter. In April, 1920, the Allied Supreme Council appointed Great Britain as the "mandatory" over Iraq and Palestine. France was given a mandate over Syria and Lebanon. The mandatory was required to act as a guardian over the mandated state and to guide it toward independent statehood. Under League of Nation rules the mandatory was required to maintain an *open door* with regard to commercial matters. In particular, concessions for the development of oil and other natural resources were to be granted without distinction to nationality and without monopolization.

The open-door policy of the mandatory was in direct conflict with the principles outlined in the Red-Line Agreement, and the U.S. State Department insisted on an open door for U.S. companies. Seven American companies—Standard of New Jersey, Socony-Vacuum, Texaco, Gulf, Standard of Indiana, Atlantic, and Sinclair—were interested in obtaining concessions in the mandated territory. However, in 1922, with the assistance of the State Department, a decision was made to cooperate with foreign concerns through TPC rather than to openly compete with them. This meant that the Americans would be required to adopt the self-denying principle of the Red-Line Agreement.

The seven American companies listed above began negotiating with Anglo-Persian for participation in TPC in 1922. These negotiations extended over six years and an agreement was finally signed on July 31, 1928. It provided for joint and equal ownership by Anglo-Persian (BP), Anglo-Saxon (Shell), Compagnie Française des Petroles (French-owned), and the American group, called the Near East Development Company. Gulbenkian was to retain his 5 percent beneficial interest. By the time negotiations were completed, Texaco and Sinclair had withdrawn and the joint venture was owned by only five American corporations. Anglo-Persian insisted that each company agree to the self-denying clause which provided that cooperation in the development of Middle Eastern reserves take place only through TPC. Standard of New Jersey and Socony Vacuum later bought out the interests of the other American companies, primarily because the self-denying principle proved too restrictive for the latter. Thus, Jersey Standard (now Exxon), Socony (now Mobil), Anglo-Persian (now BP), Shell, and the French CFP were bound together in TPC. And TPC, owned by the five largest oil companies in the world, became a joint venture for the exploration and development of Middle Eastern reserves.

The As-Is Agreement

Origin. The principal problems during the 1920s, as perceived by the companies, were "excessive competition in marketing," "overproduction," and "low prices." In September, 1928, Sir Henri Deterding hosted a grouse-shooting party for two leading oil company executives and their wives at his castle in Achnacarry, England. Walter Teagle of Jersey Standard and Sir John Cadman of Anglo-Persian were the guests. The problems of overproduction, low prices, and market shares were naturally discussed at great length. A document, variously called the "As-Is" or Achnacarry Agreement emerged from the meeting. The title on the document was simply "Pool Association," which accurately describes the nature of the agreement. It was a market sharing cartel arrangement for the distribution of petroleum products. In some respects it resembled the Asiatic Petroleum Company agreements, but the As-Is encompassed the whole world.

Major Provisions. After citing the need to conserve petroleum resources, the difficulties involved in voluntary prorationing, and the undesirable effects of competition, the document outlined seven general principles for the marketing of petroleum products:

1. To accept and maintain the *status quo* with respect to share of the market.
2. To rent or lease existing facilities from one another at cost.
3. To add new facilities only to supply increases in total demand.
4. To produce in areas close to consuming regions.
5. To minimize transport costs by purchasing from the nearest producing area.
6. To proration in each geographic area in order to maintain prices and either shut-in or offer "surplus" production at discounted prices to other members of the pool so as not to disrupt prorationing in other markets.
7. To minimize costs in providing oil at established prices.

The overall effect of the agreement was to maintain the prices and the market shares of the three international majors now known as Exxon, BP, and Shell.

National Cartels. The As-Is Agreement provided the framework within which national cartels could be organized. During subsequent years, in Great Britain, France, Germany, Sweden, the Eastern market, and most other countries outside the United States, agreements implementing the general principles of the As-Is were reached. In Great Britain, for example, subsidiaries of the majors agreed on selling prices, number of pump installations, and quotas. They even secured an agreement with the Russians fixing their share of the British market.

Quotas naturally gave rise to the problem of "overtrading" and "undertrading." Overtrading, which resulted in merger or in the financial ruin of an outsider to the cartel agreement, was rewarded by giving the "competitive" cartel member any market share it captured. Similarly, when an outsider captured part of an insider's market, the insider's company was penalized by loss of that share. This encouraged cooperation among insiders to protect established markets and to seek new outlets by merger, predatory pricing, or outright competition against outsiders. A cartel, like competition, is a delicate flower which will wither and die if not diligently protected from newcomers.

The cooperating companies met frequently to develop and preserve the cartel arrangements. In Sweden, government investigators found that the companies met on the average of once each week during the period 1937–1939 for the purpose of discussing hundreds of separate issues, including prices, quotas, market shares, new entrants, supply disruptions, and so on.

Saudi Arabia and Aramco

Early Development.   The Arabian Peninsula occupies over a million square miles of land, about one-third the area of the United States. It has always been desolate and sparsely populated, so the Arabian sheiks, or rulers of nomadic tribes, have traditionally been more interested in water than in oil. Because they also coveted gold and precious stones, they welcomed British and American oilmen who were willing to pay gold for the right to explore for and extract oil. Oil development came late in Arabia because there were few outward appearances of oil in the region. The geological traps were so ideally structured that they allowed almost no oil or natural gas to escape and cause the oil seepages and "eternal flames" so prevalent in regions that have proven less prolific. This fact and the extremely inhospitable Arabian terrain and climate explain why oil exploration was delayed until the 1920s.

The man most responsible for the discovery of oil in Arabia was Major Frank Holmes, a New Zealand adventurer and developer. Anglo-Persian officials had shown little interest in the region because there were no "oil shows," so the area was open for individuals more venturesome and less averse to risk. In May, 1923, Holmes obtained a concession for his company, the Eastern and General Syndicate, from Abdul al-Aziz ibn Saud, to explore and develop the oil resources in the al Hasa province in the eastern part of Arabia. Abdul ibn Saud later consolidated the warring tribes in Arabia and in 1932 assumed the title of King of Saudi Arabia.

Abdul ibn Saud was truly the father of his country, since subsequent leaders of Saudi Arabia have been his direct blood descendants. His exploits in the boudoir are almost as famous as those on the battle field. Holmes was less fortunate than ibn Saud, as his concession lapsed a decade before oil was discovered. However, Holmes had faith that oil would be found in Arabia, and in 1925 obtained a concession from the sheik of Bahrain, a small island in the Persian Gulf. The Eastern Syndicate had little money and Holmes continually tried to interest the major oil companies in buying his concessions or forming joint ventures. His efforts were finally rewarded in November, 1927, when the Gulf Oil Corporation purchased options to buy the Eastern Syndicate's interest in Bahrain, the al Hasa concession in Arabia, rights to a concession Holmes was negotiating in Kuwait, and rights to a concession in the Neutral Zone between Kuwait and Arabia.

When Gulf decided to exercise its option on the Bahrain concession, company officials were reminded that membership in the Red-Line Agreement required joint development through the Turkish Petroleum Company or, at least, consent by TPC. TPC refused to participate but demanded a share of any oil Gulf might produce. Gulf found these terms unacceptable and sold its Bahrain option to Standard Oil Company of California (Socal), a company not subject to the Red-Line Agreement. Socal began drilling in October, 1931, and struck oil on May 31, 1932, at a depth of 2,000 to 2,500 feet.

Encouraged by its sucess in Bahrain, Socal set about obtaining concessionary rights to additional territory in Saudi Arabia. The Turkish Petroleum Company had by then become the Iraq Petroleum Company (IPC), and was again brought into the bidding. An important provision from the standpoint of King ibn Saud was an advance payment against future royalties amounting to $480,000. Socal was willing to make the advance in gold and obtained the al Hasa concession on May 19, 1933. Drilling began in August, 1933, but oil in commercial quantities was not discovered until March 5, 1938. Then the lid was off.

Aramco.   Even before the prolific fields of Saudi Arabia were tapped, Socal was concerned about finding an outlet for its Bahrain production. Socal was primarily a producing company and needed marketing facilities to dispose of its prolific find without upsetting established markets (that is, without depressing prices). A joint venture with Texas Oil Company (Texaco) provided an interim solution. Socal and Texaco retained their independence by forming two jointly owned companies, the California Arabian Standard Oil Company (Casoc) and California Texas Oil Company, Ltd. (Caltex). The latter was a marketing concern formed largely out of Texaco's marketing companies. Casoc consisted of Socal's producing interests in Bahrain and Saudi Arabia. Casoc was the immediate forerunner of the Arabian American Oil Company (Aramco), formed on January 31, 1944.

New Partners in Aramco.   World War II retarded development of Aramco's super-giant fields by perhaps five years. However, by the end of the war there had been sufficient exploratory drilling for the company to be aware that finding additional marketing outlets was imperative if "price wars" were to be avoided. Negotiations for joint participation in Aramco by Standard Oil of New Jersey and Socony-Vacuum began in 1944. These companies were to provide Aramco money for drilling, pipeline construction, and the development of refining, storage, and marketing facilities. They were also to buy crude oil directly for refining and marketing in their own distribution channels. In exchange, Jersey Standard acquired a 30 percent share of Aramco and Socony-Vacuum a 10 percent share. Socal and Texaco each retained a 30 percent interest. The deal was finally consummated on December 2, 1948.

End of the Red-Line Agreement.   One reason negotiations for the purchase of shares in Aramco required several years was the existence of the Red-Line Agreement and the self-denying clause. In October, 1946, Jersey Standard and Socony, who were parties to the agreement, declared they were no longer bound by the Red Line. Gulbenkian and Compagnie Française des Petroles brought suit in a British court insisting that if Jersey and Socony participated in Aramco they too were entitled to a share by virtue of the self-denying clause. Ironically, Jersey and Socony filed a countersuit declaring the Red-Line Agreement was "in restraint of trade" and therefore unenforceable by law. This split among the cooperating companies put an end to the Red-Line Agreement.

Kuwaiti Concessions

The development of oil in Kuwait provides an interesting story of competition, political influence, and cooperation. Kuwait exhibited many of the same characteristics as Arabia and was under the mandate of Great Britain. Gulf Oil began negotiations for a concession in Kuwait as early as 1928. The British Colonial Office at first insisted on a "nationality clause," which, in effect, was intended to prevent anyone except a British firm from obtaining a concession in the area. Anglo-Persian had previously declared it was not interested, but Gulf's overtures caused it to reassess the situation. As negotiations dragged on, Gulf and Anglo-Persian formed a joint venture, the Kuwait Oil Company, Ltd., and finally obtained a concession on December 23, 1934. Although each company held a 50 percent interest, Anglo-Persian was in control. Anglo-Persian and Gulf each agreed not to upset or injure the marketing position of the other "directly or indirectly at any time or any place." In effect, Gulf was made a party to the cooperative agreements pursued so long by Anglo-Persian. The prolific fields of Kuwait were therefore developed at a pace consistent with the desires of Anglo-Persian.

Pause

The era of cooperation among the international majors extends beyond the Red-Line and As-Is agreements. By the end of World War II there were seven international majors. These companies would eventually become known as Exxon, Mobil, Texaco, Socal, Gulf, Shell, and BP. Exxon, Shell, and BP were the giants then and now. These seven, along with Compagnie Française des Petroles, operating through numerous subsidiaries and jointly held companies, and under the general principles which evolved from the Red-Line and As-Is agreements, dominated world oil production and marketing even beyond 1945.

Further Readings

Deterding, Sir Henry. *An International Oilman*. London: Butler & Tanner Ltd., 1934.

Engler, Robert. *The Politics of Oil*. New York: Macmillan, 1961.

Gerretson, F. C. *History of the Royal Dutch*. 4 vols. Leiden, Neth.: Royal Dutch Petroleum Company, 1953–1957.

Nash, Gerald D. *United States Oil Policy, 1890–1964*. Pittsburgh: University of Pittsburgh Press, 1968.

Stocking, George W. *Middle East Oil*. Kingsport: Vanderbilt University Press, 1970.

Shwadran, Benjamin. *The Middle East, Oil and the Great Powers*. New York: Frederick A. Praeger, 1955.

Tolf, Robert W. *The Russian Rockefellers*. Stanford: The Hoover Institution, 1976.

Evolution of OPEC Control (1945–1970)

Overview:
Role of Venezuela; Role of United States; Role of International Majors and Independents; Formation of OPEC; First Ten Years of OPEC.

Trends in Production, Consumption, and Prices:
Major Producing Countries; Major Consuming and Importing Countries; Price Trends.

Major Institutional Developments:
Principal Actors; Post-War Pricing System; Fifty–Fifty Profit Sharing.

Events Leading to the Formation of OPEC:
Effects of Profit Sharing; Iranian Nationalization; Prorationing in the United States.

Formal Organization of the Oil Producing Countries:
Origin of OPEC; Origin of OAPEC.

Epilogue and Prologue.

READER'S GUIDE TO CHAPTER 6
This chapter, which extends the analyses in Chapters 4 and 5, concludes the analytical history of world petroleum markets. It begins with a survey of the period 1945–1970 and goes on to outline the major trends in production, consumption, and prices. The next section offers an explanation of the post-war pricing system, profit sharing, and prorationing; and, to conclude, there is a historical narrative of the events which led to the formation and consolidation of OPEC.

Overview

The formation of OPEC in 1960 should be regarded in terms of an evolutionary process. It was a natural, although not inevitable, development based on the distribution of world petroleum reserves. As leaders in the host countries became aware of the potential value of their resources, they began to devise institutions that would afford them a greater share of the revenue to be derived from producing oil. The process of building these institutions involved the interaction of corporate and government officials from many consuming and producing countries.

The more important institutions leading to the formation of OPEC were *profit sharing* and *prorationing*. Voluntary prorationing had been practiced by the international majors and sporadically by producers in the United State since the turn of the century. It became official policy in the United States after 1935 and was enforced by both state and federal authorities. Prorationing had a decisive effect on the rate of production, on the pattern of resource development, and on the price of oil from 1945 until 1970, when OPEC began to consolidate its position in controlling output and prices.

Profit sharing began in Venezuela in the 1940s, and by the early 1950s it was practiced throughout the world. Profit sharing led to many subtle and complex changes in country–company relations. These changes will be surveyed in this section before the details of the story are presented later in the chapter. Following is a brief overview of the unique yet interactive roles played by Venezuela, the United States, the international majors, and the member countries of OPEC in the evolution and consolidation of OPEC control.

Role of Venezuela

The original Venezuelan profit-sharing agreement of the mid-1940s provided for a 50–50 split of the profit share between the host government and the concessionaires. It had the immediate effect of reducing the profitability of oil lifted in Venezuela, thus leading the majors to shift production to the Middle East, where oil was abundant and production costs lower. Venezuelan officials responded to the production shift in two important ways. First, they spread the news about profit sharing to the leading oil producing countries in the Middle East; and, second, they opened new areas to competitive bidding by newcomers to the international scene. The newcomers were instrumental in expanding production, thus exerting downward pressure on prices. The declining price level led to a number of fundamental conflicts between host governments and the producing companies. It was these conflicts that led directly to the formation of OPEC.

Role of United States

World oil prices during the 1950s would have declined more than they actually did had it not been for prorationing by state regulatory authorities in the United States. As oil began to flow in greater volume from Venezuela and the Middle East, American production was reduced almost barrel for imported barrel through market demand prorationing. Domestic prices were thereby maintained near $3 per barrel. However, these high prices relative to costs led to increased drilling and reserve development in the United States and the consequence was excess capacity. As imports continued to rise, the American independent oilmen increasingly cried for protection against "cheap foreign oil." "Voluntary" import controls were tried in 1957, but they failed to stem the flood of oil imports. Finally, mandatory import controls were imposed in 1959 by executive order of the president. Although this mitigated the flow of oil into the United States, imports continued to increase throughout the 1960s owing to the exceptions and appeals process.

Role of International Majors and Independents

Another factor that kept world oil prices from declining even more than they did during the 1950s was voluntary prorationing by the international oil companies. Company executives were aware that rapid expansion of output would depress prices. And low prices were undesirable both for the companies and the host countries. In reality, company and country interests were similar, if not identical, because of 50–50 profit sharing. But leaders in the host countries had little knowledge of the relation between production and prices, and they suspected the motives of the majors when reserve development and production proceeded at a pace they regarded as too slow. Their response in many cases was to invite competitive bids by newcomers who were anxious to produce incremental quantities from low-cost fields. One outcome of this series of events was the emergence, during the middle 1950s, of a form of competition between the majors and the independents.

Formation of OPEC

The major international oil companies and the state regulatory authorities in the United States were fairly successful in their efforts to restrain production and maintain prices. However, given the expansionist sentiments of the host governments, the downside pressure on prices could not be contained indefinitely. In February, 1959, the majors unilaterally reduced posted prices by about 10 percent. Leaders in the host countries were at first incensed, but since they lacked a united front, they could do little more than protest. When the First Arab Petroleum Congress met in Cairo in April, 1959, representatives from two non-Arab countries, Venezuela and Iran, were invited. Informal discussions among these leaders, especially between Sheik Abdullah Tariki of Saudi Arabia and Perez Alfonzo of Venezuela, resulted in a "gentleman's agreement" to adopt a common policy that would defend the interests of the producing countries.

The Mandatory Oil Import Control Program, which began in the United States in 1959, further reduced demand from the oil exporting countries and exerted additional downward pressure on prices. Faced with a persistent oversupply at prevailing prices, the majors unilaterally reduced posted prices again in August, 1960. This led directly to the first organizational meeting of OPEC. During September 9–14, 1960, representatives from the leading oil exporting countries—Iran, Iraq, Kuwait, Saudi Arabia, and Venezuela—met in Baghdad and founded OPEC. The immediate purpose of the meeting was to restore the posted price and to ensure that prices would not be reduced further. To accomplish these ends, the founding members agreed to stand united against the companies should the latter try to switch production from one country to another or to offer higher prices to a particular country in order to promote disunity.

First Ten Years of OPEC

OPEC was immediately successful in freezing posted prices but not in restoring actual market prices to previous levels. The fixed posted price became a "fictitious" price, relevant only for the purpose of calculating royalties and the share of profits. Actual market prices thereafter bore no relation to "posted" or "tax-reference" prices. Under these circumstances the countries received a constant amount per barrel regardless of the market price. In effect, this was a return to the fixed royalty per barrel (or per ton) regime which had prevailed prior to profit sharing— the major difference being the level of compensation per barrel. Consequently, there arose a basic conflict of interests between company and country representatives. The member countries were again receiving a "false" signal to the effect that marginal revenue was unrelated to the level of output. Thus, each country pressed its concessionaires to raise lifting levels even further. The result was greatly expanded crude oil production and continually lower market prices throughout the 1960s.

As world oil prices declined, the international oil companies received a smaller and smaller share of the revenue from each barrel. Their share approached the return which might be expected in a highly competitive industry in the late 1960s. It became evident to the producing countries that still higher revenues could not be "taken from the hide of the companies" but must be obtained by raising posted prices. Thus, a new market structure began to emerge around 1969 and extended into the 1970s. It was the beginning of the modern structure of world petroleum markets (discussed in Chapter 7), and it resulted in both higher posted prices and higher market prices.

Trends in Production, Consumption, and Prices

Major Producing Countries

Early Leaders.   The United States remained the world leader in oil production throughout the 1940s, but remarkable changes were afoot. Production in the United States increased in absolute terms from 3.7 to 11.3 million barrels a day between 1940 and 1970, but its share of world production declined from 63 to 24 percent (Table 6–1). The countries which eventually formed OPEC were beginning to emerge as major producers during this era. Venezuela was the early leader, producing as

TABLE 6–1
Crude Oil Production by Major Producing Countries and Regions of the World, 1940–1970
(million barrels per day)

			CRUDE OIL PRODUCTION			
Year	United States	Venezuela	Other OPEC Members[1]	USSR[2]	All Other	World
1940	3.7	0.5	0.5	0.6	0.6	5.9
1950	5.9	1.5	1.9	0.8	0.9	10.4
1960	8.0	2.9	5.9	3.3	1.8	21.0
1970	11.3	3.7	19.4	7.8	5.6	47.8
			PERCENT OF WORLD TOTAL			
1940	63	8	8	10	9	100
1950	51	14	18	7	9	100
1960	34	14	28	16	9	100
1970	24	8	41	16	12	100

[1]Excluding Venezuela.
[2]Includes all Sino-Soviet bloc countries—mostly USSR however.
SOURCES: American Petroleum Institute, *Petroleum Facts and Figures, 1971 ed.*, Washington, D.C.: 1971, pp. 548–57. Federal Energy Administration. Project Interdependence, *U.S. and World Energy Outlook through 1990*, U.S. Library of Congress, 1977.

much as all other OPEC members combined in 1940, more than the Soviet Union in 1950, and more than any single country outside the United States until 1960, when it was finally surpassed by the Soviet Union. These figures are important because of the prominent role Venezuela played in the events leading to the official formulation of OPEC.

Member Countries of OPEC.   The member countries of OPEC have become such an integral part of world petroleum markets that it is easy to lose sight of their inauspicious beginnings. OPEC did not come about through any sort of revolution; rather, it is a loose confederation of independent nations which evolved over the course of time. The power of individual members is mainly dependent on the magnitude of their reserves and on production. Production and reserves are closely related in the long run, but the exploration process and institutional considerations often cause reserves and production to diverge for extended periods.

Venezuela was clearly an early leader within OPEC because its relatively meager reserves were exploited first. Venezuela produced more than Saudi Arabia and Iran until 1970 and was the third-largest producer within OPEC in 1980 (Table 6–2). However, Venezuela is more typically the fourth-largest producer. It surpassed Iran in 1980, owing to revolutionary turmoil and to the war between Iran and Iraq.

Iran and Indonesia produced nearly equal amounts in 1940, even though Indonesia's reserves were about one-seventh as large and its production costs were higher. Production in Iran, Saudi Arabia, and Kuwait became more closely aligned with their reserves by 1950, and the relative importance of Indonesia declined. Production in Venezuela, Iran, Saudi Arabia, and Kuwait continued to rise during the 1950s, and Iraq also joined the ranks of the leading oil exporters. These countries became the *five founding members* of OPEC.

Algeria, Nigeria, Libya, and the United Arab Emirates are relatively recent entrants to the oil industry, but they have become important forces. Libya is particularly remarkable. Having struck oil in 1961, it became the fourth-largest producer within OPEC by 1970. Libya played an important role in restricting output and raising prices in 1970 and 1973. Qatar is a relatively small producer which has been active since 1949. Ecuador began producing in 1918, but its production remains comparable to that of Gabon, which began producing in 1957.

Major Consuming and Importing Countries

The "Communist bloc" countries consume about as much oil as they produce, so they are not generally included in the analysis of world

TABLE 6–2
Average Daily Production of Oil by Member Countries of OPEC,
1890–1980
(million barrels per day)

Year	Indonesia (1893)[1]	Iran* (1913)	Venezuela* (1917)	Ecuador (1918)	Iraq* (1928)	Saudi Arabia* (1938)	Kuwait* (1946)
1890							
1900	.006						
1910	.030						
1920	.048	.034	.001	.001			
1930	.114	.126	.374	.043	.002		
1940	.170	.182	.508	.064	.066	.014	
1950	.137	.664	1.498	.072	.136	.547	.344
1960	.423	1.057	2.854	.075	.969	1.251	1.628
1970	.855	3.831	3.708	.041	1.563	3.789	2.983
1980	1.577	1.662	2.167	.204	2.514	9.900	1.656

Year	Quatar (1949)	Gabon (1957)	Algeria (1958)	Nigeria (1958)	Libya (1961)	U.A.E. (1962)	Total
1890							.000
1900							.006
1910							.030
1920							.084
1930							.659
1940							1.004
1950	.034						3.432
1960	.173	.015	.181	.174			8.800
1970	.367	.104	.976	1.090	3.321	.780	23.408
1980	.472	.175	1.012	2.05	1.787	1.709	26.890

*Founding member

[1]Dates in parentheses indicate the year oil was first produced in commercial quantities.

SOURCES: American Petroleum Institute, *Petroleum Facts and Figures, 1971 ed.* Washington, D.C.: 1971, pp. 548–557.

Central Intelligence Agency, *Handbook of Economic Statistics, 1979,* Washington, D.C.: 1979, p. 135.

Data from CIA, *International Energy Indicators,* July 1981, p. 4.

U.S. Department of Energy, *Monthly Energy Review,* September 1981, pp. 90–91.

demand. Among the "Western" and "free world" countries, the United States, Japan, and the European countries are the leading consumers (Table 6–3). In 1950 the United States was the leading oil consuming country by a very wide margin, accounting for 68 percent of the free world total. Since 1950 the West European countries, particularly West Germany, France, Italy, and the United Kingdom, have become major consuming countries. Oil consumption in Japan increased even more remarkably, from about 100,000 barrels per day in 1950 to 4 million just 20 years later.

TABLE 6–3
Free World Consumption and Imports of Crude Oil and Refined Petroleum Products
United States, Western Europe, Japan, and All Other Countries, 1950–1970
(million barrels per day)

	CONSUMPTION OF REFINED PRODUCTS[1]				
Year	United States	Western Europe	Japan	All Other	Free World
1950	5.8	1.0	0.1	1.6	8.5
1960	10.8	3.9	0.7	3.0	18.5
1970	14.4	12.6	4.0	7.5	38.5
	PERCENT OF FREE WORLD TOTAL				
1950	68	12	—	20	100
1960	59	21	4	16	100
1970	37	33	10	20	100
	IMPORTS OF CRUDE OIL AND REFINED PRODUCTS[2]				
1950	.85	1.22	.04	1.54	3.65
1960	1.82	3.96	0.68	2.57	9.03
1970	3.42	12.94	4.28	4.96	25.60
	PERCENT OF FREE WORLD TOTAL				
1950	23.3	33.4	1.1	42.2	100.0
1960	20.2	43.9	7.5	28.5	100.0
1970	13.4	50.5	16.7	19.4	100.0

SOURCES: [1]American Petroleum Institute, *Petroleum Facts and Figures, 1971 ed.*, pp. 572–75. British Petroleum Company, *Statistical Review of the World Oil Industry*, London: 1977, p. 21.
[2]Dankwart A. Rustow and John F. Mugno, *OPEC Success and Prospects*, New York: New York Univ. Press, 1976, p. 129.

The trends in oil consumption are truly remarkable. All other countries combined used less oil than the United States in 1950, but overall consumption increased at a more rapid rate. The United States imported very little oil in 1950, but just ten years later more than one-fifth of total consumption was imported. Japan and the European countries produce very little oil, so they import the bulk of their requirements and have done so for many years. Only the United Kingdom and Norway are important oil producers relative to consumption.

Price Trends

Three price series are important in explaining the evolution of OPEC: (1) average prices in the United States, (2) posted prices in the member countries of OPEC, and (3) actual market, or spot, prices as recorded in

Italy, Rotterdam, the Caribbean, New York, and the Gulf of Mexico. Prior to 1959 these prices were closely related via the U.S. Gulf-Plus and the Persian Gulf-Plus pricing systems. Prices in the United States became insulated from world prices in 1959 by virtue of mandatory oil import controls; thus, U.S. prices remained stable but world prices declined. Similarly, after the formation of OPEC in 1960, posted prices became unrelated to world prices by virtue of OPEC's insistence that posted prices should not be lowered. Thus, posted prices also remained stable throughout the 1960s, but spot prices in the principal refinery centers declined.

Prices in the United States.   The "ratcheting" of oil prices refers to a sharp price increase followed by relative price stability. The first sharp upward movement in oil prices occurred during the period 1945–1948, when the average price per barrel more than doubled— from $1.20 in 1945 to $2.60 in 1948 (Table 6–4). After 1948, prices remained remarkably stable for more than twenty years: The average domestic price per barrel did not fall below $2.50 nor exceed $3.10 until 1970. This record of price stability in the United States is attributable to market demand prorationing as practiced by the state regulatory authorities (see Chapter 4). The extent to which prorationing was carried out is illustrated by the fact that allowable production in Texas declined throughout the 1950s to a low of 27 percent in 1962. This means that wells subject to prorationing were pumping only one day out of every four. Similar allowables are also observable in other major producing states, such as Oklahoma and Louisiana. Restrictions on output remained fairly severe throughout the 1960s, but the percent of allowable began to increase relative to capacity after the Mandatory Oil Import Control Program was initiated in 1959.

Posted Prices in the Member Countries.   Wellhead prices were not generally posted prior to 1950. Before profit sharing became widespread, the host countries received a fixed royalty per barrel (or ton) of production. Under these conditions postings were not essential. Only when sales took place among nonaffiliated entities were postings actually required. But these transactions were the exception rather than the rule before 1950.

When posted prices were first introduced, they approximated "market prices," or the price at which oil could actually be sold. Table 6–5 records the trend in posted prices for similar crude oils sold by three early leaders of OPEC. The prices show the importance of proximity to major consuming regions. Venezuela could obtain a "transport premium" because its shipping costs to the United States were lower than those for oil shipped from the Persian Gulf. Posted prices increased during the period 1950–1957, declined slightly during 1959–1960,

TABLE 6–4
Crude Oil Wellhead Prices and Percent of Allowable
Production in Texas, 1945–1970

Year	Average Domestic Price (*dollars per barrel*)	Percent of Allowable Production in Texas
1945	1.20	—
1946	1.65	81
1947	1.93	89
1948	2.60	100
1949	2.54	65
1950	2.51	63
1951	2.53	76
1952	2.53	71
1953	2.68	65
1954	2.78	53
1955	2.77	53
1956	2.79	52
1957	3.09	47
1958	3.01	33
1959	2.90	34
1960	2.88	28
1961	2.89	28
1962	2.90	27
1963	2.89	28
1964	2.88	28
1965	2.86	29
1966	2.88	34
1967	2.92	41
1968	2.94	45
1969	3.09	54
1970	3.18	71

SOURCES: U.S. Bureau of Mines, Federal Energy Administration and Energy Information Administration. Stephen McDonald, *Petroleum Conservation in the United States,* Baltimore, Md.: Johns Hopkins, 1971, p. 164.

remained constant throughout the 1960s, and increased sharply in 1971. Posted prices did not change during the intervals between the dates recorded in Table 6–5. The stability of posted prices reflected in the narrow range of movement—about 50 cents per barrel over a 20-year period—is remarkably similar to the level and trend of prices recorded in the United States. In fact, prior to 1960, OPEC postings were based on prices in the United States.

TABLE 6–5
Posted Prices in Venezuela, Iran, and Saudi Arabia,
F.O.B. Loading Port, for Comparable Crude Oils,
Measured by API Gravity
(U.S. dollars per barrel)

Date[1]	VENEZUELA Oficina (35.0° API)	IRAN Iranian Light Kharg Island (34° API)	SAUDI ARABIA Arabian Light Ras Tanura (34° API)
1950 Nov.1	2.570	n/a	1.750
1953 Feb. 5	2.820	1.860	1.930
1957 June 7	3.050	1.990	2.080
1959 Feb. 13	2.900	1.810	1.900
1960 Aug. 9	2.800	1.810	1.800
1971 Feb. 15	2.725	2.170	2.225

[1]Indicates date Saudi Arabian postings were changed. Prices in Venezuela and Iran generally move in the same direction as those of Saudi Arabia.
SOURCE: OPEC *Annual Statistical Bulletin 1976* (Vienna: 1977).

World Oil Posted and Realized Market Prices.   Posted, or "tax reference," prices and those realized by the companies downstream remained close to each other until the late 1950s, but they increasingly diverged thereafter. Average Venezuelan posted and realized prices, shown in Table 6–6, for the period 1950–1969 illustrate the general trend for all OPEC members. Average posted prices are based on all Venezuelan postings and vary slightly as the volume of each crude changes from year to year.

The stability of market prices prior to 1957 is attributable to voluntary market demand prorationing by the international majors. Realized market prices increased in 1957 when the Suez Canal was nationalized and closed; thereafter, prices declined nearly 20 percent by 1959. The lower price realizations led to unilateral reductions in posted prices by the international majors. After 1960, posted prices remained stable but market realizations continued to decline until 1970.

Major Institutional Developments

The production, consumption, import, and price trends observed from 1945 to 1970 were the result of two important institutional relations that evolved during the period 1928–1960: (1) prorationing and (2) profit

TABLE 6–6
Posted and Realized Market Prices of Venezuelan Crude Oil,
1950–1969
(dollars per barrel)

Year	Average Crude Posting	Average Realized Market Prices	Differential between Posting and Realized Prices
1950	2.27	2.11	.16
1951	2.27	2.05	.22
1952	2.17	2.14	.03
1953	2.33	2.30	.03
1954	2.40	2.31	.09
1955	2.41	2.34	.07
1956	2.45	2.36	.09
1957	2.91	2.65	.26
1958	2.83	2.50	.33
1959	2.69	2.23	.46
1960	2.70	2.12	.58
1961	2.72	2.13	59
1962	2.71	2.08	.63
1963	2.70	2.04	.66
1964	2.73	1.95	.78
1965	2.63	1.89	.74
1966	2.67	1.87	.80
1967	2.67	1.85	.82
1968	2.62	1.87	.75
1969	2.69	1.81	.88

SOURCE: Morris Adelman, *The World Petroleum Market,* Baltimore, Md.: Johns Hopkins, 1972, p. 342.

sharing. Prorationing enabled producers to limit output to "market demand" and thereby maintain prices. However, a country's revenue was based on *volume* as well as prices, and the individual leaders in the countries which would eventually form OPEC were eager to increase their revenues. They had no control over prices but could influence volume by granting additional concessions. But higher levels of production in one country required production cuts in some other country if prices were to be maintained. The country taking most of the production cuts turned out to be the United States. The limit to production cuts was approached in the United States around 1960 when "allowable" production on wells subject to prorationing fell to less than 30 percent.

Profit sharing was an important innovation because its introduction in Venezuela caused the majors to shift their production to the Middle East. Venezuela's subsequent invitation to newcomers brought about a further increase in production and set a precedent for other countries to follow. In addition, the Venezuelans provided information to other host governments and augmented the capital assets of newcomers. And once the floodgates were open there was no stopping the incessant flow of oil from fields operated by newcomers to the international oil market.

Principal Actors

The principal actors in the world petroleum industry during the period 1944–1970 include: (1) the large international oil companies, or "majors," who functioned as a corporate cartel until the middle 1950s, (2) the smaller international oil companies, or "independents," who willingly came to Venezuela and the Middle East to increase their levels of output when the international majors were voluntarily prorationing, (3) the American producers who functioned as an isolated but large cartel-type institution during most of the period, and (4) the member countries which eventually formed OPEC. The interactions of these groups were important in shaping the course of output, prices, and the development of new institutions in world petroleum markets.

International Majors and Independents.   Building on their experience in previous decades, the seven international majors remained in a dominant position throughout the 1940s and 1950s. According to a *Federal Trade Commission Report on the International Petroleum Cartel* in 1951:

> Control of the industry by these seven companies extends from reserves through production, transportation, refining, and marketing. All seven engage in every stage of operations, from exploration to marketing. The typical movement of petroleum from producer until acquired by the final consumer is through intercompany transfer within a corporate family. Outright sales, arms-length bargaining, and other practices characteristic of independent buyers and sellers are conspicuous by their absence. Control is held not only through direct corporate holdings, by parents, subsidiaries and affiliates of the seven but also through such indirect means as interlocking directorates, joint ownership of affiliates, intercompany crude purchase contracts, and marketing agreements.

In 1949 the majors owned 92 percent of known reserves outside the United States, Mexico, and the USSR. They also owned 34 percent of reserves in the United States. Although the importance of the international majors remained beyond question, their *relative* importance began to wane in the 1950s. The majors controlled 85 percent of the crude oil produced outside the United States, Canada, the USSR, and China in 1950; but only 72 percent in 1960. This decline is an outward manifestation of the profound changes that were occurring on the world petroleum market.

The decline in the majors' share of the market was caused by the substantial inroads made by smaller companies or newcomers to established markets. Production by Standard Oil of New Jersey almost doubled in absolute terms, but its share of the market declined from 25 to 17 percent. The smaller companies, on the other hand, increased output five-fold and moved from a 15 to a 28 percent market share (Table 6–7). The small companies were successful in gaining a foothold because the host governments wanted to expand output at a rate faster than that advocated by the majors.

American Producers.   By 1935 oil producers in the United States had fashioned a stable and legally sanctioned institutional structure which enabled them to limit output and maintain domestic prices. State regulatory agencies, such as the Texas Railroad Commission and the Oklahoma Conservation Commission, had uncontested control over the level of production at the wellhead in their respective states. The Inter-

TABLE 6–7
Gross Crude Oil Production,
Seven Majors and World (Excluding United States, USSR, Eastern Europe, and China), 1950 and 1960

	GROSS CRUDE OIL AND CONDENSATE			
	1950		1960	
	1,000 barrels per day	Percent	1,000 barrels per day	Percent
Standard Oil (N.J.) (EXXON)	1,020	25	1,920	17
Royal Dutch-Shell	770	19	1,600	14
British Petroleum	800	20	1,500	13
Gulf Oil	300	7	1,170	10
Texaco	240	6	790	7
Standard Oil of California	180	4	560	5
Mobil Oil	140	3	570	5
Total Seven Majors	3,450	85	8,110	72
Total Other Companies	620	15	3,120	28
TOTAL	4,070	100	11,230	100

SOURCES: Annual reports of companies and British Petroleum, *Statistical Review of the World Oil Industry.* Comp. Edith Penrose, *Senate Hearings on the U.S. Oil Import Question,* 1969. Part 1, Economists' Views. Subcommittee on Antitrust and Monopoly of the Committee on the Judiciary, 91st Cong., 1st sess., March 11–26 and April 1–2, 1969.

state Oil Compact Commission provided a forum through which the producing states could coordinate policies to promote their own interests. And the Connally "Hot Oil" Act provided for the confiscation of interstate shipments of oil produced in violation of state regulations.

Member Countries of OPEC.   In 1960 OPEC began to devise an institutional structure similar to that of the United States. Each member country now has a Ministry of Mines and Hydrocarbons (or similar authority) with the ability to control the level of production at the wellhead. And OPEC provides the forum through which the members coordinate their policies. The main difference between the OPEC and U.S. structures is that while OPEC administers prices, it has not devised a stable system of member-wide prorationing. Similarly, there is no "hot oil" agreement providing for the confiscation of oil produced in excess of agreed levels.

Post-War Pricing System

Evolution of the Gulf-Plus Pricing System.   World oil prices prior to 1945 were determined by those in the United States at the Gulf of Mexico. The first open break with "Gulf-Plus" pricing occurred in 1944 when the British Auditor General examined prices being paid for fuel oil by the Ministry of War Transport at ports in the Middle East and India. The Auditor General questioned the inclusion of phantom freight as a legitimate cost and concluded it was "no longer acceptable." Interestingly, the chief complaint was against the company owned by the British government, Anglo-Iranian. The Auditor General was successful in establishing a precedent which effectively added the Persian Gulf as a second base-point.

The first issue under the new system concerned the price which should be established at the Persian Gulf. Government negotiators tried to obtain data on production costs and profits but the companies considered this information proprietary. An agreement was eventually reached which proclaimed that the U.S. price at the Gulf of Mexico reflected the proper or fair price level. This was apparently based on the fact that the U.S. government controlled domestic prices at a level "providing a fair return to U.S. producers."

A year later the issue of phantom freight arose in the United States when a crude-supply contract was negotiated with Aramco. The oil was to be shipped from Saudi Arabia to France under a lend-lease agreement. New estimates of proved reserves in the Middle East indicated there were 18 rather than merely 5 billion barrels of oil in the region. It was therefore becoming evident that the Persian Gulf would soon replace the Gulf of Mexico as the principal exporting region. In the Aramco case the British precedent was used to conclude the deal, and most subsequent contracts applied the same principle. Thereafter, the single base-point pricing system became a dual base-point system, but prices all over the world were still based on those at the Gulf of Mexico.

Posted Prices.   Most of the oil moving in international trade prior to 1950 moved within vertically integrated international firms. An integrated company could establish relatively low prices at the wellhead and record profits at the pump; or, it could establish high crude oil prices and record profits at the wellhead. As long as sales were *within* rather than *between* companies, the practices adopted depended mainly on the tax laws.

The institution of 50–50 profit sharing altered the importance of prices as recorded at each level in the distribution chain. In 1950 Mobil was the first company to announce "posted prices" in the Middle East. According to Shell International Petroleum:

> The offer to sell to buyers generally was intended to provide an assurance to the governments of the producing countries that oil being exported at publicly posted prices to affiliated companies was not being under-valued. It was intended that posted prices to affiliates plus appropriate long-term freights would provide the basis on which oil would be imported into consuming areas.[1]

Fifty-Fifty Profit Sharing

Origins in Venezuela.   The trends in oil production and prices during the period 1951–1970 were closely related to the events surrounding the 50–50 profit sharing regime which originated during the period 1943–1948. Venezuela was a large producer in 1943 and the first country to establish profit sharing. Some writers have attributed the desire for profit sharing to a "growing nationalism," but surely the Venezuelan authorities suspected that company profits were extraordinarily large. The more than doubling of world prices between 1945 and 1948 merely reinforced this belief.

The immediate effect of profit sharing was that the Venezuelan authorities began to scrutinize information on both costs and prices and to challenge the accounting procedures of the operating companies. Before profit sharing was instituted it mattered relatively little whether

---

[1]Shell International Petroleum Co., Ltd., *Current International Oil Pricing Problem*, August, 1965, p. 6.

costs were recorded in Venezuela, at sea, or in the consuming country, because royalties were based on quantity rather than on market price. After profit sharing, a dollar recorded as a cost in Venezuela would save the company 50 cents in Venezuelan taxes. Under these circumstances, the Venezuelan government believed it had to have full information regarding costs and selling prices as well as knowledge of the volume of production.

Host Government Treatment of Royalties.   Profit sharing posed a new set of problems for the tax authorities in the producing countries. The royalty regime was simple: Royalties were paid on a per barrel or per ton basis or they were a constant percentage of an arbitrary price used for the purpose of internal accounting. Profit sharing raised the issue of whether the royalty should be expensed or credited against the producing country's share of profits. The companies argued that royalties should be credited against their tax obligation; the producing countries maintained that it should be a cost of production (that is, it should be expensed).

The importance of expensing royalties versus crediting them against income tax can be demonstrated by applying the figures in Table 6–8. Although these figures are hypothetical, they are close to the post-World War II situation for most Middle Eastern countries. Under *expensing of royalties* the host government would receive the royalty plus 50 percent of the profit in line 4, for a total of $1 per barrel; and the company would receive 75 cents per barrel. Under *crediting royalties against*

TABLE 6–8
Example of Company and Host Country Profits and Taxes
under Expensing and Nonexpensing of Royalty Payments
(in U.S. dollars per barrel)

	Expensed Royalty	Royalty Credited Against Income Tax
1. Posted Price	2.00	2.00
2. Production Cost	.25	.25
3. Royalty ($12\frac{1}{2}$% of Posted)	.25	-
4. Before-Tax Profit	1.50	1.75
5. Company Profit (50% of line 4)	.75	.875
6. Host Government "Take": of which	1.00	.875
Royalty (12½% of Posted)	.25	.25
Net Tax Receipts	.75	.625

taxes, however, the country and the company each would receive 87.5 cents per barrel. The difference of 12.5 cents per barrel represents an enormous gain or loss in profits and tax receipts, since millions of barrels were lifted each day.

When profit sharing was first established, the companies were allowed to credit the royalty against taxes. However, in the early 1950s the countries switched to expensing royalties. This was one of the early indications that the producing countries were gaining greater control over the benefits derived from the sale of their oil.

Consuming Country Treatment of Foreign Tax Obligations. Profit sharing also posed a new set of problems for the tax authorities in the countries which had chartered the international companies, principally the United States and Great Britain. Was the payment to the producing government a business expense, like any other cost of acquiring oil, or was it an income tax? This issue was important because the foreign tax credit provisions of the U.S. Internal Revenue Code allow a taxpayer to "credit" income taxes paid to a foreign government against his obligation to pay U.S. income taxes. Business expenses, on the other hand, are deductible from gross revenues but cannot be *credited* against income taxes. This distinction is subtle but important.

Royalties had long been regarded as an expense and were not an issue. Profit sharing meant that company profits which had previously been taxed by the United States (Great Britain, Netherlands, France, and so on) would now be taxed by the host governments. And a tax credit would allow the companies to reduce their U.S. taxes by almost the full amount paid to the foreign government. If the payment were treated as an expense, the U.S. tax would be higher.

Again, the issue can be illustrated by using the figures shown in Table 6–8 and an assumed U.S. corporate income tax of 50 percent. Without a tax credit, a company would be required to pay U.S. income taxes on company profits of 75 cents per barrel, or a tax of 37.5 cents per barrel. With a tax credit, the tax liability would be on before-tax profits of $1.50 per barrel; however, the income tax of 75 cents paid to the host government could be deducted from the U.S. obligation, and the effective U.S. income tax would be reduced to zero.

The U.S. Internal Revenue Service ruled that revenues paid to host governments could be used as a credit against U.S. income taxes. The tax credit results in what public finance specialists call *tax neutrality*, meaning that a company pays the same total tax regardless of where the income is earned. Since oil companies were among the leading international companies, the tax credit had the effect of encouraging investments in foreign oil and thereby increasing oil production outside the

United States. Governments are under pressure to adopt tax-neutral policies because companies subject to taxation in two countries cannot compete against those operating under tax-neutral laws.

Events Leading to the Formation of OPEC

Effects of Profit Sharing

Initial Reaction.   The principal companies operating in Venezuela at the time profit sharing began were Royal Dutch-Shell, Standard of New Jersey, and Gulf. With profit sharing, Venezuela received the traditional royalty plus one-half of the difference between the selling price and the production costs. Almost overnight its revenues tripled and even quadrupled, depending on extraction costs in individual fields. Venezuela's increased revenues were coming directly from company profits. From a company point of view, crude oil acquisition "costs" from Venezuela increased substantially because of profit sharing. However, since the operating companies had important concessions in the Middle East, where profit sharing had not yet been instituted, they naturally began to shift production away from Venezuela and toward the Middle East where costs were lower and after-tax profits greater.

Profit sharing became fully implemented in Venezuela in 1948, and by 1949 its yearly production had *declined* by 8 million barrels. On the other hand, in Kuwait and Saudi Arabia yearly production increased by 53 and 31 million barrels, respectively. In fact, oil production increased in *every* Middle Eastern country between 1948 and 1949. But, in addition to the decline in Venezuela, yearly production also declined, by 178 million barrels, in the United States. The international oil companies were lifting oil where their acquisition costs were low and restricting (that is, prorationing) their output in Venezuela, where costs were high. And in the United States, the state regulatory authorities were restricting output through market demand prorationing.

Spreading the Good News About Profit Sharing.   Venezuelan authorities viewed the companies' defection to the Middle East as an international conspiracy designed to impoverish the Venezuelan people. And in response they sent emissaries to Iran, Iraq, Kuwait, and Saudi Arabia to explain the virtues of profit sharing to authorities there. The Venezuelan story fell on receptive ears, and Middle Eastern producers soon started negotiating profit sharing agreements of their own. In

November, 1950, Saudi Arabia concluded an agreement providing for 50–50 profit sharing. Kuwait and Iraq followed a few months later; and by 1951–1952, the practice became almost universal.

Iranian Nationalization

The Takeover.   News of profit sharing had an impact on all countries, but subsequent events in Iran reflected more than simply a reaction to the developments in Venezuela. Iran was also in the forefront of company–country confrontations. In October, 1947, the Iranian Parliament enacted a law requiring the government to begin negotiations to recapture all concessionary rights granted since the 1933 D'Arcy agreement. Consequently, in early 1948, the Iranian Prime Minister, Dr. Muhammad Mossadegh, initiated negotiations with the Anglo-Iranian Oil Company. He steadfastly supported the principle of Iranian sovereignty over oil resources and, pursuing his appointed task with enthusiasm, he insisted on complete withdrawal of Anglo-Iranian claims to Iranian oil. Anglo-Iranian executives countered by offering better terms to the Iranian government, but they would not freely relinquish prior concessions, which they viewed as legal business contracts.

Events external to the negotiations were to help shape the outcome. The sharp increases in the price of oil and in the volume produced during the period 1945 to 1948 greatly increased both company profits and country revenues. However, Anglo-Iranian gained relatively more than did the Iranian government. In the years 1944–1950, Anglo-Iranian profits increased more than ten-fold, whereas Iranian tax receipts merely quadrupled. The reason is that Iranian royalties were based on a fixed payment per ton, so the price increases benefited the company but not the government. This great bone of contention is what underlay most of the Iranian hostility and their resentment of the British.

Anglo-Iranian officials and Mossadegh were equally intransigent, and negotiations dragged on for several years. The company would not even agree to 50–50 profit sharing; and Mossadegh was adamant about Iranian sovereignty over oil resources. Finally, on May 1, 1951, the Iranian government nationalized the properties of Anglo-Iranian and expelled British diplomats from the country.

But Mossadegh proved a better organizer of reactionary forces than an administrator of nationalized properties under the newly organized National Iranian Oil Company (NIOC). Indeed, the cards were stacked against the Iranians from the beginning. The majors boycotted Iranian oil and Anglo-Iranian warned prospective buyers that legal action would be taken if they bought directly from the Iranians. More importantly, oil was available in abundance from other sources. Excess capacity had been developed in the United States, Venezuela, Kuwait, Iraq, and Saudi Arabia. Consequently, Iranian oil production slowed to a trickle and oil revenues declined from $400 million in 1950 to less than $2 million during Mossadegh's reign (July, 1951, to August, 1953).

Renegotiation.   Without financial resources, it was only a matter of time before the Iranian government under Mossadegh would fall. Internal strife between the young Reza Shah Pahlavi and Mossadegh finally had resulted in the shah fleeing the country. However, a military coup under General Zahedi soon forced Mossadegh out of office and restored the shah to power in August, 1953. In October negotiations began between a consortium of oil companies and the new Iranian government.

Iranian public sentiment against the British was running so high that restoration of the previous agreement was out of the question. But a "Consortium Agreement," providing that a group of companies operate nearly all the properties of the National Iranian Oil Company (NIOC), was finally worked out. Anglo-Iranian, which changed its name to British Petroleum (BP) in 1954, was granted a 40 percent share in the Consortium. Shell had 14 percent, the Aramco partners (Exxon, Mobil, Texaco, and Socal) had 7 percent each, the French (CFP) had 6 percent, and a number of American independents shared the remaining 12 percent.

The immediate problem of the Consortium was how to work the renewed flow of Iranian oil into a world market which had learned to live without it. The answer lay in increasing output slowly. Thus the Consortium, largely under the control of old hands adept at limiting output to maintain prices, voluntarily prorationed Iranian output well into the 1950s and 1960s.

Prorationing in the United States

The Basic Position.   Price controls were removed after World War II and competition drove prices upward sharply. Fields in Venezuela and the Middle East were only beginning to supply the world market, and Europe needed large quantities of oil for reconstruction. By January, 1948, the price of crude oil had more than doubled to $2.75 F.O.B. Gulf of Mexico. This price was sufficient to stimulate additional drilling both within and outside the United States. Entry into the domestic oil industry had always been relatively easy. Even with market demand prorationing, the marketability of a new discovery was assured because new wells were generally exempt from output restrictions for the first two years so that investors could recover their initial investments. The relatively high price of crude oil stimulated domestic wildcat and exploratory drilling and caused capacity to increase sharply in the early 1950s. Foreign output could also be sold in the United States, since there were no restrictions on importation until 1959. Foreign production costs plus freight remained low relative to domestic prices throughout the 1950s, and U.S. imports increased substantially.

Economic Rent Available to Oil Importers.   Professor Morris Adelman's data on per-barrel crude oil costs, prices, and freight in September, 1949, illustrate why oilmen were so anxious to import oil into the United States. The actual Gulf of Mexico F.O.B. price was $2.71, freight from the Gulf to New York was about 25 cents and the delivered price in New York was $2.96. On the other hand, the actual Persian Gulf wellhead costs were 18 cents, the Saudi Arabian royalty was 21 cents, and the wellhead acquisition cost was 39 cents. Freight from the Persian Gulf to New York added $1.21, so the delivered price in New York was $1.60. Thus, the international oil companies stood to gain $1.36 on each barrel imported from Saudi Arabia. In an industry where output is recorded in millions of barrels per day, this offered a significant incentive to expand production and sell in the United States.[2]

Regulatory Response.   Imports into the United States increased during the years 1947–1949, but the Texas Railroad Commission and other state regulatory commissions successfully maintained the domestic prices by restricting production. The severe restriction on output required to maintain prices is well known among oilmen but is not generally appreciated by people outside the industry. The large excess capacity for the period 1948–1973 is recorded in Table 6–9. Column 7 shows the percentage of shut-in capacity. In 1948 virtually all wells were operating at capacity, but in 1949, 22.1 percent of capacity was shut-in. The difference was the result of market demand prorationing.

Clearly, the price of $2.54 per barrel could not have been maintained beyond 1949 if wells had been allowed to produce at 100 percent capacity. The average U.S. price does not reflect a price determined by market forces; it does reflect a consensus of opinion among oilmen and regulatory authorities concerning what the price of crude oil should be. It was an administered price maintained by prorationing.

Effects of Prorationing During the 1950s.   The willingness of the regulatory authorities to reduce domestic production enhanced the value of discoveries in foreign countries and made imports even more attractive. Oil produced abroad could be marketed without restrictions, whereas oil discovered in the United States would eventually be subject

---

[2]Morris Adelman, *The World Petroleum Market* (Baltimore, Md.: Johns Hopkins, 1972), p. 135.

to prorationing. Although the incentives to import were strong, the international majors voluntarily limited shipments because they feared congressional action which would establish quotas or tariffs. However, prorationing also provided an inducement for independent oil producers to go abroad. Their output was increasingly restricted at home by prorationing, their domestic costs exceeded foreign cost-plus-tax-plus-freight charges, the barriers to movement abroad were crumbling, and there were few barriers to selling foreign-produced oil in the United States. The newcomers on the international scene negated attempts by the majors to voluntarily limit oil flowing into the United States.

Oil Import Quotas. The possibility of oil import controls had been a latent threat in the United States for more than two decades. Congress imposed a tariff on imported oil in 1932, but the law was declared unconstitutional in 1935. There was little support for tariffs or quotas after 1935 because the volume of imports remained relatively small. The rising flood of oil imports during the early to middle 1950s evoked new outcries for protection from independent producers in Texas, Oklahoma, and Louisiana. In 1954, in response to such pressure, President Eisenhower appointed a committee to study the oil import question.

The committee issued a report one year later suggesting that national security would best be served if the "ratio of oil imports to production" were allowed to remain at the level prevailing in 1954. This implied that national security would not be seriously impaired if the share of imports remained around 10 percent of consumption. The committee recognized that flexibility would be required to maintain market shares while providing for fluctuations in consumption over the business cycle. They suggested that the necessary flexibility could be attained by voluntary import restraints. The American independent producers, those with no foreign interests, were unhappy with the report because the committee failed to recommend mandatory quotas.

Congress debated the oil import question in 1955 in connection with its deliberations on the Reciprocal Trade Agreements Act. The decision was against import quotas or tariffs, but the act did include a compromise clause which gave the president the option to impose quotas if imports ever became a threat to national security. The nationalization and closing of the Suez Canal in 1956 created a shortage and once again brought the national security issue to the fore. Again there were demands for a quota. After the crisis was resolved, the flood of oil imports became an even more pressing issue.

During 1957, oil imports rose sharply, whereas domestic production was curtailed. These developments prompted the director of defense mobilization to urge the president to impose oil import quotas. Eisenhower, however, still preferred voluntary restraints and encouraged industry to establish the Voluntary Import Control Program of 1957. As

TABLE 6–9

Average U.S. Prices, Consumption, Production, Imports, Productive Capacity, and Shut-in Capacity, 1948–1973

(1)	(2)	(3)	(4)	(5)	(6)	(7)	(8)
Year	Average Price per Barrel	Consumption (*million barrels*)	Production (*million barrels*)	Imports (*million barrels*)	Productive Capacity (*million barrels*)	Excess or Shut-in Capacity	Event
1948	$2.60	2,114	2,167	53	2,167	0	First Arab–Israeli War (May 1948)
1949	2.54	2,118	1,999	119	2,441	22.1	
1950	2.51	2,375	2,156	219	2,628	21.9	
1951	2.53	2,570	2,453	117	2,729	11.3	Iranian oil fields nationalized (March 1951)
1952	2.53	2,664	2,514	150	2,866	14.0	
1953	2.68	2,775	2,596	179	3,038	17.0	
1954	2.78	2,832	2,567	265	3,167	23.4	
1955	2.77	3,088	2,766	322	3,368	21.8	
1956	2.79	3,213	2,911	302	3,567	22.5	Suez Canal nationalized (July 1956); Second Arab–Israeli War (October 1956)
1957	3.09	3,219	2,912	307	3,689	26.7	
1958	3.01	3,315	2,744	571	3,789	38.1	
1959	2.90	3,450	2,896	554	3,867	33.5	

(1) Year	(2) Average Price per Barrel	(3) Consumption (million barrels)	(4) Production (million barrels)	(5) Imports (million barrels)	(6) Productive Capacity (million barrels)	(7) Excess or Shut-in Capacity	(8) Event
1960	2.88	3,536	2,915	621	3,899	33.8	
1961	2.89	3,579	2,984	595	3,993	33.8	
1962	2.90	3,736	3,049	687	4,065	33.3	
1963	2.89	3,851	3,154	697	4,112	30.4	
1964	2.88	3,959	3,209	750	4,187	30.5	
1965	2.86	4,125	3,290	835	4,274	29.9	
1966	2.88	4,325	3,496	829	4,392	25.6	
1967	2.92	4,481	3,730	751	4,549	22.0	Suez Canal closing and Third Arab–Israeli War (June 1967)
1968	2.94	4,788	3,883	905	4,641	19.5	
1969	3.09	5,249	3,952	1,297	4,600	16.4	
1970	3.41	5,463	4,113	1,350	4,553	10.7	
1971	3.41	5,638	4,072	1,566	4,385	7.1	
1972	3.51	5,990	4,037	1,953	4,352	7.8	Fourth Arab–Israeli War (October 1973)
1973	4.32	6,298	3,926	2,372	4,130	5.2	

SOURCES: American Petroleum Institute, *Petroleum Facts and Figures, 1971 ed.* p. 87. OPEC, *Annual Statistical Review*, Vienna: 1977, pp. 101, 110.

this program was pursued, it became increasingly apparent that voluntary import controls were ineffectual in excluding oil imports. Evidence of this is shown by the level of excess capacity, which rose to a high of 38.1 percent in 1958 (Table 6–9).

In March, 1959, President Eisenhower issued an executive order authorizing the imposition of mandatory controls. Enforcement was charged to the Interior Department, which was responsible for licensing imports and establishing quotas. Import quotas were based on historical levels. However, "historic" importers were restricted to 80 percent of their last allocations under the voluntary program, and 20 percent of the quota was allocated to new entrants based on their refinery runs. Preference was given to "small" refiners in the allocation formulas. Exchanges among oil producers were allowed in order to minimize transport costs. This program was known as the Mandatory Oil Import Control Program of 1959 (MOIP).

As a result of the MOIP, a license to import a barrel of oil became a valuable and coveted right. In the latter part of the 1960s it was estimated that the value of an "import ticket" (a right to import one barrel of oil) was $1.25. Thus, the quota system resulted in a substantial redistribution of income from American consumers to American producers. More importantly, from the standpoint of world markets, the MOIP reduced the demand for oil from foreign countries, exerted greater downward pressure on world oil prices, and increased capacity utilization rates in the United States. By 1970 the world oil price was $1.30 per barrel compared with a domestic price of $3.18, and excess capacity in the United States was approaching zero. The latter was important because excess capacity constrained the members of OPEC from pressing for a better deal.

Formal Organization of the Oil Producing Countries

Origin of OPEC

The seeds of the formal institution known as OPEC were sown when the Arab League held its first meeting in 1945. Almost from the beginning, the Arab League considered the possibility of forming an organization of Arab oil exporting countries. However, the representatives recognized the desirability of including the large non-Arab oil exporters as well, notably Venezuela and Iran, and plans were postponed. Then, in February, 1959, the major oil companies reduced posted prices unilaterally without consulting the producing countries. This set off a series of events that led to the first formal meeting of OPEC.

In April, 1959, the Arab League sponsored the first Arab Petroleum Congress in Cairo, Egypt, with representatives of Venezuela and Iran invited as observers. The formal agenda included only matters of interest to Arab countries, but informal meetings between Sheik Abdullah Tariki of Saudi Arabia and Perez Alfonzo of Venezuela resulted in a "gentleman's agreement" for the establishment of a formal organization of petroleum exporting countries. Having reached an agreement in principle, the two influential leaders made a joint declaration in May, 1960, urging the producing countries to adopt a common policy in defense of their interests. The atmosphere for cooperation improved when posted prices were again unilaterally reduced in August, 1960—once more, without consultation with the producing countries. This led directly to the establishment of OPEC.

On September 9, 1960, representatives of the governments of Iran, Iraq, Kuwait, Saudi Arabia, and Venezuela met in Baghdad, Iraq. Five days later, on September 14, 1960, they reached an agreement providing for a permanent intergovernmental federation to be known as the Organization of the Petroleum Exporting Countries (OPEC). The five founding member countries controlled 67 percent of known recoverable reserves, produced 38 percent of world output, and exported 90 percent of oil moving in international trade.

The original aims and objectives of OPEC were modest, as indicated by its first two "Resolutions." The first Resolution provided

> that members shall demand that oil companies maintain their prices steady and free from all unnecessary fluctuations; that members shall endeavor, by all means available to them, to restore present prices to the levels prevailing before the reduction. That they shall ensure that if any new circumstances arise that in the estimation of the oil companies necessitates price modification the said companies shall enter into consultations with the member or members affected in order fully to explain the circumstances.

The second Resolution stated OPEC's overall objectives:

> The principal aim of the Organization shall be the unification of petroleum polices for the member countries and the determination of the best means for safeguarding the interests of member countries individually and collectively.

These broad objectives were increasingly given specific content in the form of "participation" in oil company management, investment decisions, and control over prices. However, no one in 1960 conceived the magnitude of the changes which were imminent.

Membership.   Membership in OPEC now consists of the five "founding" members and eight "new" members for a total of thirteen "full" members. Eligibility for membership requires that a country be a "substantial net exporter" and show that its petroleum interests are "fundamentally similar" to those of the founding members. New membership requires approval by three-fourths of the full members and the unanimous consent of the founding members.

Three members were admitted within two years of the organizational meeting: Qatar (1961), and Libya and Indonesia (1962). In 1967 the sheikdom of Abu Dhabi was admitted. (After oil was discovered in the small sheikdoms of Dubai, Sharjah, Ras al-Khaimah, and Umm al Qaywayn, they joined Abu Dhabi to form the United Arab Emirates.) Algeria (1969), Nigeria (1971), Ecuador (1973), and Gabon (1975) round out the membership.

Initial Success of OPEC.   OPEC succeeded in preventing further reductions in posted prices, but in the process it created a subtle institutional structure which resulted in downward pressure on realized market prices. The large excess capacity which existed in many countries and the low costs meant that prices could only be maintained by restricting output. Prior to the formation of OPEC, the international majors had performed that function tolerably well from the producers' point of view, although the new concessionaires in Venezuela and the Middle East had complicated their task.

The insistence on no reductions in "posted" or "tax-reference" prices aggravated the conflict of interest between the companies and the host governments. With fixed posted prices and fixed tax rates, the tax revenue derived from each barrel of oil was the same regardless of actual market prices. So the countries pressed the concessionaires to increase their lifting levels; and when the majors balked because additional quantitities could only be sold at lower prices, the host governments offered additional fields to newcomers to the world market. Thus, member countries were receiving a "false" market signal to the effect that revenues per barrel were unrelated to the total quantity produced. The operating companies were painfully aware that their revenues were dependent on both the level of production and the market price. But their alternative was to expand output at a rapid pace or lose their market share to aggressive rivals, including the newly established national oil companies.

The downward trend in world oil prices during the 1960s is widely believed to have been the result of competition among the international oil companies. In a limited sense, this was true. More fundamentally, however, prices declined because members of OPEC had much to gain by increasing their levels of output—and the international majors were unable to prevent expansion. The new concessionaires and rapid expansion of output in Venezuela and the Middle East are testimony to the fact that the large international corporations were not producing enough to satisfy the member countries. And so control of production at the wellhead gradually passed from the international companies to the member countries of OPEC.

Origin of OAPEC

The Arab–Israeli Conflict.   The formation of the Organization of Arab Petroleum Exporting Countries (OAPEC) was the direct result of the Third Arab–Israeli War, which occurred in June, 1967. It brought about subtle but profound changes in petroleum markets. As an initial response to the conflict, representatives of the Arab oil producing and transporting countries met and decided to prevent Arab oil from reaching any country which directly or indirectly supported Israel. On June 6–7, Syria closed its oil pipelines from Iraq and Saudi Arabia; Lebanon banned the loading of Iraqi and Saudi Arabian oil tankers in her ports; and Saudi Arabia stopped loading tankers bound for countries supporting Israel. The principal countries affected were the United States and Great Britain.

The "embargo" or "boycott" was important because it signified the willingness of the Arab countries to use oil as a political weapon. However, it was not very successful in denying oil to the importing countries. The United States had large excess capacity which could be brought on stream, and there were also stockpiles in Europe. Saudi Arabia enforced the embargo for only one week; but the more "radical" countries withheld oil for between two and four weeks. In all, when judged as a single event, it was a rather dismal failure.

Formation of OAPEC.   The failure of the embargo and the dissention among the unorganized Arab oil producing countries led directly to the formation of the Organization of Arab Petroleum Exporting Countries (OAPEC). OAPEC, organized in January, 1968, was originally a "conservative" group designed to *prevent* the use of oil as a political weapon. But it was destined to play an important role in the Arab oil embargo of October, 1973.

The original intent of the founding members was to exclude the Arab countries who desired to use oil as a political weapon in their disputes against Israel. The original membership requirements were that a country must be Arab, its major export must be oil, and the three founding members—Saudi Arabia, Kuwait, and Libya—must vote favorably on a new applicant. These requirements effectively ruled out Iran,

Egypt, and Algeria. (Iraq was not interested in membership at the time because of its radical and pro-Soviet orientation.)

After the overthrow of King Idris by Colonel Qadhafi in Libya, the OAPEC meeting scheduled to take place in Tripoli in December, 1969, was postponed. Qadhafi was a radical and firmly committed to using oil as a political weapon. The Libyan foreign minister at the time stated that oil ". . . must be used against our enemies; it does not make sense to sell oil to America which supplies Phantom planes to Israel, which are aimed to kill Arabs." In April, 1970, Algeria, Bahrain, Qatar, Abu Dhabi, and Dubai applied for membership in OAPEC and in May they were accepted. Saudi Arabian leaders opposed membership for Iraq because they hoped to keep oil and politics separate. However, in late 1971 Saudi Arabia acquiesced to changes in membership requirements and in March, 1972, Iraq, Syria, and Egypt were admitted as members. Thus, OAPEC rapidly became a political institution, with a majority of its membership intent on using oil as a political weapon. The formation of OAPEC set the stage for the dramatic events in world petroleum markets which were to take place during the 1970s.

Epilogue and Prologue

Cooperation has waxed and waned throughout the history of the world petroleum market. It is certain that pure competition is a far cry from an accurate characterization of the market. The individual participants have always functioned in a historical context and have generally learned, soon or late, that sincere cooperation is a good substitute for competition. American oilmen learned this lesson in the fields of Pennsylvania, Ohio, Oklahoma, and Texas. The heads of the international oil companies learned the same lesson in the United States and from their dealings in Indonesia, Venezuela, and the Middle East. Leaders of OPEC gradually reached the same conclusion based on their experiences with the international majors.

The principal groups responsible for fashioning the important institutions in the world oil market include: (1) the large international oil companies who functioned as a corporate cartel until the middle 1950s; (2) the smaller international oil companies who were invited by the member countries of OPEC to increase levels of output when members of the corporate cartel were prorationing; (3) the American producers who functioned as an isolated domestic cartel; and (4) the member countries of OPEC who assumed control over the level of production and prices after 1970.

Using this characterization, it is clear that the world price of oil declined during most of the years between 1945 and 1970 because one cartel was losing control to its rival. There was no master plan, but an emerging OPEC increasingly constrained the prorationing activities of the corporate cartel. The conflicts of interest between the members of each group were inherent! OPEC members were operating on the assumption that their net revenues per barrel were constant, and they sought to increase output; but the whole basis of cartel profits for the international companies was the ability to *limit* output and maintain prices. The fact that member countries of OPEC permitted smaller oil companies to operate within their boundaries in competition with the international majors is evidence that the corporate cartel was losing control, and this set the stage for greater control by OPEC.

Further Readings

Adelman, Morris. *The World Petroleum Market*. Baltimore: Resources for the Future, Inc., Johns Hopkins University Press, 1972.

Bohi, Douglas R., and Milton Russell. *Limiting Oil Imports, An Economic History and Analysis*. Baltimore: Johns Hopkins University Press, 1978.

Federal Trade Commission. *Report on the International Petroleum Cartel*. Washington, D.C.: 1951.

Rouhani, Faud. *A History of O.P.E.C.* New York and London: Praeger, 1971.

Rustow, Dankwart A. "Petroleum Politics, 1951–1974," *Dissent*, 21, Spring 1974, 144–53.

U.S. Cong. Senate. *Governmental Intervention in the Market Mechanism, The Petroleum Industry*. Hearings before the Subcommittee on Antitrust and Monopoly of the Subcommittee on the Judiciary, 91st Cong., 1st and 2nd sess. Pt. 1, Washington, D.C.: GPO, March 1969 and March 1970.

Wyant, Frank R. *The United States, OPEC, and Multinational Oil*. Lexington, Mass.: Lexington Books, 1977.

Part Three

Modern Structure

During the 1950s, oil prices were stable, and during the 1960s they declined. But the 1960s are ancient history with respect to the institutional mechanisms determining oil prices and levels of output—that is, the absolute level of prices and their variability. Prices increased sharply three times after 1970, and each increase was associated either with a revolution or a war involving an important oil producing country. To summarize, average posted prices of Saudi marker crude increased from $1.80 to $2.18 per barrel in 1971 and much more sharply in 1973–1974 and 1979–1980. By October 1, 1981, the price of marker crude was set at $34 per barrel. These price trends have been brought about by changes in the market structure resulting from the actions taken by OPEC members and the inaction on the part of importing countries. Part Three explains the fundamental processes involved in the transition to a new energy environment.

Chapter 7 focuses on the process which enables prices to increase dramatically and then remain flat for several years. This is known as "the oil price ratchet process." It developed because the delivery system for oil was constructed for a world in which supply disruptions could be mitigated by opening the valves in Texas, Oklahoma, Louisiana, and in other producing countries controlled by interests in the consuming countries. These sources of incremental supply dried up after 1970. And oil inventories or surplus capacity to cope with supply disruptions have not been developed to replace this formerly available surplus. In fact, there are subtle economic incentives which encourage buyers to build inventories when prices are rising and to draw down inventories when prices are stable. Once prices rise they do not come back down, because OPEC cuts production to maintain prices achieved during the upward phase of the

157

ratchet process. Chapter 7 is devoted to an explanation of the fundamental processes involved. A major conclusion is that leaders in the oil-exporting countries are well organized and have constructed institutions to redistribute income in their favor.

Chapter 8 contains an explanation of the importing countries' reactions to higher oil prices. The initial response was shock and confusion followed by a variety of measures designed to alleviate or even solve the problems associated with "dependence" on foreign oil and high prices. The chapter stresses the problems of building institutions to cope with the new energy environment. A major conclusion is that although leaders of the oil-importing countries are not very well organized, they have nevertheless made preliminary gestures toward constructing institutions of their own to cope with OPEC.

Chapter 9 outlines the major issues and options available to the exporting countries and OPEC. Indexing of oil and natural gas prices, decisions regarding new capacities, development, and utilization, and problems in maintaining "proper" price differentials are emphasized. The political issues include the use of oil as a weapon in the Arab—Israeli conflict. A point continually stressed is that decisions of OPEC will largely determine the course of energy prices for at least the next decade.

The orientation of the final chapter is neither exclusively scientific nor policy-related. It contains an assessment of the current state of world petroleum markets and forecasts price trends for the 1980s. The forecasts also include the policies which leaders in the exporting and importing countries are likely to adopt. Assessment beyond the 1980s is more difficult. However, a major conclusion is that OPEC is not about to crumble.

READER'S GUIDE TO PART THREE

This part of the book explains the modern structure of oil markets, analyzes the policy options of the consuming and producing countries, respectively, and provides a glimpse of the future. Chapter 7 is essential to understanding the modern structure of world petroleum markets. Chapter 8 can be profitably read by those interested in consuming country responses to OPEC's expanded role in world markets and the options considered by them. The policy options for the producing countries are taken up in Chapter 9. In general, the latter two chapters are organized so that the reader can gain an overview from the material presented under major headings or delve more deeply by reading the detailed analyses under each subheading. Chapter 10 contains a discussion of anticipated developments in world petroleum markets during the 1980s and, to a lesser extent, the 1990s.

Modern Structure of the World Oil Market

Overview.

Price Determination:
Analytical Framework; The Pricing System; The Persian Gulf-Plus Pricing System; Price Movements in the 1970s.

Consumption, Production, and Inventories:
Consumption; Production; Inventories.

The Cartel Problem and OPEC:
Capacity Utilization Rates.

The "New" Market Structure of the 1970s:
The First Oil Price Ratchet; The Geneva Accords; The Second Price Ratchet; The Third Price Ratchet.

Conclusion.

READER'S GUIDE TO CHAPTER 7
This chapter describes the post-1970 world oil market. The first section outlines the modern structure and explains why prices tend to be ratcheted upward rather than to increase smoothly over time. Next, there is a graphic illustration of price movements during the 1970s and an explanation of trends in consumption and production. The following section stresses the importance of the narrow delivery system and inventory policies in ratcheting prices upward. In conclusion, there is a preview of the principal subjects of Chapters 8 and 9—the market structure's effect on OPEC stability, consumer country reactions to price increases, and a survey of policy options for the consuming and producing countries.

Overview

The price of oil could be set so low that it just covers extraction costs in the Middle East or so high that alternative forms of energy would displace oil on a massive scale. The actual price that is set depends on policies adopted by businesses and government officials in the importing and exporting countries. The fact is that oil prices increased sharply three times during the 1970s but were relatively stable between the sharp upward movements. Each round of price increases was associated either with an internal political crisis or a war in an important producing country. The narrow delivery system and the policies of the companies, the governments of the consuming countries, and the members of OPEC, played important roles in driving prices to levels actually attained.

The nominal price levels of "Saudi Light" crude oil are recorded in Figure 7–1 along with the chronology of principal events that influenced the price jumps. The first round of price increases occurred in February, 1971, after the overthrow of King Idris in Libya and the assumption of control by Colonel Qadhafi. The new regime demanded both higher prices and a 58 percent share of company profits. This was followed by a series of "leapfrog" maneuvers resulting in price increases on the order of 20 percent (Table 7–1).

TABLE 7–1
Average Posted Price and Percentage Change in Price of Saudi Light Crude Oil, 1970–1980

Date	Average Posted Price (*dollars per barrel*)	Year-to-Date Percentage Change	Principal Event
1970	1.80	0.0	
1971	2.23	24.0	Tehran–Tripoli Agreements
1972	2.48	11.1	(February, 1971)
1973	3.63	46.3	Fourth Arab–Israeli War
1974	11.45	215.7	(October, 1973)
1975	12.18	6.4	
1976	12.13	−0.5	
1977	12.40	1.0	
1978	12.70	2.4	
1979	17.26	35.6	Iranian Coup (January, 1979)
1980	28.67	66.1	

SOURCE: Exxon, *Middle East Oil,* 2nd ed., New York: 1980, p. 25. © 1980 Exxon Corporation, Reprinted With Permission.

FIGURE 7–1

Selling Price of Middle East Crude (Using "Arab Light"[1] as an Example)

Dollars per Barrel

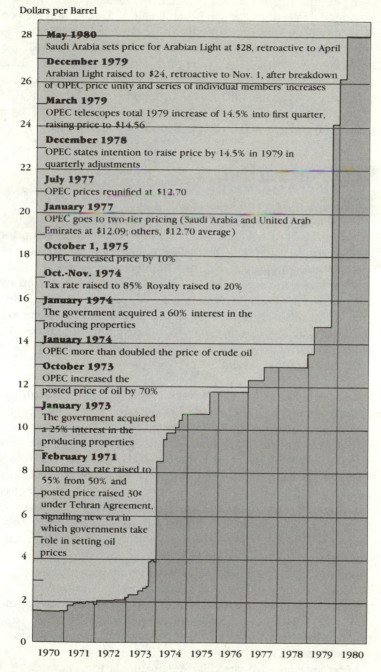

May 1980
Saudi Arabia sets price for Arabian Light at $28, retroactive to April

December 1979
Arabian Light raised to $24, retroactive to Nov. 1, after breakdown of OPEC price unity and series of individual members' increases

March 1979
OPEC telescopes total 1979 increase of 14.5% into first quarter, raising price to $14.56

December 1978
OPEC states intention to raise price by 14.5% in 1979 in quarterly adjustments

July 1977
OPEC prices reunified at $12.70

January 1977
OPEC goes to two-tier pricing (Saudi Arabia and United Arab Emirates at $12.09; others, $12.70 average)

October 1, 1975
OPEC increased price by 10%

Oct.-Nov. 1974
Tax rate raised to 85% Royalty raised to 20%

January 1974
The government acquired a 60% interest in the producing properties

January 1974
OPEC more than doubled the price of crude oil

October 1973
OPEC increased the posted price of oil by 70%

January 1973
The government acquired a 25% interest in the producing properties

February 1971
Income tax rate raised to 55% from 50% and posted price raised 30¢ under Tehran Agreement, signalling new era in which governments take role in setting oil prices

1970 1971 1972 1973 1974 1975 1976 1977 1978 1979 1980

---

[1]The term "Saudi Light" is often substituted for "Arab Light." Ed.

SOURCE: Exxon, *Middle East Oil*, 2nd ed. New York: 1980, p. 25. © 1980 Exxon Corporation, Reprinted With Permission.

More dramatic price increases occurred in association with the fourth Arab–Israeli conflict which began October 6, 1973, and the consequent Arab oil embargo extending from October, 1973 to March, 1974. The net result was a quadrupling of prices, to a level of $11–$12 per barrel. Nominal contract prices were fairly stable from 1974 until late 1978 when an Iranian *coup d'état* appeared imminent. In absolute terms the price increases during the first half of 1979 exceeded those in 1974. Prices eventually increased by about two and one-half times—to $30 per barrel in 1980 and to $34 per barrel effective October 1, 1981.

Price Determination

Analytical Framework

The absolute level of crude oil prices cannot be determined a priori, because prices depend on the interactive polices of individuals in both the exporting and importing countries. Elementary supply-and-demand theory provides a framework within which the oil market may be analyzed. However, the theory must be judiciously applied. The goal of this chapter is to explain the market structure and the actual price movements during the 1970s, rather than to ascertain what prices could or should have been relative to some normative standard. The orientation is strictly in the positive realm.

Shortages at a Price.   The definition of a "high" or "low" price is the source of much confusion in the analysis of oil prices. The question should always be: "High or low relative to what?" During the period 1950–1973 the oil importing countries bought increasing quantities from the member nations of OPEC because oil prices were low relative to prices of alternative fuels. Contrary to popular opinion, oil prices remained low during the 1970s *relative to what many consumers were willing to pay*. Consumers were clearly unable to find alternative fuels or to curb consumption significantly enough to reduce imports. This is evidence that oil prices were low relative to the alternatives of using other energy resources or doing without.

But from another perspective, oil prices were very high during the 1970s *relative to average extraction costs*. The latter ranged from less than $1 per barrel to the current market price. There is always a "marginal" barrel which costs approximately what it will fetch in the market, and many submarginal barrels which are not exploited because their costs would exceed market prices.

Oil prices were also very high relative to historical standards. In 1980 they were on the order of twenty times as high as in the late 1960s.

This accounts for the popular opinion that there is an oil shortage. There *is* a "shortage" at historical prices, but not at prevailing market prices. The problem is not, nor has it ever been, that oil is unavailable; oil always has been and will be available at a price. The problem is that many people consider the price too high. Some economists in the consuming countries believe oil prices are "too high" relative to the competitive norm; and the general public believes oil prices are "too high" relative to expectations based on historical experience.

Supply and Demand.   When a cartel forms and is in the process of consolidating its position, the market may be characterized by unused capacity. This is likely to occur because the higher prices associated with cooperation reduce consumption and increase production by the "competitive fringe" of producers who do not formally participate in the cartel agreement. Nowhere has this general pattern been more clearly illustrated than with OPEC since 1973. The residual demand model can be used to show the effect of higher prices on consumption, on OPEC and non-OPEC production, and on capacity utilization.

Residual Demand Model.   The world demand for oil is represented in Figure 7–2(a) by curve D_W; non-OPEC supply is shown by S_N.

FIGURE 7–2
OPEC Residual Demand Model

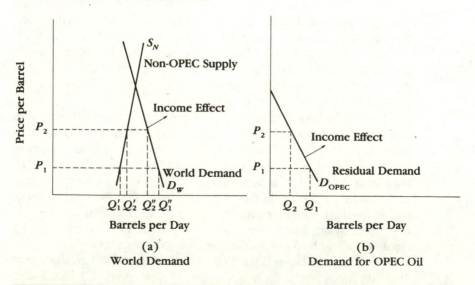

(a)
World Demand

(b)
Demand for OPEC Oil

The relatively low price, P_1, and large quantity, Q''_1, may be thought of as the pre-embargo relation. Non-OPEC producers sell quantity Q'_1 and OPEC nations sell the "residual" between Q''_1 and Q'_1. The post-embargo price is higher, P_2, and world demand is lower, Q''_2; non-OPEC producers sell more, Q'_2, and OPEC nations sell the much smaller "residual" between Q''_2 and Q'_2.

The "residual" demand for oil from OPEC is the horizontal distance between D_W and S_N; it depends on the elasticity of world demand and on non-OPEC supply. The residual demand curve derived from part (a) is shown in part (b) of the figure. The quantity Q_1 corresponds to Q''_1 - Q'_1, and Q_2 corresponds to Q''_2 - Q'_2. OPEC faces a residual demand schedule, or is the "residual supplier," for the world under the assumption that OPEC desires to maintain a specified price, such as P_2. In order to maintain a price of P_2, some producers must "shut-in" enough capacity to ensure that world output does not exceed Q''_2, otherwise the market price will fall. OPEC nations are presumably the ones willing to shut-in capacity in order to maintain the higher price.

Applicability to the World Oil Market.   The residual demand model is particularly useful in analyzing the oil market in a time frame such as a few years or a decade. But it is less applicable to the analysis of seasonal and monthly variations in output and prices. In very short time frames such as these, income changes or "income effects" can easily outweigh expected reductions in demand caused by higher prices. On the other hand, lead times required to expand output make supply highly inelastic in a time frame of much less than two or three years. The residual demand model is not particularly useful to the analysis of a longer time frame such as two decades or more, because finding additional reserves is problematic and depletion becomes a more important consideration. Therefore, it is by no means certain that higher prices will call forth larger quantities from non-OPEC producers in either a very short or a very long time frame.

The residual demand model must be used judiciously even in short- to midterm analyses because non-OPEC producers may not respond as anticipated on the basis of the model. For example, higher oil prices may be expected to call forth greater output from non-OPEC producers, but Canada reduced its oil exports after 1973 by a far greater percentage than did any of the OPEC nations. The reason was that the provincial and national governments could not agree on the distribution of income derived from oil, which caused a stalemate over how to proceed. The result was lower levels of production. Similarly, price ceilings associated with oil price regulation in the United States reduced the production of "old oil" and retarded the development of new reserves. Federal–state jurisdictional problems also played a role in slowing natural gas pipeline construction and the development of oil shale.

Nevertheless, a good theory provides the basis for predicting tendencies, and the residual demand model is a good theory when properly employed. Since oil prices increased sharply during the 1970s, the responses one would expect based on the residual demand model may be summarized below. Compared with what would have prevailed in the absence of sharp price increases, the model predicts:

1. Lower consumption
2. Higher non-OPEC production
3. Lower OPEC production

Determining what "would have prevailed in the absence of price increases" requires judgment. However, it will be shown that predictions based on the residual demand model describe actual events remarkably well.

The Pricing System

Real markets are characterized by subtle institutional relationships, and the world oil market is no exception. This market is best characterized as one dominated by a cartel which has attempted to maintain both prices and stable market shares for its members. However, there are inherent problems in the establishment and maintenance of prices for the various crudes produced by OPEC members. The pricing problem as presently constituted consists of two parts: (1) determining the absolute price of the Saudi "marker crude," and (2) establishing "differentials" around the "marker" price. The problems cannot be resolved once and for all because both objectives have a dynamic dimension involving changes in the marker price and changes in the differentials.

Marker Price and Differentials.   The pricing mechanism which evolved after 1970 is similar to previous pricing systems. It may be described approximately as follows: Saudi Arabia determines the price level by specifying the price of its most abundant crude, Saudi Light, 34° API gravity. This is the "marker crude price." Each country then selects a price for its crude. The difference between the price of a given crude and the price of the marker crude is called the "differential."

Most purchases of crude oil are made by refiners or by the refinery division of an integrated company. Refiners generally purchase on long-term contracts of a year or more. The refiners' decision to purchase one crude rather than another depends on relative prices of those available. Crudes yielding relatively large quantities of the more highly valued products, such as gasoline, command a higher price than other crudes. Similarly, crudes which have a low sulphur content are more highly valued.

Refiners' Decision Process.   Refiner buyers examine the alternative prices available and select those crudes which will maximize their profits. When prices change, they generally switch away from crudes whose *relative* price has increased and buy more of those whose price has declined. However, moderate or temporary price changes do not result in the complete loss of a market. Even more or less permanent changes do not have this result since there are established buyer–seller relationships which are not severed easily or without cost. The tendencies brought about by relative price changes may operate very slowly, as when buyers have long-term commitments and long-established relationships. On the other hand, refiners may respond quickly, as in the spot market.

As if the problem were not difficult enough, refiners differ in terms of their geographic location, refining equipment, optimal product mix, and environmental laws regulating their operation. Determining actual choices of one crude over another for a particular refiner is therefore a very complex problem. However, the broad principles are not difficult to comprehend.

Consider a refiner deciding between two crudes, Saudi Light and Iranian Light. These are approximately equal in quality and available from the same geographic region. For simplicity, suppose the quality and transport costs are identical. If the prices were also equal, the refiner would be indifferent between the two. He might even flip a coin to decide which to purchase. In other words, the probability of buying either Saudi or Iranian Light would be one-half, or 0.5. This is shown in Figure 7–3, where the price ratio of Iranian to Saudi Light is unity. Thus if Iranian Light were 4 percent cheaper than Saudi Light ($P_i/P_j = .96$), the refiner would always buy the Iranian; and, if Iranian Light were 4 percent higher, the refiner would always buy the Saudi Light.

Similar statements can be made for higher and lower quality crudes, such as Libyan "Zueitina" and Venezuelan "Tia Juana." When price differentials are sufficiently great it induces refiner buyers to switch to crudes they regard as "undervalued." It is an accurate description of the pricing system to say that sellers largely determine prices but that buyers determine volume and market shares among suppliers. Sellers influence overall volume and market shares through the price level and pattern of differentials they choose to establish.

The Persian Gulf-Plus Pricing System

The pricing mechanism outlined above is equivalent to a single base-point pricing system, with the Persian Gulf as the base point. It evolved during the 1970s because the Persian Gulf, particularly Ras Tanura, Saudi

FIGURE 7–3

Probability of Purchasing ith Crude, Libyan Zueitina, Iranian Light, and Venezuelan Tia Juana at Alternative Prices Relative to the Saudi Marker Crude (P^J)

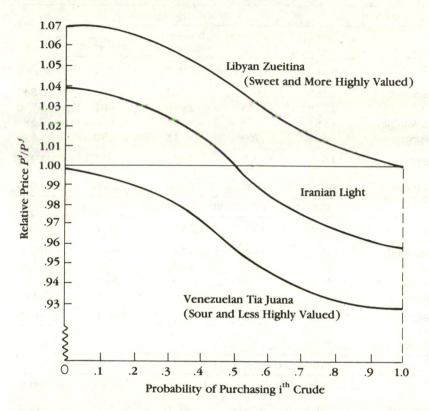

Arabia, became the leading oil exporting center. Prices are now high relative to production costs in the principal exporting countries, and the degree of cooperation among OPEC member nations is sufficiently great that all prices are based on the Saudi marker crude prices, notwithstanding disagreements within OPEC concerning the appropriate price level.

Principal Oil Movements. The importance of the Persian Gulf-Plus system may be illustrated by examining data on regional exports sent to the major consuming regions (Table 7–2 and Figure 7–4). Persian Gulf oil represented about half the total exports for 1979 and it was

TABLE 7–2

Crude Oil Exports and Imports by Principal Regions of Origin and Destination, 1979

(thousand barrels per day)

EXPORTING REGION[1]	IMPORTING REGION				
Production	United States	Japan	Western Europe	Other[2]	Total
OPEC	6,417	4,697	10,897	8,729	30,740
Persian Gulf	2,385	3,910	7,787	6,758	20,840
Africa	2,618	15	2,416	681	5,730
South America	991	8	681	900	2,580
Indonesia	423	764	13	390	1,590
Non-OPEC	1,994	940	5,337	2,955	11,226
Total Imports	8,411	5,637	16,234	11,684	41,966
PERCENT OF EXPORT REGION TOTAL					
OPEC	20.9	15.3	35.5	28.4	100.0
Persian Gulf	11.4	18.8	37.4	32.4	100.0
Africa	45.7	0.3	42.2	11.9	100.0
South America	38.4	0.3	26.4	34.9	100.0
Indonesia	26.6	48.1	0.8	24.5	100.0
Non-OPEC	17.7	8.4	47.5	26.3	100.0
Total Imports	20.1	13.4	38.7	27.8	100.0
PERCENT OF IMPORT REGION TOTAL					
OPEC	76.3	83.4	67.1	74.7	73.2
Persian Gulf	28.4	69.4	48.0	57.9	49.7
Africa	31.1	0.3	14.9	5.8	13.7
South America	11.8	0.1	4.2	7.7	6.2
Indonesia	5.0	13.6	0.1	3.3	3.8
Non-OPEC	23.7	16.7	32.9	25.3	26.8
Total Imports	100.0	100.0	100.0	100.0	100.0

[1]Regions are defined as follows:
　Persian Gulf: Saudi Arabia, Iran, Iraq, Kuwait, UAE, and Qatar.
　Africa: Libya, Nigeria, Algeria, and Gabon.
　South America: Venezuela and Ecuador.
[2]Includes oil consumed within each member country of OPEC.
SOURCE: Central Intelligence Agency, *International Energy Statistical Review,* 20 Aug. 1980, p. 4.

FIGURE 7–4
Principal Oil Movements by Sea

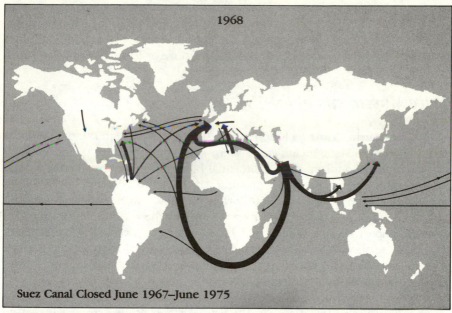

1968

Suez Canal Closed June 1967–June 1975

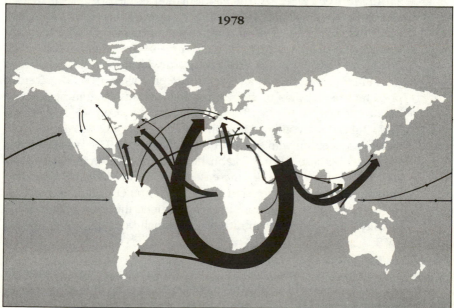

1978

SOURCE: Exxon, *Middle East Oil*, 2nd ed. New York: 1980, p. 15. © 1980 Exxon Corporation, Reprinted With Permission.

shipped worldwide. Almost no oil from Africa or South America flowed to Japan, and only a negligible quantity from Indonesia reached Western Europe. These patterns emerged because African and South American crudes were priced equal to or slightly below those from the Persian Gulf. Indonesian crudes could fetch better prices in the Far East, Japan, and California. It is a pattern compatible with a Persian Gulf-Plus base-point pricing system. It is the system more or less in effect at present.

Price Movements in the 1970s

Spot and Contract Markets.   The pricing system is more complex than the Persian Gulf-Plus system may imply, because oil can be purchased on a long-term contractual basis or on the spot market. Crude sales contracts are far from uniform but have generally become less rigid than during the 1960s; prices are now subject to change without notice. The official price is established by the producer country and is simply the price in effect on the date a tanker arrives at the loading port. Nevertheless, these prices tend to remain stable for prolonged periods whereas spot prices fluctuate daily because each tanker load or portion thereof is subject to negotiation.

Saudi Marker Price.   The Saudi marker crude price has increased sharply three times since 1970 and each upward thrust has been associated with a political crisis or a war in an important producing country. Between the sharp upward movements prices were relatively stable. The first set of price increases was associated with the overthrow of King Idris in Libya and the Tehran–Tripoli agreements in 1971. The average price increased by about 24 percent, but this was a significant change because it marked the first time prices had increased since 1957 (see Table 7–1). The second major round of price increases was the fourfold increase associated with the Arab oil embargo of 1973–1974. This was significant because it firmly established OPEC's position in regard to its ability to set prices. The price increases in 1979 and 1980 were associated with the Iranian revolution and resulted in another doubling of prices. But between the sharp upward price movements there was relative price stability—for example, contract prices actually declined in 1976 and 1978.

Spot Prices.   Spot prices are not collected by a government agency but are "estimated" by daily trade publications, such as *Platts' Oil Price Service*. The principal locations for spot price quotations are Rotterdam, New York, Italy, and the Caribbean. Spot and contract prices are generally related to one another but spot prices are more highly variable. An interesting and important aspect of the relationship between spot and contract prices is that spot prices always lead contract prices up. This happened in 1971, 1973, and 1978–1979 (see Figure 7–5).

The reason for this relationship is not hard to find. Leaders of OPEC nations are caught in a dilemma when spot prices greatly exceed contract prices, because a company buying on contract can immediately resell on the spot market and reap handsome profits. Even when a company does not or cannot resell on the spot market because of contractual agreements, it can eventually reap as much by selling to its own end-use customers downstream. These revenues could just as well be accruing to the member countries, and some leaders within OPEC naturally think they should. No producing country will tolerate spot prices greatly exceeding contract prices indefinitely. Thus, spot prices influence contract prices and generally lead them upward.

In fact, the variability of world oil prices and the price level itself have been influenced greatly by the relationship between spot and contract prices. Combined with the willingness of OPEC nations to cut production rather than prices when markets are weak, the spot and contract relationship literally explains the price trends observed. Consequently, the spot market is of far greater importance in price determination than the volume of spot trading might indicate.

Consumption, Production, and Inventories

The analysis of oil consumption, production, and inventories is important to understanding the level and stability of oil prices. The analysis is complicated by seasonal and cyclical variations in consumption, inventory speculation, and the fact that oil inventories are mostly of the working and precautionary variety (that is, oil in transit or strategic reserves). Consumption, production, and oil stocks are, of course, intricately related.

Consumption

Oil consumption is not measured as accurately as production, since basic data are collected only from producers. The cost of surveying consumers is considered prohibitive, so worldwide trends in consumption must be estimated on the basis of production figures and on measured inventory changes. Table 7–3 contains official estimates of world and free world production, inventory changes, and free world consumption for the period 1973–1980. Free world consumption declined

FIGURE 7–5

Contract and Spot Prices, 1970–1981

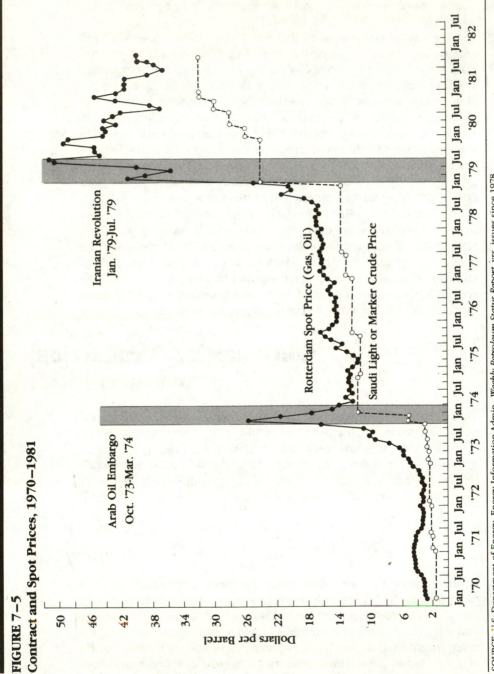

Iranian Revolution
Jan. '79–Jul. '79

Arab Oil Embargo
Oct. '73–Mar. '74

Rotterdam Spot Price (Gas, Oil)

Saudi Light or Marker Crude Price

Dollars per Barrel

SOURCE: U.S. Department of Energy, Energy Information Admin., *Weekly Petroleum Status Report*, vrs. issues since 1978.

TABLE 7–3
Production, Inventory Change, and Free World Consumption of
Crude Oil, 1973–1980[1]
(million barrels per day)

	PRODUCTION			CONSUMPTION	
Year	World	Russia and China	Free World[2]	Inventory Changes	Free World Consumption[3]
1973	55.8	9.6	46.2	N.A.	46.2
1974	55.9	10.3	45.6	1.3	44.3
1975	53.0	11.1	41.9	0.3	41.6
1976	57.4	11.9	45.5	−0.1	45.6
1977	59.6	12.6	47.0	0.7	47.0
1978	60.2	13.3	46.9	−0.3	47.2
1979	62.4	13.6	48.6	0.6	48.2
1980	59.4	13.8	45.6	0.1	45.6

[1]Comparable inventory data are not available prior to 1974.
[2]World minus Russia and China.
[3]Free world production minus inventory change.
SOURCE: U.S. Department of Energy, *Monthly Energy Review,* Sept. 1981, p. 91. U.S. Department of Energy, *International Energy Indicators,* July 1981, p. 8.

by 1.9 million barrels per day between 1973 and 1974, and by another 2.9 million barrels per day during the recession of 1975. Oil consumption rebounded in 1976 to near the 1973 level and continued to climb slowly until the price increases of 1979–1980 and the recession of 1980–1981.

Growth rate estimates vary depending on the method used in their calculation and the time period covered. Nevertheless, *the rate of increase* in oil consumption was substantially lower after 1973 as compared with previous periods. Thus, one of the predictions based on elementary supply-and-demand analysis is borne out by historical events. Consumption is substantially lower than what could reasonably have been expected in 1973.

Production

Crude oil production trends for OPEC and non-OPEC free world countries are shown in Figure 7–6. The most striking feature is the difference in the pre- and post-embargo production trends. Before the embargo, OPEC production increased at an average annual rate of about 2 million barrels per day; after the embargo, OPEC production was flat and more

FIGURE 7–6
Crude Oil Production by OPEC and Non-OPEC Free World Countries, 1970–1981

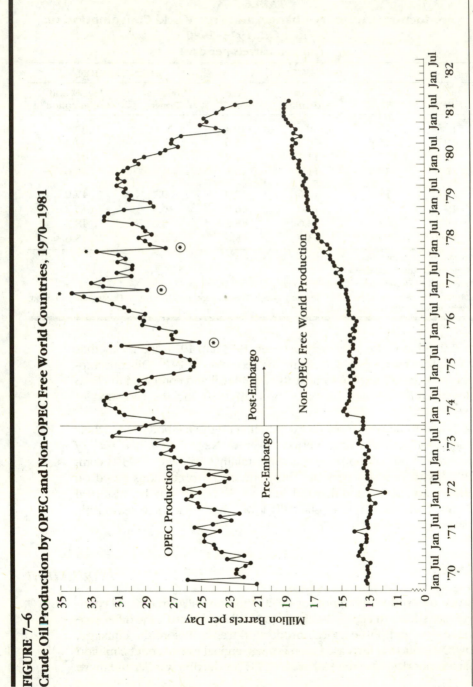

SOURCE: U.S. Department of Energy, Office of International Affairs, *International Energy Indicators*, vrs. issues since 1978. OPEC and Non-OPEC production: *Petroleum Intelligence Weekly*, 28 Sept. 1981, p. 11.

highly volatile. On the other hand, non-OPEC production was relatively flat before the embargo but increased steadily during the post-embargo period, especially after 1977. Alaskan North Slope, North Sea, and Mexican oil are primarily responsible for the increased non-OPEC production.

The production trends in the 1970s are compatible with what might be expected on the basis of the residual demand model. OPEC production was more highly variable from month to month and year to year than that of non-OPEC production, reflecting the role of OPEC as a residual supplier. OPEC production fell to the extraordinarily low level of 26 million barrels per day during the period February through May, 1975. This was attributable to the recession of 1975 and a draw-down of inventories. A similar pattern emerged in 1980 and 1981 owing to the same basic forces.

An interesting pattern of production variability emerged based on what might be called the OPEC "announcement effect." Typically, price increases are announced following an OPEC ministerial meeting. The meetings at which price increases were anticipated are shown by the symbol * in Figure 7–6. The month following the OPEC meeting is shown by the symbol ⊛. The most extreme "announcement effects" occurred in 1975, when production fell from 30.7 million to 25.3 million barrels per day between September and October; in December, 1976, and January, 1977, when production reached 34.5 million barrels per day, only to decline to 29.0; and then one year later, when production fell from 32.6 million to 27.6 million barrels per day between December and January.

The extreme variation in OPEC production during this period was due to the manner in which OPEC set prices and the fact that buyers were determining from whom and how much they would buy. The OPEC ministers learned an important lesson from these production trends and in December, 1978, they announced that prices would be raised four times "in tiers" during 1979. This was an attempt to mitigate the adverse effects of the announcement. The events of 1979 and 1980 overwhelmed this policy initiative but the lesson was clear: Buyers will build inventories to beat anticipated price increases if they are reasonably certain such increases will be implemented. This is why knowledge of inventory fluctuations is required if one is to understand the extreme variability in OPEC production.

Inventories

Definitions.   Crude oil and refined product inventories are classified as strategic, primary, secondary, and tertiary. *Strategic reserves* are held in below- and above-ground storage facilities as a contingency against supply interruptions. Primary, secondary, and tertiary reserves are "working inventories." Those held at refineries, in pipelines, and at bulk storage terminals with a capacity of 50,000 barrels or more are considered *primary*; those held by wholesalers and retailers are *secondary*; and those held at the point of consumption are classified as *tertiary*. Data on tertiary stocks are not recorded but fluctuate seasonally, cyclically, and during supply crises (for example, topping off tanks when gasoline is in short supply).

Strategic reserves traditionally have been held in the form of standby productive capacity which remains available in the event of a supply disruption—the U.S. Naval Petroleum Reserve program, operative since the early 1920s, falls in this category. Underground storage of oil extracted from one reservoir and reinjected into salt domes or other repositories became more prevalent after 1970, the U.S. Strategic Petroleum Reserve being a prime example. Strategic reserves have been built for the purpose of mitigating politico-economic embargoes as well as for purposes of national defense.

U.S. Oil Stocks.   Fairly reliable monthly data on oil stocks covering the entire 1970s are available for the United States but not for the world as a whole. Stock levels and trends in the United States are indicative of stocks held by other countries, however. Table 7–4 and Figure 7–7 show primary stocks held in the United States during the period 1970–1979. The oil embargo and price increases of 1973–1974 definitely stimulated the build-up of oil inventories. Inventories have always been highly variable, both before and after the embargo, but the post-embargo trend was upward, whereas the pre-embargo trend was flat. Since U.S. inventories represented 33 percent of the world total in 1973 and only 31 percent in 1980, other countries built inventories even more rapidly after the embargo than did the United States.

Figure 7–7 is designed to emphasize the seasonal nature of oil inventory policy. The various refined products have their individual patterns of seasonal usage but distillate fuel oil varies more than the other products and dominates the crude oil and refined product inventory series. Gasoline inventories vary by about 20 million barrels between their typical high in March and their normal low in October, whereas distillate fuel oil varies by 80 to 90 million barrels during the same period, except that the typical high is in October. Large fuel oil inventories in October are designed to meet fall and winter demands. Residual fuel oil follows the same seasonal pattern as distillate but varies by only about 10 million barrels.

With consumption growing each year, one might also expect inventories to grow. However, as can be seen from Figure 7–7, inventories were not built steadily over the entire period. In fact, consumption was

TABLE 7–4
Stocks of Crude Oil and Refined Products; United States, 1970–1980

Date	ACTUAL STOCK	STOCK BUILDUP MARCH–OCTOBER		STOCK DRAW-DOWN OCTOBER–MARCH	
	Million Barrels	Million Barrels	Million Barrels Per Day	Million Barrels	Million Barrels Per Day
March 1970	906	119	0.46		
Oct. 1970	1,025			−91	−0.60
March 1971	934	163	0.76		
Oct. 1971	1,097			−155	−1.02
March 1972	942	109	0.51		
Oct. 1972	1,051			−164	−1.09
March 1973	887	150	0.70		
Oct. 1973	1,037			−74	−0.49
March 1974	953	153	0.71		
Oct. 1974	1,106			−32	−0.21
March 1975	1,076	80	0.37		
Oct. 1975	1,156			−95	−0.63
March 1976	1,061	143	0.67		
Oct. 1976	1,204			−117	−0.77
March 1977	1,087	249	1.16		
Oct. 1977	1,336			−168	−1.11
March 1978	1,168	113	0.53		
Oct. 1978	1,281			−135	−0.89
March 1979	1,146	183	0.86		
Oct. 1979	1,329			13	0.07
March 1980	1,342	59	0.32		
Oct. 1980	1,401				
Average (1970s)	1,000	150	0.67	−75	−0.89

SOURCE: U.S. Department of Energy, Energy Information Administration, *Energy Information Administration Weekly Petroleum Status Report*, 14 Nov. 1980, p. 6.

growing at a rapid rate prior to October, 1973, but inventories were drawn down in both 1972 and 1973, just prior to the embargo. Oil inventories were built during the embargo period and the 1979 "crisis." Inventories were drawn down by only 0.49 million barrels per day during the embargo compared with the average seasonal draw-down of 0.76 million barrels per day.

The period March, 1977, to March, 1978, is noteworthy for the degree of instability in oil inventories. The build-up from March to October, 1977, was 1.16 million barrels per day compared with the average level of 0.67 million. The draw-down of 1.11 million barrels per

FIGURE 7-7
Inventories of Crude Oil and Refined Products; United States, 1970–1981

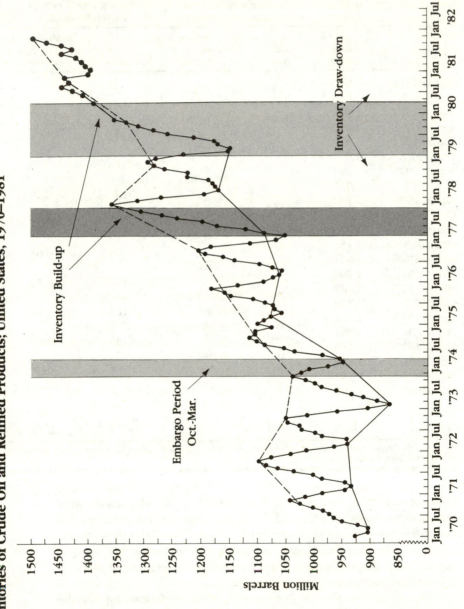

SOURCE: U.S. Department of Energy, Energy Information Admin., *Weekly Petroleum Status Report*, vrs. issues since 1978.

day during the next six months was substantially greater than the 0.89 million average. These relatively small changes in inventory build-up and drawn-down in the United States were magnified by similar swings in inventories worldwide. In fact, worldwide inventory changes can cause production to fluctuate by 1.5 million to 3.0 million barrels per day, and most of the instability falls on OPEC nations, which act as residual suppliers.

Oil Stocks in IEA Countries.   In response to the 1973–1974 Arab oil embargo, the principal oil consuming nations formed the International Energy Agency (IEA). All major consuming countries except France are IEA members, as will be explained in Chapter 8. Data for the IEA countries plus France, which are available quarterly, indicate that the same pattern of inventory build-up and draw-down emerged as in the United States. Strategic and primary inventories amounted to 2.6 billion barrels on March 31, 1973, whereas seven years later these stocks stood at 4.2 billion barrels. The build-up of 1.6 billion barrels means that production exceeded consumption by 0.63 million barrels per day over the entire period. However, the stock build-ups and draw-downs were highly variable, both seasonally and cyclically.

The seasonal nature of consumption and inventory accumulation are essentially the same for the IEA as for the United States. Crude oil consumption during the late 1970s was typically 3 to 6 million barrels per day higher in the fall and winter than in the spring and summer. Stocks were drawn down by 1 to 3 million barrels per day in the winter, built-up by 1 to 2 million barrels per day in the spring and summer, and drawn-down by 0 to 1 million barrels per day in the fall. The quantities varied slightly from year to year depending on weather conditions, the general level of economic activity, and speculative inventory changes. There is a seasonal regularity in consumption and a slow increase from year to year. However, the rate of growth was much slower than in the 1960s and early 1970s.

Effect on World Oil Prices.   As presently constituted, the delivery system contributes to the magnitude of upward price movements. The system, which was designed to accommodate an uninterrupted flow of oil from the wellhead to the final consumer, consists of tankers, barges, pipelines, and tanks containing working inventories, as well as a managerial system for deciding when and how to utilize available facilities. The average time between extraction and consumption of oil is about 70 to 80 days. There is sufficient excess capacity at all levels of the system to meet seasonal variations in demand and to allow for modest levels of inventory accumulation. However, since there is relatively little slack in the overall system, virtually any interruption in supply is sufficient to provoke a short-term supply crisis.

Spot prices are sensitive to anticipated shortages because the delivery system was constructed for a "business as usual" environment and therefore contains relatively little surplus to cope with a supply cut-off. Since inventories are costly to build and carry it pays to minimize them when prices are constant or declining. It only pays to build inventories when prices are expected to increase at a rate greater than the opportunity costs of money (for example, the market rate of interest).

The system OPEC nations employ to establish prices ensures that prices will rise during a political crisis or after an OPEC ministerial meeting. The inventory build-up in anticipation of periodic OPEC price increases can be seen from the high OPEC production figures in December compared with January, when new prices go into effect. This announcement effect is well-known in oil circles. The inventory build-up associated with political crises was particularly evident in 1973 and 1979. It is a predictable market phenomenon—one that will become more evident when the specific events of the 1970s are recounted.

Seasonal inventory policies tend to stabilize oil production. However, the stock draw-down would be greater in the fall and smaller in the winter if it were not for the OPEC announcement effect. The international oil companies increase stocks in December to "beat" the price increase and work them off in January, February, and March. The inordinate fall quarter buying is a form of inventory speculation which destabilizes OPEC production. OPEC production is typically 2 million barrels per day higher in the fall than in the winter quarter, and the December level is often 4 to 5 million barrels per day higher than the following January. This is in sharp contrast to the small variation in production by non-OPEC members.

The Cartel Problem and OPEC

Oil prices are high relative to historical standards and to production costs because OPEC members have gained control over the rate of exploration, development of reserves, and capacity utilization. The capacity utilization rate is the single most important determinant of the crude oil price level in the short run, whereas reserve development and capacity utilization codetermine prices in the long run. The members of OPEC developed reserves slowly during the 1970s in the name of conservation and were able to maintain prices far above competitive levels. Production generally averaged about 80 to 85 percent of sustainable capacity for OPEC as a whole during this period and was flexible enough to accommodate substantial fluctuations in world consumption and inventory demand. Nevertheless, maintaining prices and cartel discipline was by no means easy. The cartel problem regarding who shall take production cuts to maintain prices was ever present, but a reasonably satisfactory solution was worked out through the differentials and the Persian Gulf-Plus pricing system.

Capacity Utilization Rates

Market Shares.   According to former OPEC Secretary General Ali Jaidah, an avowed goal of the member countries is to establish differentials which will maintain stable market shares within OPEC. However, this goal is difficult to achieve under present pricing practices because most of the member countries have established prices relative to the marker crude, which leaves them with considerable excess capacity. In addition, the marker crude itself has been elevated to such a high level that there is typically excess capacity in Saudi Arabia. Under these circumstances buyers generally determine the quantity bought from each country and, therefore, buyers—not sellers—determine market shares. This corresponds to the general principle that a monopolist (or a cartel) can select either quantity or price, but not both. The difference between this and a more competitive market structure is that the competitive firm has no control over prices; it can only determine quantities brought to market.

Definition of Capacity.   The term *capacity* has at least three distinct meanings: (1) installed, (2) maximum sustainable, and (3) available. According to the U.S. Central Intelligence Agency:

> Installed capacity, also nameplate or design capacity, includes all aspects of crude oil production, processing, transportation, and storage. Installed capacity is generally the highest capacity estimate.
>
> Maximum sustainable or operational capacity (also referred to as technical capacity) is the maximum production rate that can be sustained for several months; it considers the experience of operating the total system and is generally some 90–95 percent of installed capacity. This capacity concept does not necessarily reflect the maximum production rate sustainable without damage to the fields.
>
> Available or allowable capacity reflects production ceilings applied by Abu Dhabi, Kuwait, Iran, and Saudi Arabia. These ceilings usually represent a constraint only on annual average output, and thus production may exceed the ceilings in a given month.[1]

---

[1] Central Intelligence Agency, *International Energy Statistical Review*, 25 November 1980, p. 3.

Technical and available capacity are the most relevant concepts from the standpoint of assessing "excess capacity" in the member countries. A country operating near available capacity is under little or no pressure to lower prices. When all countries are operating near available capacity, the market is said to be "tight." A country operating with considerable excess available capacity is under pressure to lower prices; it can do so quite easily by adjusting its differentials. When all or most countries are operating below available capacity there is said to be an "oil glut."

OPEC Capacity Utilization.   The importance of capacity utilization rates can be illustrated by a recent example. In 1979, a reduction of oil exports from Iran and the resulting inventory accumulation made oil markets extraordinarily tight. Thus, the utilization of available capacity outside Iran increased to an inordinately high level (Table 7–5). Eighty-nine percent of "maximum sustainable capacity" and 99 percent of "available" capacity were utilized in 1979. However, these figures represent an average for the whole year and are not typical of utilization rates for individual countries. Capacity utilization is highly variable from month to month for OPEC considered as a whole, and even more highly variable for individual countries. Figures 7–8(a), (b), and (c) show "technical" capacity, production, and the difference between the two, called "shut-in capacity," for Saudi Arabia, Iran, and other OPEC members. Saudi Arabia had large shut-in capacity during the 1975 recession and during the 1978 period when inventories were drawn down to very low levels. Since later 1978 there has been little excess capacity in Saudi Arabia. A similar, although less pronounced, pattern is observable for the other OPEC members, especially during 1979. Capacity utilization outside Saudi Arabia has declined since mid-1979 because of dissention within the ranks of OPEC regarding the proper price and differentials. The variability of capacity utilization is a reflection of the cartel problem and is a testament to the difficulty of maintaining stable market shares.

The "New" Market Structure of the 1970s[2]

OPEC now functions as a price-setting and output-limiting institution, and it has opted for a policy of high prices relative to those prior to 1970. The delivery system for oil contributes to the periodic upward movement of prices, and the relation between the spot and contract

---

[2]Portions of this section are based on "World Oil Price Increases: Sources and Solutions," *The Energy Journal*, Oct 1980.

TABLE 7–5
Crude Oil Productive Capacity for Member Countries of OPEC, January 1, 1980
(million barrels per day)

Country	Concepts of Capacity			Cumulative Total of Available Capacity	Average Production in 1979	Percent Utilization of Available Capacity
	Installed	Maximum Sustainable	Available			
Saudi Arabia[3]	12.5[6]	9.5	9.5	9.5	9.2	97
Iran	7.0	5.5[1]	3.5[2]	13.0	3.0	86
Iraq	4.0	3.5	3.5	16.5	3.4	97
Kuwait[3]	2.9	2.5	1.5	18.0	3.3	147
Neutral Zone[4]	0.6	0.6	0.6	18.6	0.5	90
Venezuela	2.6	2.4	2.2	20.8	2.4	107
United Arab Emirates	2.6	2.4	1.8	22.6	1.8	100
Libya	2.5	2.2	2.2	24.8	2.1	94
Nigeria	2.5	2.2	2.2[5]	27.0	2.3	105
Indonesia	1.8	1.7	1.7	28.7	1.6	94
Algeria	1.2	1.2	1.2	29.9	1.1	95
Qatar	0.6	0.6	0.6	30.5	0.5	83
Gabon	0.2	0.2	0.2	30.7	0.2	100
Ecuador	0.2	0.2	0.2	30.9	0.2	100
TOTAL	41.4	34.7	30.9	30.9	30.7	99

[1] The precise loss in sustainable capacity remains uncertain.

[2] This figure represents the upper end of the range of available capacity, according to government statements.

[3] Excluding share of capacity in the Neutral Zone, shown separately.

[4] Capacity and production is shared about equally between Kuwait and Saudi Arabia.

[5] Estimated production ceiling effective August 1, 1979, based on announced average 10 percent cutback.

[6] In Saudi Arabia, the concept of "facility," rather than "installed," capacity is used. Facility capacity refers to the total installed capacity of gas–oil separating plants, main trunk pipelines, and oil-load terminals; it does not include the capacity of salt water–oil separators or flow lines.

SOURCE: Central Intelligence Agency, *International Energy Statistical Review*, 26 Aug. 1980, p. 3. U.S. Department of Energy, *Monthly Energy Review*, October 1980, pp. 88–89.

prices is important. The relations among these variables and institutions are still being debated by professional economists, but the broad outlines of the new market structure have become reasonably clear. Prices are periodically ratcheted to higher levels by the interaction of buyers and sellers.

The year 1970 was pivotal for OPEC, because it marked a significant change in the structure of the world oil market. Prior to 1970 there was excess capacity available outside OPEC, so that potential supply disruptions resulted in only modest price increases. The Suez Canal crises in

184

FIGURE 7–8(a)
Saudi Arabia—Capacity, Production, and Shut-In, 1974–1981
(Million Barrels per Day)

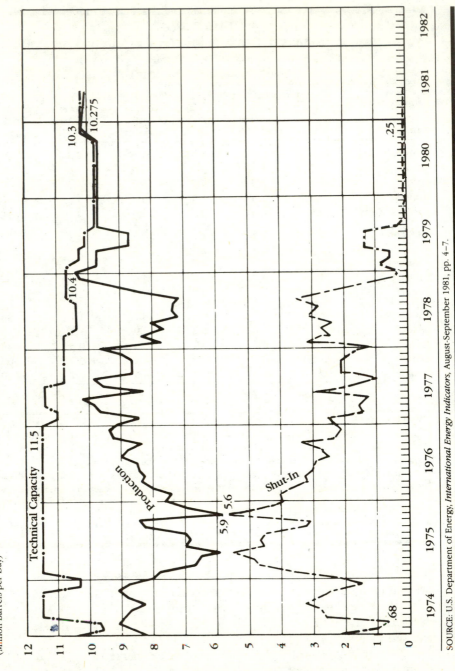

SOURCE: U.S. Department of Energy, *International Energy Indicators*, August–September 1981, pp. 4–7.

FIGURE 7–8(b)

Iran—Capacity, Production, and Shut-In, 1974–1981
(Million Barrels per Day)

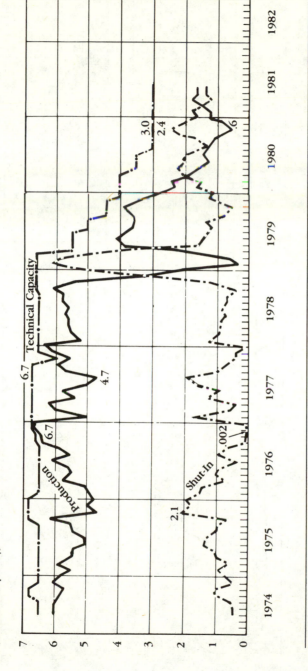

SOURCE: U.S. Department of Energy, *International Energy Indicators*, August-September 1981, pp. 4–7.

186

FIGURE 7–8(c)
OPEC (Ex-Iran and Saudi Arabia) Capacity, Production, and Shut-In, 1974–1981
(Million Barrels per Day)

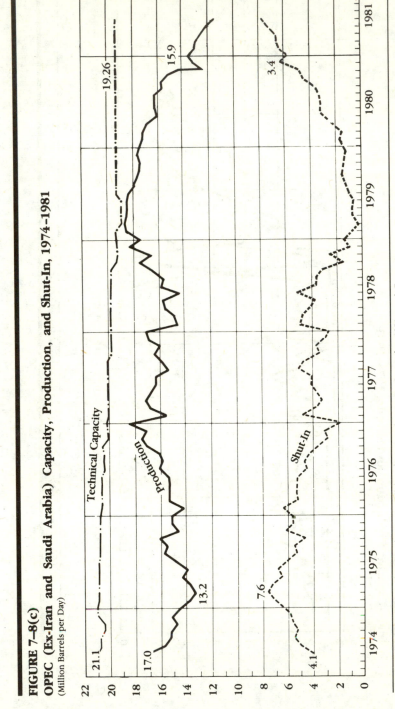

SOURCE: U.S. Department of Energy, *International Energy Indicators*, August–September 1981, pp. 4–7.

1956 and 1967 illustrate the point. During these episodes there was large excess capacity in both the United States and Canada due to market demand prorationing. In addition, there was an institutional peculiarity during the 1960s which led the member countries to expand output at a rapid rate and thus hold prices down. This was the practice of basing taxes on fixed posted prices which bore no relation to actual market prices. But the market structure of the 1970s was fundamentally different.

The first round of price increases was associated with the overthrow of King Idris in Libya and the assumption of control by Colonel Qadhafi. Although prices were raised by only about 20 percent, this was significant because it reversed the long-term decline which had begun in the middle 1950s. The second round was the quadrupling of prices associated with the Fourth Arab–Israeli War and the Arab oil embargo of 1973–1974. This was significant in that OPEC had now firmly established its position as the primary price-setting institution in world petroleum markets. The price increases during 1979 and 1980 were associated with the Iranian revolution and the attendant production cutbacks by Iran. Between the upward price movements of 1974 and 1979 there was relative price stability. During this period various OPEC members cut production when necessary to prevent prices from falling. Since January, 1981, contract prices have been relatively stable whereas spot prices have fallen. Again, OPEC members were willing to take production cuts rather than reduce prices much below levels previously attained.

The First Oil Price Ratchet

Libya Takes the Lead.   Libya played an important role in reversing the long-term decline in world oil prices which had begun in the mid-1950s. The reasons are fairly obvious, in retrospect. Libya differed from the other leading oil producers in two important respects. First, Libya had rapidly become a major oil producer only in the 1960s. Libyan output averaged 180,000 barrels per day in 1962; by 1970, it had soared to 3.3 million barrels per day. Second, King Idris had invited many small companies to drill in Libya and fully 55 percent of Libyan output in 1970 was produced by independents. The Libyan prime minister during the 1960s, Mustafa Halim, later explained the policy of inviting many independents into the country as follows: "I did not want Libya to begin as Iraq or as Saudi Arabia or as Kuwait. I didn't want my country to be in the hands of one oil company." Two other important considerations were that Libya was favorably located to the European market and the quality of its oil was higher than most OPEC crudes. The quality and transport cost differentials made oil produced in Libya extremely profitable for the companies fortunate or wise enough to hold Libyan concessions.

The political developments which took place in Libya in 1969 were also important. On September 1, 1969, the regime of King Idris was overthrown by a revolutionary council headed by Colonel Muammar al-Qadhafi. After studying oil prices and concessionaire agreements, Qadhafi told representatives of the oil companies that Libyan oil prices were too low. The assertion was based on new assessments of production costs, on transport costs to Europe, and on the quality of Libyan oil. In effect, the companies had been receiving much of the "economic rent" derived from a favorable geographic location and from the Libyan quality differential. Qadhafi sought to appropriate that economic rent for the Libyan government. It was the first inkling of the "differentials problem" which emerged full-blown in the 1970s. The specific demand was to increase prices from $1.80 to $2.20 per barrel. The companies made a counter-offer of a 5-cent increase, but it was rejected.

Next, the Libyan government instituted a policy of divide and conquer. The majors had interests in other countries and were so large that should the Libyan government cut their "allowable" production it would have had little impact. The largest of the independents, Occidental Petroleum Company (OXY), was therefore singled out for production cuts. During the summer of 1970, OXY's daily allowable was reduced from 800,000 to 440,000 barrels. OXY president, Armand Hammer, appealed to the majors for relief, proposing that they sell him oil "at cost" from alternative sources. Unsuccessful in this effort, OXY signed a contract on September 4, 1970, providing for a price increase of 30 cents, to be increased to 40 cents in 1975.

Spot and Contract Interactions.   The Libyan initiative was no doubt aided by developments which affected spot prices. In 1966 the U.S. Congress enacted the Environmental Protection Act (1966), thus restricting the use of high sulphur coal and oil in the generation of electricity. This greatly increased the demand for low-sulphur fuel oil and enhanced the value of higher quality oils such as those produced in Libya. More important, it increased the overall demand for oil and helped drive tanker rates to unprecedented levels. Tanker rates were also influenced by Syria's closing of the Trans-Arabian pipeline in May, 1970. The result was that Rotterdam product prices rose by about $1 per barrel, to $3.33 during the second half of 1970.

The companies benefited enormously from these developments, particularly those with low transport costs and favorably located to the European market. The countries also benefited from increased production but not from increased prices, since royalties and the profit share were based on posted prices which bore no direct relation to realized product prices. Under these conditions the countries felt entitled to a larger share of the revenue accruing to the producing companies. Since

OXY had no other major source of crude oil, and since prices in Europe were more than sufficient to cover the Libyan demands, OXY capitulated.

Leapfrogging—The Tehran and Tripoli Agreements.　　Soon after OXY gave in to the Libyan demands, the other companies operating in Libya and Algeria agreed to the same terms. Then the Persian Gulf countries demanded similar increases. The operating companies suggested "joint negotiations" to include both North African and Persian Gulf countries. They hoped to settle the "differentials problem" once and for all by restoring "stability" and "unity" to the pricing structure. However, Iran opposed "joint negotiations" and so did Libya. The result was that "separate but necessarily connected negotiations" were scheduled in Tehran and Tripoli.

The Persian Gulf negotiations resulted in the Tehran Agreements on February 14, 1971, whereas negotiations for the African countries were concluded by the Tripoli Agreements on April 2, 1971. The net result of these meetings was to boost Persian Gulf prices by about 46 cents per barrel, with additional increases of 20 cents scheduled to take place by 1975. Libya and Algeria received increases of about 80 cents over the same period, thus vindicating Qadhafi's belief that the companies had been receiving economic rent which "rightfully" belonged to Libya.

Participation.　　The Tehran and Tripoli agreements were intended to be long-term, extending over five years; but on September 22, 1971, the OPEC ministers decided that member countries should "... establish negotiations with the oil companies, either individually or in groups, with a view to achieving effective participation ... " in company operations. Within one month Libya outlined its demands for "participation." In December, 1971, Libya nationalized BP's interest in the Sarir field in retaliation for the British role in permitting Iran to occupy Arab-controlled islands in the Persian Gulf. This represented one of the first overt uses of *oil as a political weapon*. Libya and Iraq subsequently nationalized the entire oil industry.

Events in other Persian Gulf countries paralleled those in Iraq and Libya. Joint negotiations with representatives of Saudi Arabia, Kuwait, Abu Dhabi, and Qatar led to a General Participation Agreement in December, 1972. This agreement provided for 25 percent participation to take effect immediately with scheduled increases leading to 51 percent by 1982. The companies agreed to purchase a portion of the governments' newly acquired oil, known as "buy-back" oil, and the governments agreed to compensate the companies for unrecovered investments. Kuwait did not ratify the agreement, holding out and obtaining a 60 percent ownership share effective January 1, 1974.

An Exxon report released in September, 1980, describes subsequent developments succinctly.

> The rapidly changing events of the 1970s were mirrored in the fragility of these participation agreements. The OPEC countries were quick to take advantage of their new bargaining strength vis-a-vis the oil companies. Participation levels called for in the 1972 agreement were deemed unsatisfactory less than a year later, and were escalated so that most of the other Gulf states joined Kuwait in achieving 60 percent ownership effective January 1974 (*Middle East Oil*, p. 32. © 1980 Exxon Corporation, Reprinted With Permission).

Participation and nationalization in the member countries represented a continuum rather than a cataclysmic change, and the private companies generally continued to operate under a new contractual arrangement known as "service contracting." Companies are now paid a fixed price per barrel of output regardless of the market price. Exploration, drilling, road construction, and other investment activities are financed by the producing country on a contractual basis. Thus, the concession era came to an end.

The Geneva Accords

Although the Tehran–Tripoli agreements were intended to last until 1975, the countries became dissatisfied before the end of 1971. The principal reason was worldwide inflation and depreciation of the dollar relative to other major currencies. The companies and countries met in Geneva, Switzerland, in January, 1972, to hammer out an agreement which would compensate the countries for their consequent loss of purchasing power. The first "Geneva Agreement" was important because it marked the first time that OPEC nations were able to adjust prices in order to maintain the *real price* of oil. Prices were raised 20 cents per barrel in January, 1972, to compensate the oil producers for inflation. In June, 1973, the second Geneva Accord provided for another 15-cent per barrel increase and it was agreed that adjustments would be made monthly thereafter. Subsequent pricing events soon made the Geneva agreements obsolete, but the issue of maintaining real oil prices remains a critical issue within OPEC.

The Second Price Ratchet

Arab Oil Embargo.   The worldwide demand for crude oil increased at such a rapid rate in 1973 that there was upward pressure on spot prices and much talk of an energy crisis. In April and May, 1973, congressional hearings were held in the United States on the issue of "oil short-ages" and the energy crisis. The oil shortages were typical "shortages at a price" and were attributable to price controls which had been in effect in the United States since August, 1971. In the spring and summer of 1973 there were localized shortages, gasoline lines, voluntary allocations by companies, limited fuel supplies, recriminations against oil compa-nies, and much discussion of the "energy crisis." Interestingly, during September 25–27, 1973, the American Enterprise Institute for Public Policy Research held a symposium on *The Energy Crisis*. This was prior to the Arab–Israeli War and the Arab oil embargo of 1973. During this same period negotiations between Israel, Egypt, and Syria continued in an effort to resolve the territorial claims dispute which had resulted from the Six Day War in 1967.

Unable to settle their differences at the negotiating table, Egypt and Syria invaded Israel on October 6, 1973, setting off the "Yom Kippur" War. On October 8 a previously scheduled meeting between represen-tatives of OPEC and the major oil companies was held in Vienna. The principal item on the agenda was the price of oil. More important, on October 16, 1973, the oil ministers of the Organization of Arab Oil Exporting Countries (OAPEC) gathered in Kuwait to discuss war issues. On the following day they unanimously agreed to cut oil supplies by 5 percent each month and to impose a total embargo on certain countries who were supporting Israel. The embargo and supply reductions were to continue until Israel withdrew from all occupied territories, including Jerusalem, and until Palestinian rights were restored. It was also agreed that posted prices should be increased from $3 to $5.12 per barrel, or about 70 percent.

For purposes of the embargo OAPEC classified the consuming coun-tries as "friendly," "neutral," or "hostile" to Arab interests. Britain, France, and Spain were classified as "friendly," Japan and Germany as "neutral," and the United States and the Netherlands as "hostile." A total embargo was to be selectively carried out against "hostile" countries. However, there was much controversy within OAPEC on how to implement a selective embargo and there was no administrative machinery for mon-itoring oil shipments once tankers were loaded. On November 5 the Arab countries agreed to speed up the production cutback by reducing liftings by 25 percent from September levels. Implementation of these production cuts resulted in unprecedented spot price increases. Con-tract prices remained in the $5 to $6 per barrel range.

Reports that the hostile countries were still receiving oil from Arab sources through transshipping and that non-Arab oil was being diverted to "hostile" countries greatly aggravated the Arab leadership. On Decem-ber 9, 1973, OAPEC members decided that January production cuts would apply to *all* countries. At a meeting held in Tehran during December 22–24 the six Persian Gulf states decided to raise the marker crude price to $11.65 effective January 1, 1974. However, Saudi Arabia lost much of its enthusiasm for the embargo after then and continually advocated that it be ended. After much diplomatic maneuvering, the embargo was officially ended on March 17, 1974.

The Arab oil embargo can be counted a success only in terms of its effect on world oil prices. It did not significantly reduce oil imports into the United States or the Netherlands as compared with the other import- ing countries since transshipping and rerouting effectively undermined the selectivity of the embargo. Even the USSR apparently rerouted oil so as to fetch the highest price possible. In addition, free world oil production increased toward the end of the embargo period (refer back to Figure 7–6).

Actions within OPEC also helped undermine the selectivity of the embargo and hold oil prices down. Iran, which had argued for higher oil prices throughout the embargo, was nevertheless one of the principal countries to increase production and thus to undermine the effects of production cutbacks by the Arab countries. Iraq shipped more than had been overtly agreed on and there were charges and countercharges of overlifting. The embargo period emphasized the conflicts as well as the harmonies of interest within the Arab world and within OPEC.

The price increases achieved during the embargo were due to the reduced level of production rather than to the selectivity of the embargo. The Arab countries reduced production and caused panic buying on the spot market. Production by non-Arab OPEC and non-OPEC countries increased, thus mitigating the Arab production cutbacks somewhat. Inventories are normally drawn down between October and March; however, during 1973–1974 inventories were drawn down less than nor- mal, so that some of the additional non-Arab production was used to build inventories (refer back to Figure 7–7). This was a rational response on the part of the buyer-refiners who anticipated price increases greater than inventory carrying costs.

The contract price increases made effective January 1, 1974, lagged behind spot price increases by several months. This was the most dra- matic percentage increase in contract prices to date. Production was unstable during 1974 and especially during 1975, as the OAPEC mem- bers sought to restore production and market shares to pre-embargo levels. The higher prices proved an incentive for member countries to expand output.

Inventories were built substantially in 1974, as over a million barrels per day were stockpiled. This helped hold up the level of OPEC pro- duction and prices. However, tight money policies and uncertainty about the future caused a severe economic recession in 1975 and a lower level of demand for oil. The question arose concerning who would shut in production to maintain prices. In fact, actual prices paid were frequently only 80 percent of the posted price and there was great dissention within the ranks of OPEC during this period. Saudi Arabia was particularly aggrieved as production fell to 5.9 million barrels per day in late 1975 and the Saudi market share fell to 22 percent of the OPEC total. But an OPEC ministerial meeting in October, 1975, restored unity within OPEC, and Saudi Arabia subsequently was able to restore its market share to the more normal 28–29 percent range. Contract and spot prices were relatively stable throughout this time period.

Split-Level Price Increase.   The December, 1976, OPEC ministerial meeting in Doha, Qatar, marked the first open split within OPEC on oil prices since the 1973 embargo. Saudi Arabia and the UAE argued that prices should only increase 5 percent effective January 1, 1977, whereas the other member countries advocated a 10 percent increase. The result was the famous "split-level" price increase of January 1, 1977. The Saudi position was partially based on the large excess capacity it had held in 1975 and the belief that consuming countries might learn to live without their oil. Countries with large reserves have relatively more to lose from "conservation" and from long-term substitution of alternative energy resources for oil.

The split-level price increase resulted in much higher lifting levels for Saudi Arabia and the UAE during the first half of 1977 and lower production in Iran and other member countries. Reduced shut-in capacity by Saudi Arabia and corresponding increases by Iran and other OPEC members in early 1977 were the result of "undervalued" Saudi and "overvalued" non-Saudi (and UAE) crudes [see Figure 7–8 (a)]. Saudi production declined from 10.2 to 8.5 million barrels per day in May, 1977, owing to a fire and to a pipeline accident, which account for the higher shut-in capacity in that month. "Pricing unity" was restored in June, 1977, when the Saudi price was raised another 5 percent. Saudi production subsequently declined, but it increased for other member countries in the latter half of 1977 as "pricing unity" restored more normal market shares. The uncertainty about prices caused substantial increases in the level of inventories throughout 1977.

The Saudi marker crude price remained at $12.70 per barrel throughout 1977 and 1978, and spot prices generally declined. One reason for the price decreases was the low level of OPEC production as inventories were drawn down. OPEC shut-in capacity increased in 1978 and oil markets were thought to be in a glut during this period. It was generally believed that oil supplies were "adequate" and that another oil crisis would not occur until the middle 1980s. This led to an inventory draw-down and set the stage for the dramatic price increases of 1979 and 1980.

The Third Price Ratchet

Iranian Revolution.   Evidence indicating severe political problems in Iran began to emerge in September, 1978. There were strikes in the oil fields and refineries and riots in some of the major cities. The government responded by declaring martial law; but, within weeks, oil deliveries became subject to *force majeure,* or reductions due to circumstances beyond the control of the companies. This sent buyers to the spot market, with predictable effects on spot prices. Table 7-6 shows the resulting spot and contract prices. The price differential for June, 1978, when Libyan Amna commanded a 59-cent differential over Saudi Light, may be regarded as fairly normal. Gasoil, which is a partially refined product, was $4.10 higher in Rotterdam. These prices move in tandem under normal market conditions. However, the events since late 1978 have been far from normal, so the price differentials have been very unstable. The general relation shown in Table 7-6 indicates that spot prices led contract prices upward. The reasons behind this relation make a fascinating story which reveals much about the modern structure of petroleum markets.

The Abu Dhabi Meetings.   The OPEC ministerial conference in Abu Dhabi in mid-December, 1978, took place against a background of imminent revolution in Iran and rising spot prices. Faced with uncertainty about the events in Iran, the OPEC ministers decided on a moderate course of action, proclaiming that contract prices would be increased in quarterly "tiers" during 1979 by a total of only 14.5 percent. This would have increased the marker crude price to $14.55 per barrel by October 1, 1979.

The political situation in Iran was deteriorating rapidly as abdication by the shah appeared imminent. On December 26, 1978, Iranian exports were suspended entirely, resulting in a decline in production from a pre-revolutionary level of 5.5 to 0.5 million barrels per day in January and February, 1979. But it is false to assume that the Iranian reduction in itself caused the sharp price increases of 1979. There were disruptions in normal sources of supply and in the distribution systems; but other OPEC member countries increased production almost enough to fully offset the Iranian cutback. A major problem was that refiner buyers, anticipating higher prices, built inventories during 1979. This increased short-term demands and drove spot prices much higher. On February 21, 1979, the spot price for gasoil in Rotterdam reached $44.24 per barrel.

A Saudi Miscalculation.   Iran restored exports to a level of 2.2 million barrels per day in March, 1979, but due to technical difficulties

TABLE 7–6
Evolution of Official Prices for Arabian Light and Libyan Amna Compared to Gasoil Prices at Rotterdam, June 1978–October 1981
(U.S. dollars per barrel)

Date	Saudi Arabian Light (34° API)	Libyan Amna (36° API)	Gasoil in Barge Lots at Rotterdam
1978			
June (Avge.)	$12.70	$13.19	$16.80
Nov. 3	•	•	23.12
1979			
Jan. 1	13.34	14.03	24.03
Feb. 1	13.51	•	32.04
Feb. 21	•	14.71	44.24
Mar. 3	•	15.41	40.55
Apr. 1	14.55	17.60	35.92
May 15	•	18.30	43.90
May 27	•	20.61	47.92
June 1	18.00	•	51.34
Oct. 15	•	25.57	44.30
Nov. 1	24.00	•	47.45
Dec. 13	•	29.30	47.59
1980			
Jan. 1	26.00	34.02	49.06
Apr. 1	28.00	•	37.94
May 20	•	36.02	42.63
July 1	•	35.30	41.29
Aug. 1	30.00	•	37.60
Oct. 1	•	•	40.35
Nov. 1	32.00	•	43.57
1981			
Jan. 2	•	40.30	40.35
Apr. 3	•	•	40.75
May 1	•	•	36.86
June 5	•	39.20	35.99
Sep. 4	•	•	40.08
Oct. 2	34.00	•	40.62

SOURCES: Petroleum and Energy Intelligence Weekly, Inc., "Updated Price Scoreboard for Key Export Crudes," *Petroleum Intelligence Weekly,* Supplements 5 February 1979, 3 March 1980 and 23 February 1981. See also, "Spot Price Review for Key World Markets", 2 February 1981, p. 8. *Platt's Oil Price Handbook and Oilmanac,* 57th ed., McGraw-Hill, Inc., 1981, pp. 45–69. U.S. Department of Energy, *Weekly Petroleum Status Report,* Washington, D.C., various issues, 1978–1981.

and the chaos associated with the assumption of control by the Khomeini regime, this was far below pre-revolutionary levels. Saudi Arabia sought to "accommodate" the higher level of Iranian production by lowering its own output by one million barrels per day. In retrospect this was a miscalculation, because Iranian production has never reached its pre-revolutionary levels. Given the lofty spot prices, Saudi Arabia decided to raise its prices, effective April 1, 1979, the full 14.5 percent agreed to at the Abu Dhabi meeting. Libya increased its prices even more and could find buyers for its near-capacity output without difficulty. Spot prices for gasoil were receding from $44 per barrel, but the price differential still made Saudi and Libyan oil a bargain.

The Saudi cutbacks made markets so tight that spot prices escalated again in April and May. Consequently, Libya, Algeria, and other "hawks" within OPEC started to base their prices on an *assumed* Saudi marker crude price of $18 per barrel, even though the actual price was $14.55, and they were still able to produce at capacity. "Pricing unity" or "disunity" thus became a central issue within OPEC. Saudi Arabia remained a "dove," or "price moderate," but tried to restore unity by raising the marker crude price to $18 effective June 1, 1979. In addition, the Saudis recognized the April production cutback as a miscalculation as spot prices for gasoil rose above $50 per barrel; and they restored their production ceiling to 9.5 million barrels per day effective July 1, 1979.

Numerous Attempts to Restore Pricing Unity.   Saudi Arabia remained a reluctant follower in all of the subsequent price increases during 1979 and 1980. The pattern of price adjustments was repeated almost quarterly until January, 1981. This can be observed by tracing the pattern of Saudi and Libyan contract prices in Table 7-6. Libya or one of the other "hawks" would take the lead by assuming the Saudi marker crude price was $24, then $30, and eventually $36 per barrel. These "notional" prices were in all cases far above the actual marker crude price. After several months, Saudi Arabia would try to "restore pricing unity" by increasing the marker price to the previously assumed level. This would precipitate even higher assumed Saudi prices. The result was great uncertainty among buyers, large inventory accumulations, and much higher oil prices.

The specifics of the case bear reiteration. On October 15, 1979, Libya raised its price for Amna to $25.57 based on an assumed Saudi marker price of $24. Saudi Arabia followed by raising its price to $24 on November 1. On December 13, 1979, Libya raised its prices again, based on an assumed Saudi price of $28, and on January 1, 1980, Saudi Arabia raised its prices to $26. And so it went, until the Saudi marker crude price was raised to $32 on November 1, 1980. After that time the Saudis were adamant that they would not raise prices further, although another

$2 per barrel increase was made effective October 1, 1981. During all this time the spot price differentials from the Saudi marker price far exceeded what may be considered normal. In fact, the spot differentials even from Libyan contract prices far exceeded what may be regarded as normal levels until the middle of 1980.

Effects of Higher Prices on OPEC Production.   Economic theory suggests that higher prices will reduce overall demand and cause buyers to switch to lower-cost alternatives. Both have occurred in a dramatic fashion since 1979, but inventory build-ups and draw-downs have complicated the picture. OPEC production remained at a very high level throughout 1979 as inventories were built up, but declined precipitously during 1980 and 1981 to reach a low of 22 million barrels per day in October, 1981, (see Figure 7-6). Figure 7-7 shows the pattern of inventory build-up and draw-down during this period.

Effects of Price Differentials on Production Shares within OPEC.   The countries within OPEC who have maintained their price differentials far above normal levels vis-à-vis the Saudi marker crude price have been the ones who have taken the largest production cuts during 1980 and 1981. In particular, it has been Kuwait, Libya, Nigeria, Iran, and Iraq who have been unable to sell enough to sustain production at near capacity levels. The extent to which Iranian and Iraqi production has been reduced, due to the Iran–Iraq war, which began in October, 1980, or to the high asking price, is subject to conjecture. In any case, these countries were producing at less than half their technical capacity in the latter half of 1981.

Saudi Arabia has been producing at capacity since July 1, 1979, but recently (October, 1981) it has announced plans to reduce output to 9.5 million barrels per day. This represents an effort to maintain prices at prevailing levels as inventories are drawn down worldwide. An interview with Saudi Oil Minister, Ahmed Zaki Yamani, on September 23, 1981, indicates that he has a clear understanding of the current issues. When asked whether the world could accommodate a resumption of 3 to 5 million barrels per day from Iran and Iraq without lowering prices, he replied that world demand will be substantially higher by the time they come back on stream. Asked about the magnitude and effects of inventory draw-downs, he replied

We think that it is in the range of 2 million barrels per day. And this is very natural, even probably against the will of the IEA [International Energy Association—see Chapter 8], because the commercial companies which are holding stocks will find it very expensive to keep that oil because it costs them, with the very high interest rates prevailing right now, more than 75¢ per barrel per month. And the price of oil is not going up, it is coming down—I mean the weighted average price. Therefore they have to draw from these stocks.[3]

Asked whether Saudi Arabia would raise prices to restore unity, he replied that the pressure will be on other OPEC members to lower their prices. And when asked if Saudi Arabia would increase production to prevent further spot price increases, he replied, "I might envisage that countries like Libya, Nigeria, Algeria, Venezuela, and the others might increase a little bit. They're dying to increase their production. Why should it be Saudi Arabia alone?"[4]

With such a clear perception of the issues, one might anticipate a reunification of prices and related policies within OPEC. But not all the oil ministers perceive the issues in this light, and some who do are constrained from aligning (that is, lowering) their prices to the marker crude because of internal political pressures. For countries such as Libya, Mexico, and Nigeria, it is a matter of national honor that prices be maintained at existing levels, a throwback to the fourteenth-century conception of a "just" price. In addition, many political leaders have very little understanding of market processes; instead, they observe gasoline in principal European countries at $3 per gallon, which amounts to $126 per barrel, and cannot conceive how $40 per barrel for their crude is unreasonable. Their basis for comparison is of course wrong, since Saudi oil is the next-best alternative to their own. But not everyone has that perception of the pricing problem.

Conclusion

The energy crises of the 1970s were oil crises. The 1973–1974 and 1979–1980 oil crises did not involve physical shortages independent of the price level. The central issue was not the *availability* of oil; it was the *price* at which oil would sell. There will always be a market clearing price for oil as with any other commodity. Under present market arrangements, the nominal price could be established at any level over a fairly broad range, depending upon the interactive policies between OPEC and the importing countries. OPEC is a price setting cartel which seems to be cohesive enough to prevent nominal contract prices from declining when markets are weak, but apparently it is not strong enough to substantially raise prices except when political turmoil brings about sharp production cutbacks. It is this degree of cohesion which has resulted in the relative success of OPEC.

---

[3]"Yamani Sees Rise in 'Real' Prices Unlikely in '80s," *Petroleum Intelligence Weekly—Supplement,* 5 October 1981, p. 3. Reprinted with permission.

[4]Ibid.

Further Readings

Danielsen, Albert L. "The Role of Speculation in the Oil Price Ratchet Process." *Resources and Energy,* 2 September 1979, 243–263.

⸻, and Edward B. Selby, Jr. "World Oil Price Increases: Sources and Solutions." *The Energy Journal,* 1 October 1980, 57–74.

Edens, David G. *Oil and Development in the Middle East.* New York: Praeger, 1979.

Krapels, Edward N. *Oil Crisis Management, Strategic Stockpiling for International Security.* Baltimore: Johns Hopkins University Press, 1980.

OAPEC, Department of Information. *Basic Facts About the Organization of Arab Petroleum Exporting Companies.* Kuwait: 1976.

Roeber, Joe. "Dynamics of the Rotterdam Market." *Petroleum Economist.* Three-Part Series beginning February 1979, 49–52.

Consuming Country Reactions and Policies

8

READER'S GUIDE TO CHAPTER 8

This chapter deals with consumer country reactions to and policies for coping with the new oil-market structure outlined in Chapter 7. As usual, the first section is an overview of the chapter. The next section explains the political, socioeconomic, and energy goals of the consuming countries and their diverse patterns of consumption. The following section considers reactions among the elite groups who largely determine policy. It shows that their reactions are conditioned by various perceptions of the problem, ranging from the idea that prices and quantities are determined by supply and demand to the notion that consumers are the victims of a grand conspiracy. The fourth section deals with cooperative efforts among the consuming countries; and the final section describes the specific program of the International Energy Agency (IEA). The concluding section contains an evaluation of consumer country policies.

201

Overview

Everyone agrees that world oil markets have changed remarkably since 1960. The old order, based on the military and technological superiority of Western powers, has given way to the new reality of OPEC. In 1960, six of the thirteen present member nations of OPEC were protectorates, or colonies of European countries. Oil flowed through the Suez Canal; and the Strait of Hormuz was controlled by European and American interests. The world petroleum market was regulated by the international majors through marketing agreements and voluntary prorationing. Although market "control" was never absolute and was gradually eroded by an emergent OPEC, the influence of the majors and their governments remained pervasive.

Some of the complex developments leading to the assumption of greater control by OPEC have been recounted in previous chapters. To recapitulate: The political influence of the British, French, and U.S. government officials began to erode as leaders in the oil producing nations sought greater autonomy and self-determination in their internal affairs. The changes that took place during the 1960s were subtle, so that many individuals both inside and outside the industry perceived that oil was abundant and would remain cheap. This perception, though illusory, provided the basis on which fuel choices were made. Hence, there were decisions to invest in oil-fired power plants and heating units, and a determination that fuel efficiency was a less desirable characteristic in transport equipment than was comfort and environmental quality. These choices dictated the characteristics of the stock of fuel-using equipment, and consequently committed consumer countries to the use of a relatively large amount of fuel-intensive capital equipment. Then, in the 1970s, when oil prices became relatively high, decisions had to be made whether to utilize or scrap equipment already in use. The choices were based on marginal cost calculations, which is a primary reason why adjustments require a prolonged period of time—such as a decade or more. Viewed in this perspective, the effects of the 1973–1974 oil price increases are still being worked out through the system. The changes which will result from the 1979–1980 increases have barely begun.

Consumer country responses to higher oil prices and less-secure supplies have been numerous and diverse; but in general they may be analyzed in terms of the following classification: (1) internal programs of individual consuming countries; (2) multilateral consumer country cooperation; (3) bilateral consumer–producer cooperation; and (4) multilateral consumer–producer cooperation. The first category, internal programs of the consuming countries, is so diverse that no attempt will be made to survey programs of individual countries. Instead, the program of the International Energy Agency (IEA), which is a creation of the major consuming countries, will be outlined in detail. It will be shown that the IEA program is largely a slate of recommendations for action by individual countries. As such, it represents a consensus among them regarding what actions would promote their own interests. The latter two categories, bilateral and multilateral consumer–producer cooperation, will be considered in less detail in Chapter 9. It will be shown that few tangible results have come from these efforts and that little can be expected of them.

The major effort to secure cooperation among the consuming countries resulted in the formation of the International Energy Agency (IEA) in November, 1974. This agency is important to the consuming countries and appears destined to remain a viable international organization. Its main objective is to reduce dependence on foreign oil and vulnerability to supply disruptions, primarily through policies to substitute alternative energy and nonenergy resources for imported oil. The relative success of these efforts is best judged by observing the changes in consumption patterns outlined in Chapter 7. Based on this criterion, the consuming countries have not substantially altered their *patterns of energy consumption* or significantly reduced their *level of economic well-being*. On the other hand, the rate of growth in *oil consumption* has declined remarkably since 1973, and economic growth rates are also lower. If pre-embargo trends had continued, total oil consumption in 1980 would have been on the order of 90 million barrels per day rather than the 60 million actually recorded. Most of this reduction in consumption can be attributed to slower economic growth and to the substitution of non-energy for energy resources.

Whether the consuming countries are judged to have been moderately successful or unsuccessful in adjusting to higher energy prices depends on one's assessment of the trade-offs they have made between their energy, economic, and political goals. One reason *patterns of energy consumption* have changed no more than they have, is that substitution requires a long period of time. The other is that choices are made on the basis of *relative* prices. Not infrequently, political leaders in the consuming countries have announced goals whose attainment would require the substitution of alternative energy resources for oil while they have simultaneously adopted policies which practically guarantee that such substitutions will not take place. In the United States, price controls on oil and the "entitlements program" represent prime examples of the conflict between goals and means of attainment. An evaluation of actual consumer policies therefore reveals that goals, priorities, and actual policies frequently appear inconsistent.

Consuming Countries

Goals and Priorities

Political Goals.   A primary goal of political leaders in all countries is to maintain or increase their degree of control over internal and external affairs. In most cases this requires military capability and alliances with other nations. Defense against external aggression is foremost among nearly all nations. But almost equally important is the goal of maintaining internal political stability. In countries that are politically unstable this means preventing revolutions; in more stable countries it involves a more nebulous pursuit, often summed up as "defending our way of life." Internal and external security are closely related, since internal strife complicates national defense, and losing a war invariably changes power relations.

Given a degree of political stability, the primary goal of the ruling elite is to remain in power. This can be accomplished either by economic or military means. The larger and more politically stable nations are secure enough from the threat of a *coup d'état* that those in power generally rely on economic means to maintain control. In practice, this means being "attuned" to the desires of the electorate. It is particularly important that the political elite ensure that the distribution of income be considered "equitable" by the vast majority of people, since sudden changes in the distribution of income are frequently regarded as "inequitable." Thus, leaders in such countries as the United States, Japan, and those in Western Europe have directed their efforts toward maintaining the status quo with respect to income distribution. This overriding goal or priority has been extraordinarily important in shaping energy policy in most of the consuming countries.

Socioeconomic Goals.   The economic goal sought by the political elite in virtually all countries is a high and rising standard of living for all or nearly all of the nations' inhabitants. Subsumed under or implied by this goal are: (1) a rapid rate of economic growth, (2) a high level of employment, (3) a stable price level, and (4) an equilibrium in the balance of payments. Means for achieving these goals, and to some extent separate goals in themselves, are: (5) maintenance of individual freedom, (6) efficiency in the production and distribution of goods, (7) equity in the distribution of income, and (8) maintenance or improvement of environmental quality.

Governments are often pressured by individual citizens, either on their own or through various interest groups, to pursue one or another of these goals. Public sentiment is particularly strong about such issues as a clean environment, elimination of poverty, equal income distribution, efficient production, individual freedom, full employment, and more rapid economic growth. However, these goals are often in conflict, and trade-offs in attaining them are required. The sort of trade-offs that are made reflect the degree of influence enjoyed by one or another of the special interest groups.

Energy Goals.   Energy goals are related to the more general political and socioeconomic ones. The broadest energy goals are: (1) to achieve a high degree of security in regard to supply, and (2) to minimize costs. These may conflict with each other and with the stated political and economic goals. The specific goals which have dominated energy policy in the consuming countries since 1973 include:

1. Maintenance of supply sources which are secure enough to ensure adequate national defense capabilities.
2. Maintenance of the distribution of income which prevailed prior to 1973.
3. Utilization of resources which minimize damage to the environment.
4. Maintenance of "free enterprise" in the production and distribution of energy resources.
5. Utilization of resources which can be obtained at relatively low real costs.

These goals obviously conflict with one another and not all of the consuming countries have pursued them with equal vigor. In terms of priorities, the United States has adopted policies which appear more or less in accord with the order listed. Japan has been less concerned with security of supply and with the environment than has the United States. France has not been highly concerned with maintaining free enterprise. Germany has been less concerned with maintaining the status quo with respect to income distribution than have most other countries. Nevertheless, an assessment of goals and priorities for each of the consuming countries would include all those listed.

Trade-offs in goal attainment depend on a variety of considerations, including the availability and cost of alternative energy resources; the influence of elite groups, such as domestic energy producers; and the relative power of the major international oil companies. In France and Germany, where domestic coal-producing interests have been strong and the international majors relatively weak, it has been possible to impose high gasoline taxes. This has had the effect of limiting ownership and size of automobiles and holding down miles driven (gasoline consumption). France has pursued an active nuclear program in an effort to minimize dependence on foreign energy, in part because domestic producer interests in oil and natural gas are weak. Japan is in a similar position, since it has few indigenous energy resources and the international majors have little political clout. Great Britain and Norway have large oil interests in the North Sea, and the outlook for even more oil in that region is bright.

All these factors make the energy situation in each country somewhat unique. Accordingly, each country will have rather different goals, priorities, and costs of attaining specific targets. It is therefore inevitable that the result will be a certain amount of conflict, as well as harmony, of interest among the various consuming nations.

Basic Patterns of Energy Consumption

Major Energy Consuming Countries.   The United States, with only 5 percent of the world's population, consumes more than one-quarter of the energy produced worldwide each year. The Soviet Union also consumes a disproportionately large share of energy compared with its population. Together, the two nations consume about 44 percent of the primary energy produced worldwide. The other large consuming countries are a distant third and fourth; the People's Republic of China consumes about 7 percent, and Japan about 5 percent. Germany, the United Kingdom, Canada, France, Italy, and the Netherlands round out the top ten. These ten countries consume about three-fourths of all energy produced each year.

The major energy-consuming countries differ in their political, sociological, economic, and geographic conditions. The most notable political distinction is that of "communist" versus "free world" nations, although even within these political camps there are subcategories. Free world countries consume about 70 percent of the world total, whereas communist-bloc countries account for 30 percent. The USSR and its European satellites consume 74 percent of the communist total (see Table 8–1).

The largest group of consuming countries in the free world is the Organization for Economic Cooperation and Development (OECD).[1] The OECD was set up under a convention signed in Paris on December 14, 1960, for the purpose of achieving higher levels of economic growth, full employment, financial stability, and expansion of world trade. Member countries are committed to multilateral and nondiscriminatory trade relations in the pursuit of these goals.

---

[1]The member countries of OECD include Australia, Austria, Belgium, Canada, Denmark, Finland, France, the Federal Republic of Germany, Greece, Iceland, Ireland, Italy, Japan, Luxembourg, the Netherlands, New Zealand, Norway, Portugal, Spain, Sweden, Switzerland, Turkey, the United Kingdom, and the United States.

TABLE 8–1
Primary Energy Consumption, Percent of Free World and
World Total, and Energy-Dependence Ratio, World and
Regional Groupings, 1980

Country or Region	Primary Energy Consumption[1]	Percent of Free World	Percent of Total World	Energy Dependence Ratio[3]
FREE WORLD				
United States	37	39	27	16
Western Europe	26	27	19	47
Japan	7	7	5	85
Canada	5	5	3	(7)
Middle East	2	2	2	(767)
Other	18	19	13	(29)
Free World Total	96	100	69	1
COMMUNIST COUNTRIES				
Soviet Union	23	55[2]	17	(12)
People's Republic of China	10	24[2]	7	4
Other Communist	9	21[2]	7	20
Communist Total	43	100[2]	31	(1)
WORLD TOTAL	138	—	100	0

[1]Million barrels per day oil equivalent.

[2]Percent of communist total.

[3]Ratio of primary imports to primary consumption expressed as a percent. Figures in parentheses indicate net exports.

SOURCES: British Petroleum, *BP Statistical Review of the World Oil Industry–1980,* London: 1981, pp. 16, 32. U.S. Department of Energy, *1980 International Energy Annual,* September 1981, p. 6.

The OECD represents a very broad grouping of energy-consuming countries. A more detailed geographic breakdown includes the United States and Canada as the major consuming countries in North America, Japan and Australia in the Far East, and the European countries. The United States consumes almost as much energy as all other OECD countries combined.

On the other hand, although OPEC member nations produce very large quantities of energy, they consume relatively little. Not surprisingly, less developed countries (LDCs) which are not members of OPEC also consume comparatively little. Furthermore, about two-thirds of the energy consumption in all LDCs combined is attributable to only eight nations: Brazil, Chile, Cuba, Jamaica, Korea, Singapore, Taiwan, and

Turkey. Clearly, then, energy resources, production, and consumption are distributed very unevenly across the globe.

Patterns of Primary Energy Utilization

The more highly developed countries use large amounts of primary energy per capita, and most of it is derived from petroleum. The levels of energy resource consumption for the principal consuming countries and regions are shown in Table 8–2; the percentage distributions are recorded in Table 8–3. The data in Table 8–3 are comparable to the energy "dependence ratios" discussed in Chapter 1.[2] They indicate that 44 percent of world energy consumption is derived from liquid petroleum, 29 percent from coal, 19 percent from natural gas, 2 percent from nuclear fission, and 6 percent from other means, such as hydroelectric, geothermal, and solar sources.

Among OECD members, Japan is highly "dependent" on liquid fuels and particularly on oil imports. The European countries are only slightly less dependent on oil imports than Japan, but they also use relatively larger amounts of coal. The United States has struck a balance between domestic oil, imported oil, natural gas, and coal, and is relatively self-sufficient. Nuclear, hydroelectric, and geothermal sources constitute a comparatively small proportion of primary energy in virtually all countries. Natural gas is an important source of energy for space heating, and coal is used to generate electricity; but it is not much of an exaggeration to assert that the world runs on oil. The only large country which derives a large proportion of its primary energy from hydroelectric power is Canada.

Alternative Perceptions of the Energy Problem

Any attempt to appraise the policies that have been proposed and/or adopted by the consuming countries requires knowledge of the paradigms, or broad views, held by policymakers. The dominant paradigms may be classified according to:

1. Supply and demand analysis.
2. Depletion of oil resources.

---

[2]It should be reemphasized that "dependence" is an unfortunate term, since the ratios reflect choices made by individuals in each country concerning the utilization of alternative energy resources.

TABLE 8–2
Primary Energy Consumption[1] Derived from Domestic Energy Resources and Imported Oil, World and Regional Totals, 1980[1]
(million barrels per day oil equivalent)

Country or Region	CRUDE OIL AND NATURAL GAS LIQUIDS			OTHER FOSSIL FUELS		OTHER SOURCES		TOTAL PRIMARY ENERGY CONSUMPTION
	Domestic	Imported[2]	Total	Natural Gas	Coal	Nuclear	Hydro, Other	
FREE WORLD								
United States	9.7	6.2	15.9	9.9	8.2	1.4	1.6	37.0
Western Europe	2.4	11.3	13.7	3.7	5.4	0.9	2.1	25.8
Japan	negl.	5.0	5.0	0.4	1.2	0.4	0.4	7.3
Canada	1.6	(0.2)	1.8	1.0	0.4	0.2	1.2	4.5
Middle East	18.8	(17.2)	1.6	0.7	negl.	negl.	0.1	2.4
Other	13.4	(3.5)	9.9	1.9	4.9	0.1	1.7	18.5
Free World Total	45.7	2.0	47.7	17.6	20.1	3.0	7.1	95.5
COMMUNIST COUNTRIES								
Soviet Union	12.2	(3.4)	8.8	6.6	6.9	0.3	0.9	23.4
People's Republic of China	2.1	(0.4)	1.7	0.2	8.1	—	0.2	10.3
Other Communist	0.3	1.8	2.1	1.3	5.5	0.1	0.1	9.1
Communist Total	14.6	(2.0)	12.6	8.1	20.5	0.4	1.2	42.8
WORLD TOTAL			60.3	25.7	40.6	3.4	8.3	138.3

[1] Rows and columns may not add to total due to rounding.
[2] Figures in parentheses denote exports.

SOURCES: British Petroleum, *BP Statistical Review of the World Oil Industry—1980*, London: 1981, p. 16. U.S. Department of Energy, *1980 International Energy Annual*, September 1981, p. 7

TABLE 8–3
Percent of Primary Energy Consumption Derived from Domestic Energy Resources and Imported Oil, World and Regional Totals, 1980

Country or Region	CRUDE OIL AND NATURAL GAS LIQUIDS			OTHER FOSSIL FUELS		OTHER SOURCES		TOTAL ENERGY CONSUMPTION[2]
	Domestic	Imported[1]	Total	Natural Gas	Coal	Nuclear	Hydro, Other	
FREE WORLD								
United States	26	17	43	27	22	4	4	100
Western Europe	9	44	53	14	21	3	8	100
Japan	negl.	68	68	5	16	5	5	100
Canada	36	4	40	22	9	4	27	100
Middle East	783	(716)	67	29	negl.	negl.	4	100
Other	72	(19)	54	10	26	1	9	100
Free World Total	48	2	50	18	21	3	7	100
COMMUNIST COUNTRIES								
Soviet Bloc	52	(15)	38	28	29	1	4	100
People's Republic of China	20	(4)	17	2	78	—	2	100
Other Communist	3	20	23	14	60	1	1	100
Communist Total	34	5	29	19	48	negl.	3	100
WORLD TOTAL			44	19	29	2	6	100

[1] Figures in parentheses denote exports.
[2] Rows may not add to total due to rounding.
SOURCE: Table 8–2.

3. "Overdependence" on oil imports and vulnerability to embargoes.
4. Conspiracy doctrines.

These are not mutually exclusive views, but policymakers tend to adopt one over another when evaluating energy problems. A description of each of these analyses follows.

Supply-and-Demand Analysis

Economists, and the policymakers who are persuaded by their arguments, contend that prices and the rate of use of natural resources respond to the same laws of supply and demand as do other goods. Thus, they turn to supply-and-demand analysis, which provides them a way to assess the effects of a given change in circumstances on a good's price and the quantity of it that is supplied and demanded. In a free market economy, a good's price and quantity will tend to seek an equilibrium, so that the quantity supplied is just equal to the quantity demanded. In markets influenced by a few large producers, prices may be established far above costs, and consumers are obliged to take it or leave it. Their decisions depend on such factors as income, the prices of other goods, and so forth (internal market forces). Energy problems, then, may be characterized as resulting from a disruption of the price–quantity relations brought about by both internal (price) and external (policy) changes in circumstances. They also depend on collective actions of individuals as implemented through government policy.

Market-Induced Demand Changes.　　The fundamental "law" of demand states that consumers buy less when prices are high and more when prices are low. The essence of this law has to do with choice and substitution. Holding other things constant, higher oil prices, for example, induce consumers to adjust their habits by using less oil. And since oil is an intermediate good (that is, one used to produce a variety of other goods and services), a rise in its price will increase the costs of producing other goods, reduce the amount of these goods supplied, and raise their prices. Consumers are thus induced to make still additional adjustments by switching to substitute goods, that is, to goods which can be used in place of oil or oil-using equipment. The result is less demand for goods containing oil and increased demand for oil-substitute products—coal and natural gas are examples.

Market-Induced Supply Changes.　　The fundamental "law" of supply states that firms produce more when prices are high and less when prices are low. Again, the essence of this law relates to choice and substitution. For example, since higher oil prices offer firms a greater profit on oil-producing equipment, they respond by bringing more of these goods onto the market. At the same time, a decline in the price of, say, trucks, diesel locomotives, and other transportation equipment, will induce these producers to bring less onto the market. The result is an increased supply of oil and a decreased supply of equipment which requires the intensive utilization of oil products. Both tend to reduce the residual demand on OPEC for more oil.

Policy-Induced Demand Changes.   Policies intended to change the demand for oil may be classified into two broad categories: (1) those that seek to substitute alternative energy resources for oil and (2) those that seek to substitute nonenergy resources for oil. The latter are frequently labeled "conservation" measures, but "nonenergy resource substitution" more accurately describes the choices involved.

Policies designed to promote the use of alternative energy resources to displace oil include favorable taxation and direct subsidization of research and development (R & D), demonstration, and deployment. The alternative energy resources toward which these activities are directed include coal; nuclear fission and fusion; coal gasification; and solar, geothermal, and tidal power. Within each of these broad categories there are many alternatives. For example, the use of solar energy requires R & D on hot water heaters, solar cells, wind, biomass, and hydroelectric power.

Policies designed to promote the substitution of nonenergy for energy resources require R & D and the imposition of rules and standards which force new choices on energy consumers. Examples are lower speed limits, maximum and minimum thermostat settings, enforcement of automobile and appliance efficiency standards, more stringent building codes, and prohibitions on the use of oil in the generation of electricity. All these involve the use of more labor and capital and some sacrifice of comfort and convenience. Resource substitution is evident in nearly all of these so-called "conservation" measures. For example, consumers have responded to a maximum winter thermostat setting of 65°F in public buildings by wearing more clothes, installing auxiliary electrical heating appliances, or simply avoiding public buildings. Similar responses have been made to other mandated programs designed to "conserve" energy.

Policy-Induced Supply Changes.   Policies intended to increase the supply of non-OPEC oil include subsidization and/or favorable taxation of conventional oil resources. Direct subsidy and tax incentives may be used to encourage production or promote R & D of secondary or tertiary recovery techniques. Examples are the oil depletion allowance and the expensing of capital outlays for exploration and drilling.

Depletable Resource Doctrine

The *depletable resource doctrine* may be based on sound economic analysis as developed in Chapter 2, but it has a much less rigorous meaning when applied to policy matters. According to a popular version of the doctrine, oil prices increased during the 1970s because petroleum reserves are about to run out. Oil and natural gas were being produced and consumed too rapidly, and the consequent "shortages" are what drove prices up. Thus, prevailing market prices are essentially competitive prices, and OPEC is little more than the bearer of the bad news that oil reserves are about to be depleted. The U.S. government agency most responsible for propagating this view was the Central Intelligence Agency. Similar versions of the depletable resource doctrine have also dominated the thinking of some leading officials in the International Energy Agency. A few outsiders contend that these groups have a vested interest in promoting the idea that an energy crisis is imminent. And what greater crisis could befall a nation than running out of resources?

The analysis often used to dramatize the depletable resource doctrine is a variation of the supply-and-demand analysis called "gap analysis." It states that gaps or "shortages" arise when *domestic* energy consumption ("demand") exceeds *domestic* production ("supply"). The terminology is borrowed from conventional economics, but here the terms "supply" and "demand" mean quantity supplied and demanded at an *assumed price*. The assumption which generates the "gap" is that the growth rate of "demand" exceeds the growth rate of "supply." The logic is as simple as the proposition that nonparallel lines extended to infinity must cross. In the energy context, if the growth rate of "demand" exceeds the growth rate of "supply," then "demand" will eventually exceed "supply." Figure 8–1 provides a graphic illustration of gap analysis.

Gap analysis logically leads to the question of how to "fill the gap." The obvious answer is to increase "supply" and/or reduce "demand." Such changes can be accomplished by what has been called policy-induced changes in supply and demand. The remaining "gap" will be filled by higher oil prices or by market-induced changes in quantities supplied and demanded. The central thrust of gap analysis is that policy-induced changes in supply and demand are required to prevent higher oil prices.

Economists are almost universally critical of gap analysis because of its inherent weakness as a tool for analyzing market-induced changes

FIGURE 8–1
Gap Analysis

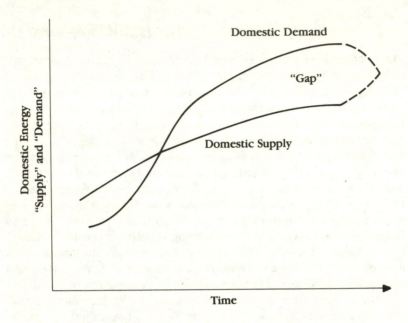

in quantities supplied and demanded. Nevertheless, gap analysis has been used extensively by analysts in the consuming countries and it underlies most of the policies adopted since 1973.

Dependence and Vulnerability Doctrines

Vulnerability to short-term supply interruptions and too much dependence on foreign energy resources are related problems. A war in an important producing country, an embargo, or a natural disaster can precipitate a major reduction in the availability of oil within a short period of time. There is little or nothing an importing country can do to prevent these events, but a country self-sufficient in energy would be relatively unaffected by external supply disruptions. High levels of "dependence" are therefore associated with vulnerability to interruptions in supply.

Dependence and vulnerability doctrines have been influential in determining policy in all the major consuming countries. The U.S. Federal Energy Administration's "Project Independence" specified a goal of energy independence for the United States by 1980. This was an ambitious attempt to achieve energy self-sufficiency within six years. But it was mostly rhetoric, since the policies required to achieve the lofty goals were barely on the drawing board. Pronouncements by the International Energy Agency to limit oil imports to a specified level are in about the same category.

Proponents of isolation and protection have often framed their arguments in terms of a nation's vulnerability to supply disruptions. Other analysts recognize vulnerability as a legitimate problem from the standpoint of national defense but they prefer to use supply and demand, rate of return, and related analyses to evaluate optimal levels of oil imports for the various consuming countries.

Conspiracy Doctrines

Conspiracy doctrines abound in the popular press and in public debates on the energy problem. The most prevalent conspiracy doctrine in late 1973 was that the major oil companies had conspired with OPEC to withhold supplies and raise prices, and, in the process, to limit competition by driving independent refiners and marketing firms out of the industry. It was further held that in order to strengthen their hold on energy markets, the majors were buying up coal and uranium reserves in order to also withhold these products from the market. Those promoting conspiracy doctrines raised the twin issues of vertical and horizontal divestiture of the international oil companies.

Under *horizontal divestiture* the companies would be prohibited from investing in the development of alternative energy resources and be ordered to divest themselves of present interests. The principal alternative resource most critics had in mind was coal. Horizontal divestiture would presumably speed up development of coal reserves and thereby promote greater competition with oil. Under *vertical divestiture*, the international companies would be broken into smaller producing, refining, transport, and marketing companies. This would reduce their profit margins in each sector and help hold down the price of refined products. Based on the idea that the companies were conspiring among themselves and with OPEC to limit competition and raise prices, the horizontal and vertical divestiture issues were hotly debated in 1974 and 1975.

Other conspiracy doctrines pertained to the federal government's influence over petroleum prices. According to the most highly publicized of these, then Secretary of State Henry Kissinger supposedly encouraged Reza Shah Pahlavi of Iran to raise oil prices in order to transfer income to the Iranian government. Kissinger's motives were presumably both professional and personal. Specifically, more revenue would enable the shah to purchase weapons from the United States so that Iran could defend important U.S. Middle Eastern interests, and, incidentally, the shah could deposit surplus revenues in the Chase Manhattan Bank, controlled by Rockefeller interests, who were important benefactors of Kissinger.

A long discourse on the merits and demerits of the conspiracy doctrines would serve no useful purpose here. In general, economists place little credence in them because of the degree of control that would have been necessary to secure such cooperation. Furthermore, conspiracy doctrines have not been particularly influential in mainstream political circles, and relatively little consumer-country policy has been based on them.

Cooperative Efforts

The oil embargo against the United States and the Netherlands in 1973 made the consuming countries painfully aware that they had no formal multinational institution to cope with a supply disruption. The oil sharing that took place during the embargo occurred through established markets and was organized by the international oil companies. France and the United Kingdom sought "special relations" with Middle Eastern governments and there were fears among many Western political leaders that "access" to oil supplies would be denied. Consequently, in December, 1973, Secretary Kissinger proposed that the United States, Japan, and the nations of Western Europe form an international organization of consumer countries in order to promote united actions on energy problems. The first meeting was held in Washington, D.C., in February, 1974.

The principal results of the Washington Conference were (1) nearly unanimous agreement that joint actions were desirable, and (2) the establishment of an Energy Coordination Group (ECG). The responsibility of the ECG was to work toward forming a permanent organization of the energy consuming countries. Agreement was reached among all participants except France that consumer-country cooperation was required to promote (1) conservation, (2) research and development of alternative energy resources, and (3) oil sharing in the event of an embargo. It was also agreed that charges against the major oil companies to the effect that they had withheld supplies, colluded with OPEC, and engaged in profiteering during the embargo, should be more closely investigated. The French rejected oil sharing as "aggressive" toward OPEC and refused to sign the joint communique emanating from the Washington Conference.

Formation of the International Energy Agency

The work of the ECG bore fruit on November 15, 1974, when the International Energy Agency (IEA) was formally organized. The IEA is an autonomous agency within the Organization for Economic Cooperation and Development (OECD) with its own board of directors and executive director. The IEA member countries are listed in Table 8–4.

Organizational Structure.   The IEA consists of a governing board, a secretariat, and a number of standing committees (see Figure 8–2).

TABLE 8–4
Voting Weights for IEA Governing Board, 1980

	General Voting Weights	Oil Consumption Voting Weights	Combined Voting Weights
Australia	3	1	4
Austria	3	1	4
Belgium	3	2	5
Canada	3	5	8
Denmark	3	1	4
Germany	3	8	11
Greece	3	1	4
Ireland	3	0	3
Italy	3	5	8
Japan	3	15	18
Luxembourg	3	0	3
The Netherlands	3	2	5
New Zealand	3	0	3
Portugal	3	0	3
Spain	3	2	5
Sweden	3	2	5
Switzerland	3	1	4
Turkey	3	1	4
United Kingdom	3	6	9
United States	3	47	50
TOTALS	60	100	160

Note: A majority requires 60 percent of the combined voting weights and 50 percent of the general voting weights cast. Special majorities are required for specific types of decisions.
SOURCE: International Energy Agency, "Agreement on the International Energy Program (as amended to May 19, 1980), Paris: June 1980, p. 12.

FIGURE 8–2
The International Energy Agency

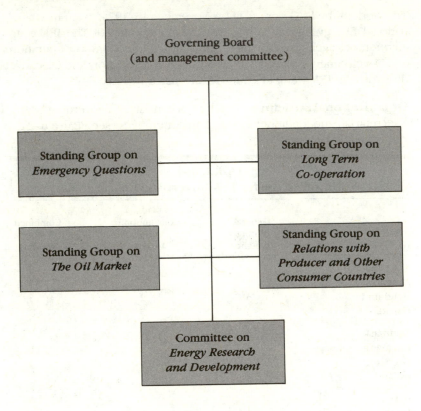

SOURCE: IEA, *The International Energy Agency,* Paris: October 1977, p. 10.

Major decisions are made by the governing board, which is composed of ministers or their representatives from each participating country. The functions of the governing board include:

> Adoption of decisions and making recommendations necessary for the proper functioning of the International Energy Program. Such decisions are adopted by majority vote.

> Periodically reviewing and taking appropriate action concerning developments in the international energy situation.

> Delegating powers to other organs of the Agency.

> Appointing the executive director of the IEA.

Any new obligations by member countries must be approved by unanimous vote of the board of directors. The IEA secretariat, headed by the executive director, has about 110 staff members, who also serve as the energy staff of the OECD. Four standing groups, each dealing with a principal area of the IEA program, report to the governing board. These include the standing groups on:

Long-term Co-operation

The Oil Market

Relations with Producer and other Consumer Countries

Emergency Questions

In addition, the Committee on Energy Research and Development was created to promote cooperation on energy R & D among participating countries.

Voting procedures are democratic but take account of each member's position as an energy consumer. In other words, each country receives an equal number of *general* voting weights, but other votes are weighted in proportion to a country's consumption of oil. Combined voting weights are the sum of the general and consumption-weighted votes (see Table 8–4). The United States has almost one-third of all votes—nearly three times as many as Japan. In general, decisions such as whether to implement prior commitments—the adoption of emergency procedures, for example—require a 60 percent majority of the "combined voting weights" for passage. This virtually enables the United States to exercise a veto power. In fact, the United States, Japan, and Germany combined have the power to defeat any measure. Other types of decisions, such as whether or *not* to activate emergency sharing measures, require special higher majorities for passage. And decisions regarding new commitments require unanimity—a policy which ensures that new IEA programs will be noncontroversial.

International Energy Program

On November 18, 1974, the IEA member countries adopted the International Energy Program (IEP). The program's basic aims were stated as follows:

To reduce "excessive dependence" on oil through energy conservation, development of alternative energy sources, and energy research and development.

To develop an information system on the international oil market, including a system for consultation with oil companies.

> To promote cooperation with oil producing and non-IEA oil consuming countries with a view to developing a stable international energy trade and the rational use of world energy resources.
>
> To prepare participating countries against a major disruption of oil supplies and to share available oil in the event of an emergency.

These broad tasks were given more explicit content as the agency became more fully staffed and operational.

Group Objective

In October, 1977, the ministers of the IEA established a "group objective" to lower oil imports to 26 million barrels per day by 1985. In addition, they directed the agency's standing group on Long-Term Co-operation to (1) review each member country's contribution to the "group objective," (2) assess the continuing validity of the "group objective," and (3) consider the need to establish objectives for later years. These directives have been carried out annually since 1978.

The procedure adopted to assess progress in achieving the group objective involves a review of the performance, programs, and policies of each IEA country. The criteria for judging progress toward achievement of the group objective are spelled out in the agency's "Principles of Energy Policy" and "Principles for Action on Coal," both of which are outlined below. At their December, 1979, meeting the IEA ministers reduced the group objective for 1985 oil imports to 24.6 million barrels per day. And IEA countries further committed themselves to limit oil imports in 1980 and to pursue the country-specific goals for 1980 and 1985. (See Table 8–5.)

Principles of Energy Policy[3]

Introduction.   In October, 1977, the governing board of the IEA adopted twelve principles of energy policy. These principles were designed to provide a framework for national policies and programs with a view to expanding indigenous energy supplies, lowering energy demand, and developing new energy technologies. The principles represent a mixture of goals and recommendations for market- and policy-induced supply and demand changes. The setting of priorities is left to the discretion of each participating country.

The IEA principles can be presented broadly within a supply–demand framework. Four of the twelve principles are simply goals to be sought,

---

[3]This section is based on IEA, *Energy Policies and Programmes of IEA Countries, 1979 Review,* Paris: 1980, pp. 225–230.

TABLE 8–5
Oil Import Goals and "Group Objective" for Specific IEA Countries, 1980 and 1985

Country	Import Goal (*million barrels per day*)[1] 1980	1985	Increased Allowable Imports
United States	8.9	8.9	0
Japan	5.4	6.3	.9
Germany	2.9	2.9	0
Italy	2.1	2.5	.4
Spain	1.0	1.1	.1
Netherlands	.9	1.0	.1
Belgium	.6	.6	0
Switzerland	.3	.3	0
Australia	.3	.3	0
Austria	.3	.3	0
Canada	.2	.6	.4
Ireland	.1	.1	0
New Zealand	.1	.1	0
Luxembourg	.1	.1	0
United Kingdom[2]	.3	(.1)	(.4)
Norway[2]	(.3)	(.4)	(.1)
IEA Total	24.5	26.2	1.7
Less Bunkers	1.4	1.6	.2
IEA GROUP OBJECTIVE	23.1	24.6	1.5

[1]Converted to million barrels per day from "million tons oil equivalent per year," (*MTOES*): one million barrels per day = 49 *MTOES*.

[2]Net exporters in 1985.

SOURCE: IEA, *Energy Policies and Programmes of IEA Countries, 1979 Review,* Paris: 1980, p. 14.

seven of them deal with policy-induced changes in demand, and the other pertains to a market-induced change in supply and demand. The IEA principles which cannot be neatly categorized are cross referenced where appropriate.

Goals.   The following four IEA principles may be regarded as general goals of the energy policies which participating countries should pursue.

IEA Principle No. 1 *Conservation and Oil Import Reduction.* Each participating country is encouraged to develop a national energy program which includes the objective of *limiting* future oil imports through conservation of energy, expansion of indigenous energy sources, and substitution of alternative energy sources for oil. (See also IEA Principle No. 10.)

IEA Principle No. 2 *Environmental Concerns.* Each country is encouraged to devote careful attention to environmental, safety, regional, and security concerns to which the production, transportation, and use of energy give rise. Improvements in the consistency and speed of implementation of public procedures for resolving conflicts between environmental concerns and energy "requirements" is an important priority.

IEA Principle No. 11 *Energy Planning.* Each country is encouraged to plan alternative means, other than those which increase oil consumption, for meeting a supply shortfall or a failure to attain conservation objectives, taking into account the appropriate requirements of economic development and social progress.

IEA Principle No. 12 *International Cooperation.* Countries are expected to cooperate in the field of energy. Such cooperation includes providing information useful for evaluating the world energy situation, engaging in energy research and development, and contributing technical and financial data. Cooperation is to take place among developed and developing countries and international organizations.

Market-Induced Changes in Supply and Demand.   Only one IEA principle is clearly in this category.

IEA Principle No. 3 *Higher Energy Prices.* IEA countries are to allow domestic energy prices to reach a level which encourages energy conservation and the development of alternative energy resources.

Policy-Induced Changes in Supply.   None of the IEA principles deal explicitly and primarily with policy-induced supply changes. However, see IEA Principle No. 10(a).

Policy-Induced Changes in Demand.

IEA Principle No. 4 *Nonmarket Incentives to Conservation.* IEA countries are to reinforce energy conservation with a view to (1) limiting growth in energy demand relative to economic growth, (2) eliminating inefficient energy use, and (3) encouraging the use of substitutes for fuels in shortest supply. Recommended measures for accomplishing these objectives include:

Establishing pricing policies which give incentives to conservation.

Setting minimum energy efficiency standards.

Encouraging investment in energy-saving equipment and techniques.

IEA Principle No. 5 *Discouraging the Use of Oil.* Countries are encouraged to progressively replace oil in electricity generation, space heating, and other sectors by:

Discouraging the construction of new, exclusively oil-fired power stations.

Encouraging the conversion of existing oil-fired capacity to more plentiful fuels.

Encouraging structural adjustments in the refinery sector to avoid an excess of heavy fuel oil.

Directing efforts to reduce the use of heavy fuel oil as a primary energy source in sectors where fuel efficiency is low.

IEA Principle No. 6 *Encouraging the Use of Coal.* Members are encouraged to develop a strong steam coal utilization strategy and to actively promote international trade in steam coal. Specific policies toward these goals include:

Rapid phasing-in of steam coal as a major fuel for electric power generation and as an industrial fuel.

Development of steam coal policies within producing, exporting, and consuming IEA countries to support increased utilization by enhancing market stability. This should be done through reliable export and import policies and under reasonable commercial terms.

Development of policies to remedy anticipated infrastructure bottlenecks.

IEA Principle No. 7 *Encouraging the Use of Natural Gas.* Participating countries are encouraged to use natural gas for premium purposes, such as petrochemical manufacture and residential space heat. Consequently, they are to develop the infrastructure necessary to expand the availability of natural gas.

IEA Principle No. 8. *Encouraging Nuclear Generation of Electricity.* The IEA has proclaimed that the steady expansion of nuclear generating capacity is an indispensable element in attaining the group objective. Thus, members are to encourage the use of nuclear energy in a manner consistent with accepted safety, environmental, and security standards, and with the need to prevent proliferation of nuclear weapons. To provide for this expansion, members are to assure reliable availability of:

Adequate supplies for nuclear fuel (uranium and enrichment capacity) at equitable prices.

Adequate facilities and techniques for development of nuclear electricity generation, for dealing with spent fuel, for waste management, and for overall handling of the back end of the nuclear fuel cycle.

IEA Principle No. 9   *Promoting R & D.* IEA countries are expected to place a stronger emphasis on energy research, development, and demonstration. This effort should include more intensive national efforts and greater coordination among participating countries. Each member should contribute to energy research and development, with emphasis on: (a) technologies that can have a relatively short-term impact, (b) policies that facilitate the transition of new energy technologies from the R & D phase to the point of utilization, (c) technologies for broadly applicable renewable energy sources, and (d) investigations into the technological possibilities of significant contributions from other renewable resources. The latter should include:

Providing financial support for energy research, development, and demonstration.

Encouraging investment through appropriate tax incentives and subsidies.

Ensuring that R & D policies remain consistent with the objective of ongoing energy policy.

IEA Principle No. 10   *Promoting a Favorable Investment Climate.* Participating countries should strive to establish an investment climate that encourages the flow of public and private capital to the development of energy resources. This requires appropriate pricing policies, minimizing uncertainties about the general directions of energy and other policies, such as mentioned in IEA Principle No. 2, and providing government incentives where necessary. The primary objectives are (a) to give priority to exploration activities, including those in offshore and frontier areas, and (b) to encourage rates of exploration and development of available capacities which are consistent with the optimum economic development of resources.

These IEA principles represent a consensus among political leaders in the consuming countries regarding ways to deal with the "energy problem." The resolution of conflicting goals, the means of attaining the goals, and the development of specific programs are left to the individual countries.

Principles for Action on Coal

At its October, 1977, meeting the IEA governing board adopted a broad set of recommendations for increasing the mining, transport, and utilization of coal. In general, the board advocated a "market" solution aided by minimal government restrictions. It proposed that subsidies be provided for "infrastructure" but not for electrical utilities or for end-use energy products. The specific recommendations for mining, transport, and utilization are summarized below.

Coal Mining.   Recommendations regarding coal mining deal with broad policy issues. The IEA stressed that participating countries should ensure that:

> Government royalties and severance taxes for transportation tariffs do not adversely affect the mining of coal.

> Programs are adopted to train labor, improve community infrastructure, and otherwise promote policies to increase production.

> Conditions for leasing government lands and for licensing encourage coal production.

> Mining regulations related to environmental safety and health regulations take account of available technologies.

Coal Transportation.   The governing board also emphasized the need to develop efficient and environmentally acceptable transportation systems with adequate capacity and flexibility. These include inland transportation facilities, ocean port facilities, and seagoing carriers—all of which are necessary for handling the expected increases in coal trade.

Coal Utilization.   The major thrust of the IEA recommendations concerned coal utilization. Countries are encouraged to *prohibit* the use of oil in the generation of electricity and in industrial uses. More specifically, they are to prohibit construction of new or replacement base-load power plants fired exclusively or mainly by oil. Exceptions may be permitted only where:

> National action has been taken to restructure refinery yield patterns toward light products but the country has not yet been able to eliminate excess quantities of residual fuel oil which cannot be used for other purposes.

> Economic or supply conditions, including remoteness of location, are such that use of fuels other than oil is unreasonably expensive in comparison with oil.

> Because of local climatic or demographic conditions it is impossible or unreasonably expensive to use fuels other than oil in an environmentally acceptable way even with advanced technology.

Furthermore, participating countries should require that existing oil-fired base-load power plants be progressively limited to only middle- or peak-load demand use. Dual-fired power plants should not be fired with oil unless other fuels are unreasonably expensive in comparison with oil or unless it is temporarily necessary for environmental reasons. Construction of coal-fired power plants should be facilitated by improving existing siting and licensing procedures; a secure coal supply for electric utilities should be promoted by encouraging coal producers to supply coal for power generation under long-term arrangements; and institutions should be established to facilitate negotiation between electric utilities and coal producers.

The substitution of coal for oil in both new and existing industrial facilities for production of steam and process heat should also be encouraged. Exceptions may be granted where costs, including those for environmental protection, would be unreasonably high in comparison with oil. The use of large coal-fire boilers should be encouraged when planning new industrial parks, district heating facilities, and cogeneration projects. Research, development, and rapid commercialization of improved technologies for coal combustion, including means for keeping the coal combustion cycle environmentally acceptable, should receive high priority. Commercialization of technologies and demonstration plants for converting coal into gas or liquid fuels should be encouraged.

In general, coal mining, transportation, and utilization should be taxed no higher then other economic activities, and end-users should be required to pay the full cost of bringing the coal to market. Government support in providing infrastructure is appropriate. And regulations should be used to prohibit the use of oil and natural gas for the generation of base-load electricity and for raising steam for industrial purposes. In most cases this would leave coal as the least costly alternative; however, environmental constraints are recognized as "legitimate" reasons for the continued use of premium fuels.

The IEA Emergency Preparation Program

The IEA program for emergency preparedness against a major disruption of oil supplies includes demand-restraint policies, target stockpile requirements, and an oil-sharing system. Operationally, two levels of emergency are defined—a 7 percent and 12 percent shortfall from normal supplies. The plan calls for each country to maintain a stockpile of at least 90, and eventually 120, days' net oil imports. And while the specific "demand-restraint" program is left to the individual countries, the goal is for each to be capable of quickly reducing demand by at least 10 percent.

The IEA Standing Group on Emergency Questions administers the emergency oil-sharing program. In the event of a shortfall ranging in magnitude from 7 to 12 percent, each country is expected to restrain demand by 7 percent. Countries are expected to draw down emergency stockpiles as necessary to maintain consumption at 93 percent of normal levels. In the event of a 12 percent or greater shortfall, each country is expected to restrain demand by 10 percent and draw upon stocks to maintain consumption at 90 percent of normal levels.

Emergency Oil-Sharing Program. In case of an emergency, a program has been worked out by which participating countries can share oil. The Standing Group on The Oil Market collects data on oil movements, production, and consumption from the participating countries and the oil companies. Should a crisis arise, the IEA secretariat will use this information to ascertain the quantity of oil available. The secretariat will then apply an allocation formula contained in the International Energy Program Agreement to determine how the available oil will be shared. Each country's fair share, its so-called "supply right," will be compared against available supplies as reported in the emergency information system. Differences between available supplies and supply rights—termed "allocation rights" and "obligations" for deficit and surplus countries, respectively—will be balanced out by reallocating quantities as necessary among the countries. This will be achieved by redirecting oil company shipments under the guidance and supervision of the IEA secretariat.

Supply and demand for the various oil product groups will be taken into account in the allocation process, since the system is designed to avoid unnecessary disturbances in normal commercial operations. Although oil will continue to be traded at prevailing market prices, the IEA will monitor the prices to ensure that principles of "fair treatment" and nondiscrimination are observed. Members of the IEA pledge that during a supply disruption they will not seek to increase their normal share of world oil supplies.

A state of preparedness is maintained through periodic tests—a procedure which also enables the IEA to help participating countries arrive at practical solutions to any problems that may arise in connection with maintaining emergency reserves, preparing demand-restraint measures, or improving international or national components of the system.

Politics of the Oil-Sharing Program. The emergency program was drafted in such a way as to minimize the overt appearance of confrontation with OPEC and OAPEC. Oil supplies "for the group as a whole" must decline by 7 percent before an emergency is declared, and selective embargoes are not mentioned. Thus, a total and effective embargo against, say, the Netherlands or any other single small country would not trigger the emergency sharing program; but one against the United States, Japan, or West Germany would almost certainly do so. In reality, however, the probability of OAPEC using oil as a political weapon solely against a small consumer is practically nonexistent, since small countries have little political or economic power. Thus, although not explicitly stated, it is believed that the emergency sharing program exists to provide a degree of protection against a selective embargo against the larger countries.

Evaluation of Reactions and Policies

The oil price increases of 1973–1974 created many problems for which the consuming countries were ill prepared. They perceived the increases as inflationary, as the cause of unemployment, and as the cause of disequilibrium in the balance of payments. And thinking that traditional monetary and fiscal policies were inadequate to cope with the problems, they tried a variety of "demand-management" programs, including direct allocation, price controls, tariffs, and quotas. Since the effects of these oil policies are difficult to isolate, the overall performance of IEA countries will be evaluated. First the "economic" and "energy" performance is assessed, followed by an evaluation of consumer-country cooperation.

Economic Performance

There is a great deal of controversy over the effects of higher oil prices on the consuming countries. At one extreme is the view that "only oil prices matter," and at the other extreme, "oil prices matter not at all." The latter view is held by those who believe that "only money matters" in determing rates of inflation. For example, well-known conservative economist Milton Friedman contends that higher prices for any single commodity or group of commodities do not constitute inflation if other prices decline enough to offset those price increases. Put another way, the general price level cannot increase unless the money supply increases by more than the rate of increase in real output. The alternative view is that prices are "sticky" (resistant to change) in a downward direction, so that higher prices of one commodity are not offset by a lowering of other prices. Thus, an austere monetary policy will simply cause unemployment and a slower growth rate.

The indisputable facts are that higher oil prices have indeed made the average consumer a little poorer and altered the distribution of income in favor of industries associated with energy production. The contrast in economic performance between the pre-embargo (1963–1973) and post-embargo period (1973–1978) is remarkable. For the twenty IEA countries, gross domestic product (GDP) grew at an annual rate of 5 percent before the embargo but at a rate of only 3.4 percent thereafter. The inflation rate averaged 4.3 percent before and 8.1 percent after the embargo; and the unemployment rate increased from 3.0 to 5.0 percent. Thus, the so-called "misery index," the sum of the unemployment and inflation rates, was 7.3 percent before but 13.0 percent after the embargo (see Table 8–6).

Given the severity of the oil price increases, it is highly probable that they did contribute to the poor economic performance. The magnitude of funds required to pay for the imbalances in oil trade have placed severe strains on capital markets. And regardless of the merits of the case, banks were allowed to create money to finance the deficits. The policy did temporarily hold interest rates down, but the increased money supply drove prices up, and nominal interest rates soon followed.

TABLE 8–6
IEA Economic Performance

	Real GDP Growth Rate (*percent*)[1]	Inflation Rate (*percent*)[2]	Average Rate of Unemployment (*percent*)[3]	Misery Index (*percent*)[4]
1974	0.6	11.8	3.3	15.1
1975	−0.5	7.3	5.4	12.7
1976	5.2	7.7	5.3	13.0
1977	3.7	7.8	5.3	13.1
1978	3.9	7.4	5.2	12.6
1979*	3.4	8.1	5.1	13.2

[1]Main economic indicators, OECD, constant 1975 prices and exchange rates.
[2]National accounts of OECD countries.
[3]OECD economic outlook.
[4]International energy trends. CIF prices of the seven major OECD countries, average over the year.
*Estimated.

SOURCE: International Energy Agency, *Energy Policies and Programmes of IEA Countries, 1979 Review*, Paris: 1980, p. 20.

The end result was slower growth, higher rates of inflation, more unemployment, and domestic and international redistribution of income. The part played by oil prices in all this is subject to individual interpretation.

Energy Performance

Since oil and other primary energy resources are used to produce a substantial amount of other goods and services, there is a positive relationship between energy use and gross domestic product (GDP). In fact, prior to the embargo there was about a one-to-one relationship between the rate of growth in GDP and the rate of growth in energy consumption—that is, about the same amount of energy was used to produce additional output as had been used to produce each previous unit. In fact, in some circles it was thought that the 1:1 ratio was a kind of "law" or required relationship comparable to a law of physics. Naturally, energy usage is dependent on relative prices, but the importance of prices was not clearly perceived by many policymakers until the late 1970s.

Table 8–7 shows the growth rates of real GDP, of total primary energy (TPE), and of oil consumption for 18 IEA countries during the periods 1960–1973 and 1973–1978. The rate of growth in oil consumption and TPE declined markedly after the embargo in virtually every country, with the sole exception being the TPE growth rate in Australia. Furthermore, although the growth rate of oil consumption generally exceeded the growth rate of TPE prior to the embargo, it was less after the embargo. Economic growth rates were also substantially lower in all countries after the embargo. These trends are what might be expected on the basis of conventional supply-and-demand theory. Individuals in the consuming countries are made a little poorer, alternative energy and nonenergy resources are substituted for oil, and less primary energy is used overall.

Despite the apparent success in reducing overall energy consumption, patterns of primary energy usage are difficult to alter during a short time period. This can be illustrated by examining coal utilization in the principal oil consuming countries. The United States is by far the largest coal user in the free world, but the pattern of production and consumption changed only modestly during the five years after 1973 (see Table 8–8). Germany, Japan, the United Kingdom, and all other IEA countries combined actually used less coal in 1978 than in 1973. Thus, although the IEA principles for action on coal are very ambitious, it is doubtful that actual utilization will increase dramatically in the near future. The IEA program should be viewed as goal-directed, and perhaps

TABLE 8–7
Growth Rates of Real Gross Domestic Product (GDP), Total Primary Energy (TPE), and Oil Consumption for 18 IEA Countries, 1960–1973 and 1973–1978
(percent per year)

	PRE-EMBARGO 1960–1973			POST-EMBARGO 1973–1978		
	GDP	TPE	Oil	GDP	TPE	Oil
Australia	5.0	5.7	8.0	3.0	5.6	4.3
Austria	5.0	5.0	11.2	3.0	1.0	−0.1
Belgium	5.0	4.8	10.9	2.5	0	0
Canada	5.6	5.5	5.8	3.3	1.4	1.0
Denmark	4.5	6.2	9.0	2.5	0.8	−1.5
Germany	4.6	4.7	13.1	1.9	0.5	−0.8
Greece	6.6	12.0	13.3	3.5	4.5	3.6
Ireland	4.1	4.6	11.9	3.8	1.9	2.2
Japan	10.4	10.3	17.9	3.6	1.2	0.4
Luxembourg	3.2	2.2	16.6	0	−2.1	3.7
Netherlands	5.2	8.3	8.4	2.5	1.0	0
New Zealand	4.0	4.4	7.3	1.2	2.7	0.6
Norway	4.9	6.2	6.3	4.7	1.8	−0.5
Spain	9.8	8.4	17.2	2.5	4.6	4.4
Sweden	4.1	4.3	6.4	1.3	0.8	−1.7
Switzerland	4.2	5.4	11.0	−1.0	0	−2.4
United Kingdom	3.3	2.1	7.4	0.8	−1.0	−2.9
United States	4.0	4.3	4.3	1.7	1.2	2.4

SOURCE: International Energy Agency, *Energy Policies and Programmes of IEA Countries, 1979 Review,* Paris: 1980.

these are very desirable goals; but implementation of suggested policies is in the hands of the individual countries.

Consumer Country Cooperation

The IEA provides a forum for the consuming countries similar to that of OPEC for the producing countries. The IEA has little power to require its members to conform to agreements, since its recommendations are strictly advisory; the group objective for oil imports provides a case in point. Attainment of the 1985 objective for each country will require reduced oil consumption relative to what would have prevailed if past

TABLE 8–8
Coal Production, Exports, Imports, and Consumption for
Principal IEA Countries, 1960, 1973 and 1978
(million tons)

Country	Production	Exports or Imports	Consumption	Percent of IEA Total
1960				
United States	434	38	396	40.1
Germany	201	23	178	18.0
Japan	72	(11)	83	8.4
United Kingdom	210	8	202	20.5
Other			128	13.0
1973				
United States	599	56	543	48.5
Germany	157	18	139	12.4
Japan	27	(72)	99	8.8
United Kingdom	134	4	130	11.6
Other			209	18.7
1978				
United States	634	32	602	54.1
Germany	145	23	122	11.0
Japan	20	(66)	86	7.7
United Kingdom	122	4	118	10.6
Other			105	9.4

SOURCE: International Energy Agency, *Energy Policies and Programmes of IEA Countries, 1979 Review,* Paris: 1980.

trends had continued. Patterns of energy consumption depend on relative prices, taxation, mandatory allocation rules, prohibition orders, regulations, and so forth. These options are the prerogatives of private individuals and the legislative, judicial, and executive branches of individual governments. There are many controversies surrounding the formulation and implementation of specific policies, and there is no assurance that the decisions reached by individual countries will be compatible with the group objective.

The IEA oil-sharing program provides another illustration. The program was designed to allocate limited oil supplies on an "equitable" basis; it was not designed to influence oil prices. The influence of the 1973–1974 embargo on the design of the program is evident. Clearly, the IEA views "availability" of oil as a more severe problem than the "price" of oil: But it has police powers over neither. More important, there are real questions concerning the need for a government sponsored oil-sharing program and about the effectiveness of the IEA emergency sharing program in particular. During the relatively "tight" oil markets of 1979, oil supplies from OPEC were nevertheless greater than they had been in 1978, and so the IEA's oil-sharing program was not invoked; and it could do nothing about oil prices. Nor is the oil-sharing program likely to have an important influence on prices in the future. A 7 percent supply shortfall would send spot prices so high that organized sharing would become almost academic. Markets will always clear at a sufficiently high price. Discrimination in the provision of oil among countries will cause disparity of prices among countries; and if price differentials are great enough, "unscrupulous" traders will move oil where it will fetch the highest price. This will tend to equalize prices and reduce shortages or excesses at a price. In short, if the pricing system is allowed to operate, the IEA emergency allocation program will be largely redundant. Nevertheless, the oil-sharing program serves notice on OPEC that a selective embargo will not be accepted by IEA participating countries, and it reduces the probability that another embargo will be attempted.

Further Readings

General

Dunkerley, Joy, ed. *International Comparisons of Energy Consumption.* Washington, D.C.: Resources for the Future, 1978.

Federal Energy Administration. *National Energy Outlook.* Washington, D.C.: GPO, 1976.

──────────. *Project Independence.* Washington, D.C.: GPO, November 1974.

Krueger, Robert B. *The United States and International Oil.* A Report for the Federal Energy Administration on U.S. Firms and Government Policy. New York: Praeger, 1975.

Landsberg, Hans H., et al. *Energy: The Next Twenty Years.* Cambridge: Ballinger Publishing Company, 1979.

Organization for Economic Cooperation and Development, *Energy Policies and Programs of IEA Countries.* Paris: OECD, 1980.

──────────. *The International Energy Agency.* Paris: OECD, 1974.

Schurr, Sam H., Dir. *Energy in America's Future, The Choices Before Us.* Washington, D.C.: Resources for the Future, 1979.

Stobaugh, Robert, and Daniel Yergin, eds. *Energy Future.* New York: Random House, 1979.

Regional and Country-Specific Studies

Alting von Geusau, Frans A.M., ed. *Energy in the European Communities*. Leiden: John F. Kennedy Institute Center for International Studies, 1975.

Ausland, John C. *Norway, Oil, and Foreign Policy*. Boulder: Westview Press, 1979.

Cook, P. Lesley, and A. J. Surrey. *Energy Policy*. London: Martin Robertson & Co. Ltd., 1977.

Frank, Helmut J., and John J. Schanz, Jr. *U.S. Canadian Energy Trade: A Study of Changing Relationships*. Boulder: Westview Press, 1978.

Goodwin, Crauford D. ed. *Energy Policy in Perspective*. Baltimore: Johns Hopkins University Press, 1981.

Lucas, N. J. D. *Energy and the European Communities*. London: Europa Publications, 1977.

Mendershausen, Horst. *Coping with the Oil Crisis, French and German Experiences*. Baltimore: Johns Hopkins University Press, 1976.

Williams, Edward J. *The Rebirth of the Mexican Petroleum Industry*. Lexington: Lexington Books, 1979.

Exporting Country Options

Introduction.

Goals and Priorities:
Individual Exporting Countries; OPEC as a Formal Organization.

Organizational Structure and Functions of OPEC:
The Conference; Board of Governors; The Secretariat; Member Country Governments.

Major Economic Issues:
Pricing Issues; Capacity, Production, and Stockpiling Issues; Relations with Other International Actors.

Political Issues:
Arab–Israeli Conflict.

Conclusion.

READER'S GUIDE TO CHAPTER 9

This chapter considers the major issues and options available to the oil exporting countries, both individually and collectively, through OPEC. Because a comprehensive treatment would require several volumes, the topics selected for inclusion—as well as the extent of coverage—are necessarily limited. The organizational structure of OPEC is included to emphasize the range and limits of member country cooperation in resolving their political and economic objectives. The major economic issues considered are (1) petroleum pricing issues, such as indexing oil prices to the price level in the industrial countries and indexing natural gas to oil prices, (2) the capacity, production, and stockpiling issues which are inherently related to one another, and (3) relations with other principal actors, such as the oil companies, industrial countries, and non-OPEC less developed countries. The only political issues considered are those related to the use of oil as a weapon in the Arab–Israeli conflict and the use of embargoes and boycotts to accomplish political objectives.

235

Introduction

The individual members of OPEC share many goals and problems because of their common status as petroleum exporters, and they enjoy the advantage of coordinating their common interests through OPEC. However, OPEC members are also sovereign nations with individual goals, aspirations, and perceptions of their role in the international community. This duality creates conflicts as well as harmonies of interest among them. The importance of OPEC as a unifying force is difficult to overemphasize; but it is also true that OPEC is a bureaucratic institution with weaknesses as well as strengths in its influence over oil affairs.

OPEC is first and foremost an organization designed to accomplish a limited range of objectives related to the level of oil prices and to the distribution of revenue derived from oil production. Pricing issues are therefore of primary concern, although they cannot be comprehended independent of capacity, production, and stockpiling decisions, nor of their effects on relations with foreign countries. The principal pricing issues concern the indexing of oil prices to prices in the industrial countries and the indexing of natural gas prices to oil prices. A related issue is the currency or currencies in which payment shall be required. These are extraordinarily important problems both for OPEC and for the importing countries. Unfortunately, they are so thorny that there is no real hope for any final resolution.

Some of the OPEC countries feel the institution should expand its range of objectives and play a more important role in the conduct of international economic and political affairs. In particular, they would like to move downstream into refining and marketing, become philanthropists to the less developed countries, and provide military support to nations in direct conflict with Israel. The success and prospects for OPEC depend on how the leadership resolves these important issues during the 1980s and beyond.

Goals and Priorities

Individual Exporting Countries

The political and economic goals of the individual oil exporting countries are similar to those of the consuming countries. Their primary political goal is to remain sovereign. This implies a degree of security from external aggression, harmonious internal relations, and the ability to prevent revolutions. These goals can be achieved by economic and/ or political means.

Economic Goals. Primary economic goals of the oil exporting countries include attaining a sustained rate of economic growth, price-level stability, and a high level of employment. They also seek a *favorable* balance of trade. The latter is emphasized because oil in the ground is a capital asset, which leaders of the OPEC nations hope to replace with financial assets and with physical and human capital.

The importance of replacing oil with other assets may be illustrated by the parable of a Saudi prince whose grandfather rode a camel and whose father drove an automobile; the prince flies a jet plane; and his son, it is said, will ride a camel. Leaders in Saudi Arabia and in other oil exporting countries would like to leave their grandchildren a more substantial inheritance. They are aware that their oil will one day be depleted, and so they seek to replace it with more durable earning assets. This can only be done by running a favorable balance of trade in oil.

Politico-economic Objectives. Because all the leading oil exporting countries were once part of a colonial empire dominated by Western powers, it is natural that OPEC leaders place much emphasis on gaining permanent sovereignty over their natural resources. In the United States and Western Europe this goal was achieved many years ago. Sovereignty over natural resources of course includes control over their rate of exploration, development, and production; but within OPEC the meaning has been extended to include obtainment of "equitable" prices. The definition of "equitable" has also been extended. Originally it simply was to maintain the *status quo* with respect to posted prices, then it was to maintain *real prices*, and, finally, it was to obtain prices comparable to the amount which must be paid for the next best alternative to oil and natural gas. The latter is comparable to obtainment of a monopoly price.

The exporting countries do not view the attainment of their political and economic goals as being incompatible with the obtainment of monopoly prices. National defense is costly, internal strife can be quelled by a wealthy elite more easily than by a poor one, and oil revenue can be used to accumulate capital. Revenue derived from oil can be spent as readily as revenue derived from other resources or from human ingenuity. Similarly, internal investment projects and control over real assets in foreign lands are facilitated by obtaining monopoly rather than competitive prices. The only goal which may possibly conflict with obtaining monopoly prices is that of price-level stability. However, higher general price levels in foreign countries are primarily monetary phenomena not subject to direct control by OPEC leaders.

Diverse Priorities.   The oil exporting countries are sufficiently diverse from one another demographically, socially, and economically that their priorities in attaining alternative goals can and do differ considerably. Leaders in the more populous countries, such as Indonesia and Nigeria, place great store in using oil revenues to stimulate sustained economic growth. These nations are still relatively poor even though they are important oil exporters. On the other hand, leaders in oil-rich countries such as Kuwait and Abu Dhabi seek to utilize their oil revenues to provide housing and "public goods," such as free schooling, medical services, improved communications, air terminals, and deep-water ports.

OPEC as a Formal Organization

The goals of OPEC as a formal organization are not identical to those of its individual members. OPEC was established in 1960 to resist oil price reductions; but, more fundamentally, its leadership seeks to promote cooperation among the exporting countries in attaining objectives deemed to be in their mutual self-interest. The goals of OPEC are expressed in its Solemn Declarations and Resolutions. They have evolved over time, but in a logical progression of a basic theme. In general, the Resolutions focus on sovereignty over petroleum resources with an emphasis on "equitable" prices.

Oil Price Objectives.   The First OPEC Resolution, drafted in September, 1960, illustrates the initial concern with maintaining nominal oil prices, stating emphatically that:

> Members can no longer remain indifferent to the attitude heretofore adopted by the oil companies in effecting price modifications; that members shall demand that oil companies maintain their prices steady and free from all unnecessary fluctuations; that members shall endeavor, by all means available to them, to restore present prices to the levels prevailing before the reduction; that they shall ensure that if any new circumstances arise that in the estimation of the oil companies necessitate price modifications, the said companies shall enter into consultation with the member or members affected.

Thus, the initial concern was simply to maintain nominal prices. The Second OPEC Resolution outlined a more general objective:

> The principal aim of the Organization shall be the unification of petroleum policies for the member countries and the determination of the

best means for safeguarding the interest of member countries individually and collectively.

The means of attaining these objectives have always been through cooperation or "solidarity." According to the Second Resolution:

> If as a result of the application of any unanimous decision of the Conference any sanctions are employed, directly or indirectly, by an interested company against one or more of the member countries, no other member shall accept any offer of a beneficial treatment, whether in the form of an increase in exports or an improvement in prices, that may be made to it by any such company or companies with the intention of discouraging the application of the unanimous decision reached by the Conference.[1]

In June, 1968, the OPEC ministers adopted a "Declaratory Statement of Petroleum Policy," which broadened the objectives of OPEC to include the maintenance of *real oil prices*. More specifically, the objective was to prevent any deterioration in the relationship between nominal oil prices and the prices of manufactured goods traded internationally. The pricing goal continued to evolve throughout the 1970s, and in 1980 the secretary general of OPEC, Rene Ortiz, flatly stated that, "Oil prices should *rise in real terms* . . . until they reach a level which approximates . . . the cost of alternative energy resources."[2]

Natural Gas Price Objectives.   The goal with respect to natural gas prices has also evolved over time. The issue was not of great significance prior to the sharp price increases of 1973, but it will become one of the more important issues in the future. OPEC would like to equalize the price of oil and natural gas on an energy-content or BTU basis. Thus, the intent is to obtain a monopoly price for natural gas as well as for oil. But stating a goal is not equivalent to attaining it, and realization of monopoly prices remains more a dream than a reality for the member countries of OPEC.

Organizational Structure and Functions of OPEC

The formal bureaucratic structure of the Organization of the Petroleum Exporting Countries (OPEC) consists of three main components: (1) the conference, (2) the board of governors, and (3) the secretariat. The conference is the supreme authority and makes all of the important

---

[1] Faud Rouhani, *A History of OPEC* (New York: Praeger, 1971), p. 78.
[2] Rene Ortiz, "Facing up to the Energy Crisis," *OPEC Bulletin*, September 1980, p. 10.

policy decisions. The board of governors manages the affairs of the organization and carries out the orders of the conference. The secretariat organizes day-to-day activities and carries out directives of the conference and the board of governors. An overview of the organizational structure is shown in Figure 9-1.

The Conference

The conference is composed of a delegation from each member country. Each delegation includes one or more "delegates," or oil ministers, along with their consultants and observers. Two ordinary meetings are held each year (summer and winter), but extraordinary meetings may be requested to deal with special problems. It has become customary to hold the summer meeting in Vienna, which is headquarters for OPEC, and to rotate the winter meetings among the member countries. Each country is entitled to representation at the meetings, but only a three-fourths majority is required for a quorum. Each member has one vote, and all decisions, except for routine procedural matters, require a unanimous vote. Resolutions become effective thirty days after they are adopted. However, if a member country is not represented at a ministerial meeting, it has the right to file disagreement with any resolution adopted in its absence. Such disagreement must be filed with the secretariat within ten days after the meeting has adjourned.

The officers of the conference include a president, alternate president, secretary-general, and chairman of the board of governors. The president, who serves a one-year term, chairs sessions of the conference. The alternate president serves when the president is absent. The secretary-general (see The Secretariat on page 243) functions as the secretary of the conference; and the chairman of the board of governors represents the board at the conference.

All major OPEC decisions are made by the conference, whose functions and responsibilities are spelled out explicitly in Article 15 of the statutes. These include:

1. Formulation of general policy and determination of appropriate means for implementation.
2. Approval of applications for membership.
3. Approval of members of the board of governors.
4. Issuing directives to the board of governors concerning the presentation of reports or recommendations regarding matters of interest to the organization.

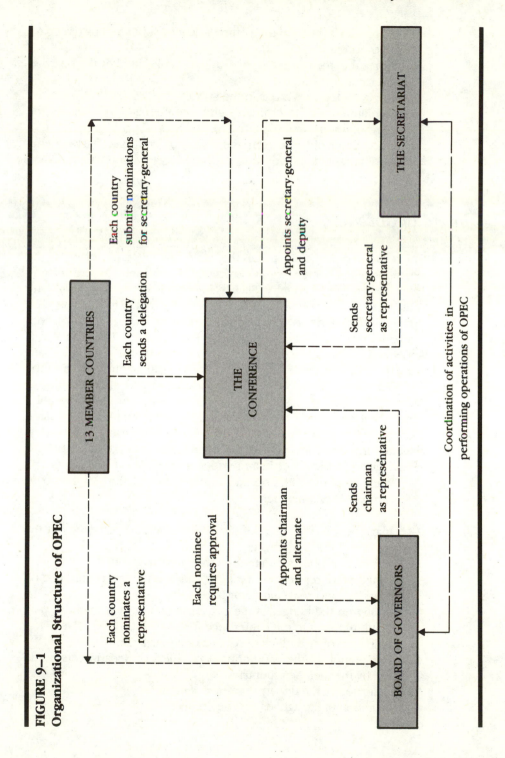

FIGURE 9–1
Organizational Structure of OPEC

5. Approval of reports and recommendations submitted by the board of governors.
6. Approval of the organization's budget as submitted by the board of governors.
7. Approval of any revisions in the statutes.
8. Appointment of the chairman and the alternate chairman of the board of governors.
9. Appointment of the secretary-general and deputy secretary-general.
10. Appointment of an auditor to audit the organization's accounts.

Board of Governors

The board of governors manages the affairs of OPEC and carries out the decisions of the conference. It is composed of thirteen governors, one from each member country. Each governor serves for two years and must be approved by the conference. Each is entitled to one vote, and a two-thirds majority is required for a quorum. If a governor cannot attend he may send an ad hoc governor in his place. The chairman is appointed by the conference and serves a term of one year. The chairman's position rotates among the countries by alphabetical order of the member countries, but seniority of membership is also considered. Meetings are held at least twice a year, generally a few days before the semiannual meeting of the conference. However, extraordinary meetings may be held at the request of the board chairman, the secretary-general, or a two-thirds vote of the board. Meetings are held at OPEC headquarters in Vienna or in a member country.

Article 20 of the OPEC statutes outlines the functions of the board of governors. These include:

1. Management of the affairs of the organization and carrying out the decisions of the conference.
2. Approval of reports submitted by the secretary-general.
3. Submission of reports and recommendations to the conference on matters of concern to the organization.
4. Drawing up the budget of the organization for each calendar year, and submitting it to the conference for approval.
5. Nomination of an auditor to serve a one-year term.
6. Consideration of the appointment of chiefs of departments nominated by the member countries.
7. Nomination of the deputy secretary-general.
8. Preparation of the agenda for the conference.

The Secretariat

The secretariat organizes and administers the work of OPEC in accord with OPEC statutes and directives from the conference. Its activities are coordinated with those of the board of governors. The secretariat is composed of a secretary-general, deputy secretary, department heads, and staff. The secretary-general is the chief administrative officer and appointed by the conference to serve a three-year term. Statutory requirements for the position of secretary-general ensure that only an experienced individual will be selected: The person must be at least thirty-five years old, hold a university degree, and have not less than fifteen years' experience in petroleum matters. He must be unanimously approved by the conference. If a nominee is not unanimously approved, the secretary-general is selected from among the nominees submitted by each member country. In such a case, the term rotates among the nominees every two years, based on alphabetical order of the member countries. So far, most secretary-generals have been selected in this manner.

The departments within OPEC—economics, legal, information, and technical—reflect the principal concerns of the organization (see Figure 9-2). A statistical unit is responsible for collection and compilation of data. Consultants and other professionals commissioned for special studies are appointed as needed by the secretary-general. Given the administrative framework, the secretary-general is charged with organizing and administering the work of the organization, preparing reports for board meetings, and informing the chairman and members of the board as to the activities of the secretariat. In terms of power, the secretariat is subordinate to the board of governors and to the conference.

Member Country Governments

The organizational hierarchy within each member country also has some influence in the organization's decision-making process. Bureaucratic structures among the exporting countries are similar to those in the importing countries. And OPEC member nations experience the same differences in power and the same sort of conflicts as well as harmonies of interest as do the importing nations. In addition, they share the universal bureaucratic problem of lags between the discovery and resolution of problems. Saudi Arabia, which has a particularly autocratic form of government, is typical of the organizational structure of the most important member countries. Others have even more cumbersome hierarchical structures.

FIGURE 9-2
Organizational Structure of the OPEC Secretariat

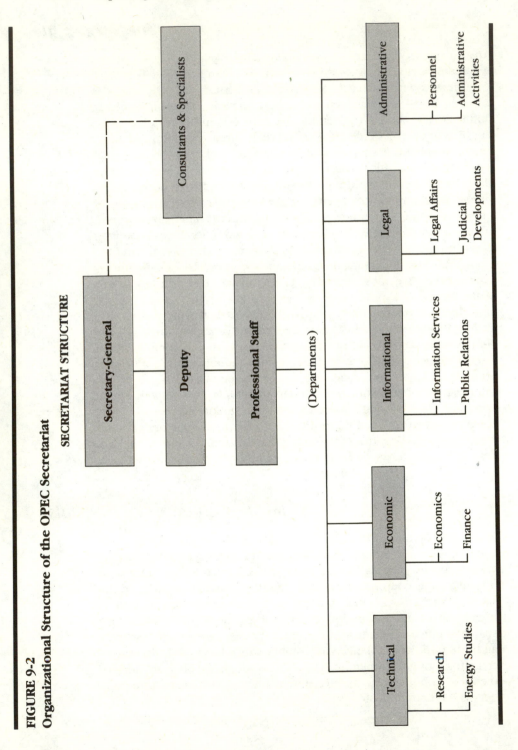

Saudi Arabia.   The Saudi Arabian government is organized by function in the areas of policy, funding, and operations. The leadership consists of a king, a crown prince, and the Supreme Petroleum Council. The king is the supreme authority and a member of the Royal House of Saud. He delegates powers to the crown prince and to the Supreme Petroleum Council, but he retains veto power over both. Figure 9-3 shows the Saudi organizational structure in further detail.

The crown prince is chairman of the Supreme Petroleum Council and is responsible for establishing petroleum policies in consultation with other Council members. He also assists other ministries in implementing their daily operations. The Supreme Petroleum Council makes recommendations to the crown prince concerning petroleum and economic policy on such issues as oil pricing, production levels, marketing strategy, and petroleum and economic development. The Council has the power to approve or disapprove policy.

Other important organizational units include the Royal Commission for Industrialization, responsible for the development of new petroleum-related industries; and the Ministry of Petroleum and Mineral Resources, charged with the implementation of petroleum policies and with daily operational decisions. The latter is responsible for sending a representative to the OPEC ministerial meetings, deciding on short-term production levels, setting prices, and allocating oil revenues. The petroleum minister reports directly to the crown prince and the king. Any new policy initiatives must be sent to the Council for approval, but the king maintains veto power. The Ministry of Petroleum deals directly with Petromin, which is Saudi Arabia's national oil company, and with the operating companies, primarily Aramco.

Major Economic Issues

The principal economic issues both for the individual exporting countries and for OPEC relate to (1) pricing of oil and natural gas; (2) capacity, production, and stockpiling decisions; and (3) relations with other international actors. Of these, pricing and production decisions require coordinated actions, whereas the other issues are the prerogatives of the individual countries and require little cooperation.

Efforts to maintain or increase the real prices of oil and natural gas have centered around "indexing" oil prices to those in the industrial countries and denominating oil prices in special drawing rights (SDRs). These issues are treated at length in this section. The issues requiring less cooperation will not be considered in detail, but they are nevertheless important to the individual countries. In particular, decisions to

FIGURE 9-3
Saudi Government Petroleum Policymaking Structure

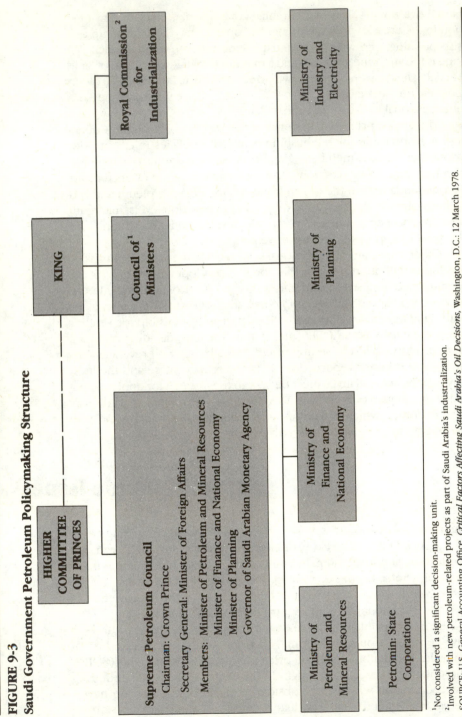

HIGHER COMMITTEE OF PRINCES

KING

Royal Commission[2] for Industrialization

Council of[1] Ministers

Ministry of Industry and Electricity

Ministry of Planning

Supreme Petroleum Council

Chairman: Crown Prince

Secretary General: Minister of Foreign Affairs

Members: Minister of Petroleum and Mineral Resources
Minister of Finance and National Economy
Minister of Planning
Governor of Saudi Arabian Monetary Agency

Ministry of Finance and National Economy

Ministry of Petroleum and Mineral Resources

Petromin: State Corporation

[1]Not considered a significant decision-making unit.

[2]Involved with new petroleum-related projects as part of Saudi Arabia's industrialization.

SOURCE: U.S. General Accounting Office, *Critical Factors Affecting Saudi Arabia's Oil Decisions*, Washington, D.C.: 12 March 1978.

invest in downstream petroleum activities related to refining and marketing and decisions to buy financial assets or to provide aid to less developed countries are considered vital to the countries' interests.

Pricing Issues

Overview.   The most important problem of the OPEC conference is to determine the appropriate target price for Saudi Arabian marker crude. The marker price is ultimately determined by Saudi Arabia, but in consultation with other member countries through the conference. However, since the conference meets at least twice annually and since Saudi Arabia can unilaterally change its prices at any time, the conference's decision is not carved in stone.

But the commitment to maintain or increase real oil prices raises problems inherent in target pricing. There are three variables that determine the real price of oil: (1) the nominal price of oil, (2) the nominal prices of goods purchased by OPEC member countries, and (3) the currency exchange rates. And although Saudi Arabia and the OPEC conference can strongly influence if not determine nominal oil prices, they have little or no control over nominal prices of imported goods or over exchange rates. Thus, the maintenance of real oil prices can be accomplished only by altering nominal oil prices.

Maintenance of real prices is further complicated by two facts. First, oil prices are quoted in U.S. dollars. Second, different member countries purchase different market baskets of goods from a variety of countries. The specific issues spawned by these factors are indexation of oil prices to prices of goods imported by OPEC members and denomination of oil prices in a composite currency, such as SDRs, rather than the dollar. A closely related issue which is destined to become increasingly important is the indexing of natural gas prices to oil prices.

Indexing Oil Prices.   The desire to index oil prices to the prices of goods and services exported by industrialized countries (or imported by OPEC members) is based on the normative belief that the purchasing power of revenues received by the oil exporting countries should not be allowed to deteriorate. The operational goal is to ensure that oil prices increase at a rate comparable to the price of a market basket of goods purchased by an oil exporter. The prescribed rate is usually defined as being equal to that of a selected market basket of goods. Of course, oil prices could be indexed to increase more rapidly than prices of other goods. Among the questions that must be considered in any indexing scheme are: What set of commodities to include in the market basket—U.S., Japanese, German, or a composite of these and other countries' goods? Whose prices should be used? Should the weights be revised every time exchange rates change? How should transportation costs be handled? And, which country of origin and which destination should be used? Thus, although the concept of indexing is quite simple, the mechanics are rather complicated. It is basically a dynamic form of target pricing or price control, with all the problems inherent in fixing prices.

OPEC could index prices to a market basket of goods in the industrialized countries if its members were willing to accept the level of output determined by buyers. However, if initial prices are too high, OPEC members will find the demand for their oil declining to a level which may prove unacceptable. On the other hand, if initial prices are too low, or if there is a supply interruption, prices will be driven beyond those called for by indexing. As shown by experiences during the 1970s, spot prices will invariably pull contract prices up in a tight market and mitigate price increases when markets are weak.

Member countries cannot each index their oil prices to the commodity bundle they import because the price differentials resulting from such a practice generally will not correspond with the market appraisal of values. Countries trying to sell undervalued crudes would find a ready market, and they would be able to produce at full capacity. Conversely, countries with overvalued crudes would find their oil difficult to sell and thus operate far below capacity. So, individual indexing will not accomplish important objectives related to market sharing and the distribution of oil revenues.

Despite all its advocacy by spokesmen in the OPEC countries, actual experience with indexing is extremely limited. In 1972 and 1973, oil prices were adjusted for inflation by virtue of the Geneva Accords; but otherwise, prices have never been formally indexed. Indexing became a moot point after the embargo of 1973–1974, because "shortages at a price" drove prices far above those warranted on the basis of price increases in the consuming countries. The issue of indexing will remain important within OPEC as an ideal and as a moving target, but as a practical matter it is impossible to fix prices with the degree of precision contemplated by its advocates. In fact, prices are established and revised in light of "market conditions," including real price targets, quantities produced, and market shares within OPEC.

Pricing in SDRs.   Under current practice, the nominal price of oil is expressed in U.S. dollars per barrel and accounts are settled in U.S. dollars. Thus, a Japanese buyer exchanges yen for dollars to pay for his oil; and the producing government may either use the dollars to buy goods, services, or securities from the United States or exchange the dollars for currency of any other country from which it wishes to buy goods. Similar statements hold for all other countries. The problem as viewed by OPEC is that the value of the dollar has depreciated relative to many of the other leading currencies. In this regard, the method most frequently proposed to maintain the purchasing power of revenues received by OPEC is to denominate oil prices in special drawing rights (SDRs).

SDRs were created by the International Monetary Fund (IMF) in 1968 as a way to increase the liquidity with which money flows throughout the world. They were initially given a value equal to ⅓₅ of an ounce of gold, which was the official exchange rate of the dollar for gold until December, 1971. The valuation of SDRs in terms of gold was dropped after 1974, and thereafter they were defined as the weighted value of sixteen major currencies. The original currency basket included those currencies which accounted for at least 1 percent of free world merchandise trade during the period 1968–1972. On July 1, 1978, the currency basket was redefined to reflect trade patterns during the period 1972–1976. New weights to become effective July 1, 1983, will be assigned based on 1976–1980 trade patterns. The following weights are effective until that date:

Country	Percent	Country	Percent
United States	33	Belgium	4
Germany	12.5	Saudi Arabia	3
United Kingdom	7.5	Iran	3
France	7.5	Sweden	2
Japan	7.5	Australia	1.5
Canada	5	Spain	1.5
Italy	5	Norway	1.5
Netherlands	5	Denmark	1.5

From OPEC's perspective, the desirability of pricing oil in SDRs depends on the relative strength of the dollar. When the dollar depreciates relative to other major currencies, individuals who hold dollars lose purchasing power. For example, if Saudi Arabia sells 1,000 barrels of oil at $34 per barrel, government revenue is $34,000. When used in Germany at an exchange rate of 2.5 DM = $1, the Saudi buying agent can command 85,000 DM worth of German goods. If the dollar depreciates against the mark to the extent that 2.0 DM = $1, the Saudi buyer can only purchase 68,000 DM worth of German goods. In this case, a 20 percent depreciation of the dollar would lower the purchasing power of Saudi revenues spent in Germany by 20 percent. This is comparable to receiving 20 percent less for a portion of their oil. From the German point of view, the price of oil drops from 85,000 DM for 1,000 barrels of oil to 68,000 DM following the depreciation of the dollar.

Exchange rate fluctuations are obviously a double-edged sword, since the dollar can appreciate as well as depreciate against other currencies. For example, if the dollar appreciates against the mark to 3.0 DM = $1, Germans would have to pay 102,000 DM to acquire 1,000 barrels of oil and the Saudi buyer could purchase 102,000 DM worth of German goods. However, exchange rate variations have no effect on the purchasing power of oil revenues spent in the United States, since the price is quoted and payment is made in dollars. In other words, the 1,000 barrels of oil will buy $34,000 worth of American goods regardless of currency exchange rates.

The history of exchange rate movements since the creation of SDRs highlights the problem of deciding if and when to shift from pricing in dollars to pricing in SDRs. It is essentially the difficulty of predicting future trends in the dollar/SDR exchange rate. From the time the dollar was devalued in 1970 until creation of the SDR currency basket in mid-1974, the dollar depreciated more than 20 percent against the SDR. This was the result of two separate dollar devaluations as well as depreciation under an exchange rate system known as the "dirty float." After 1974 the dollar performed somewhat better, increasing against the SDR in 1975 and 1976, declining during 1977–1979, but increasing again in 1980 (see Table 9-1).

If OPEC had switched to SDR pricing in mid-1975, its members would have experienced a considerable drop in purchasing power in 1976 and buyers in the United States would have benefited. If OPEC had switched to SDR pricing at the end of 1976, its members would have been the ones to benefit and buyers in the United States would have suffered a loss in purchasing power. The problem of deciding whether and when to switch to SDR pricing is similar to that of deciding whether and when to purchase a stock or bond. Of course, the buyer would like to buy when it is cheap and sell when the price goes up; the problem is in deciding when the high or low has been attained.

Another thing that makes shifting to SDR pricing relatively costly for OPEC is the fact that OPEC members have many monetary investments in the United States. "Abandoning" the dollar in favor of SDRs might further reduce the exchange value of the dollar and inflict great losses on those who hold dollars or dollar assets and who wish to exchange them for other currencies. Because of these circumstances, the conference has decided to stay with the dollar, at least for the time being.

Indexing Natural Gas Prices.   A central issue from the point of view of buyers is whether natural gas prices should be indexed at all. The question is: What effect does indexing have on prices, interfuel substitution, and patterns of energy-resource trade? Indexing natural gas prices to the price of oil is different from indexing oil prices to prices in the industrial countries. The reason is that oil and natural gas

TABLE 9-1
Value of the Yen and Deutsche Mark Relative to Special
Drawing Rights (SDRs) and the Dollar, 1970–1980
(year-end exchange rates)

Date	Number of SDRs Required to Buy		Number of Yen Required to Buy		Number of Deutsche Marks Required to Buy	
	One U.S. Dollar	One SDR	One U.S. Dollar	One SDR	One U.S. Dollar	
1970	1.000	358	358	3.65	3.65
1971	.921	342	315	3.55	3.27
1972	.921	328	302	3.48	3.20
1973	.829	338	280	3.26	2.70
1974	.817	368	301	2.95	2.41
1975	.854	357	305	3.07	2.62
1976	.861	340	293	2.75	2.36
1977	.823	291	240	2.56	2.11
1978	.768	254	195	2.38	1.83
1979	.759	316	240	2.28	1.73
1980	.784	258	203	2.50	1.96

SOURCE: International Monetary Fund, *International Financial Statistics, Yearbook 1980*, pp. 430–431. International Monetary Fund, *International Financial Statistics*, September 1981, pp. 160, 222–223, 409.

are direct substitutes, so the maximum price an end-user will pay for natural gas is the price of the next best alternative fuel. This value is relatively high when gas is used for so-called "noble" or "premium" purposes, such as for manufacturing petrochemicals or for residential and commercial heating. But the value is relatively low when gas is used in place of residual fuel oil or coal in generating electricity. While the OPEC conference has not taken a position on indexing natural gas to oil prices, the position of the OPEC secretariat is that the price of natural gas should be set so high that it will be used only as a premium fuel. This will prolong the lifetime of natural gas reserves and enhance the value of oil. In June, 1980, after four years of study, OPEC's Natural Gas Committee asserted that gas prices should be "in line with" or "indexed to" crude oil prices on a BTU (British thermal unit) basis. A more precise definition of BTU "parity" pricing was left to the individual countries.

There are two major considerations in establishing initial natural gas prices and indexing them to oil prices. The first and most important is deciding which crude oil should be used as a reference crude. The second is whether gas prices should be indexed to crude prices on a C.I.F. or an F.O.B. basis. Both decisions will influence the level of and rate of increase in natural gas prices.

The choice of a reference crude and of C.I.F. versus F.O.B. pricing are related issues. Light crudes contain relatively few BTUs but command a higher price than heavy crudes. For example, the relatively light North Sea Ekofisk (42° API) contains only 5.65 million BTUs per barrel, whereas the heavier Venezuelan Tia Juana (24° API) contains 6.07 million BTUs. In September, 1980, the F.O.B. price of Ekofisk was $37 per barrel, whereas Tia Juana could fetch only $27. If natural gas prices had been indexed to Ekofisk, the price would have been $6.58 per million BTUs; indexing to Tia Juana would have resulted in a price of only $4.27. So, in general, indexing to sweet crudes will result in higher natural gas prices.

Whether to index to the C.I.F. or F.O.B. price is important because transport and handling costs are typically seven to eight times as high for natural gas as for oil. For example, expressed in 1980 dollars, it costs approximately $1 to transport a barrel of oil from Algeria to New York; the cost of transporting a BTU-equivalent amount of natural gas over the same route is about $7.50. The cost per million BTUs works out to be 16 cents for oil but $1.20 for natural gas. These costs naturally vary somewhat depending on origin, destination, crude quality, and conditions in transport markets. However, using Ekofisk as an example, C.I.F. pricing would yield an indexed natural gas price to the consumer of $6.58 per million BTUs; and F.O.B. pricing would result in a price of $7.78 ($6.58 + $1.20). Comparable figures for Tia Juana are $4.27 (C.I.F.) and $5.47 (F.O.B.). In general, indexing to F.O.B. prices will result in relatively high natural gas prices.

The Natural-Gas Exporting Countries.   The international market for natural gas is small, but it has great potential for growth. Thus, the relative importance of the indexing issue is greater than the current volume of natural gas trade might lead one to believe. The principal natural-gas exporting countries in 1980 were the Netherlands, the USSR, Canada, and Algeria. These four countries accounted for about two-thirds of total natural gas trade.

Most natural-gas exports at present are via pipeline. The Netherlands and the USSR supply Western Europe, and Canada and Mexico export gas to the United States via pipeline. Algeria is the largest supplier of liquefied natural gas (LNG), shipping to France and the United States. The LNG trade is extremely limited and specialized. In 1980 there were only nine LNG processing plants worldwide. High shipping costs and evaporation losses incurred in transit make LNG shipments from the Persian Gulf to the principal markets in Europe and the United States unprofitable as compared with oil, which is the primary reason OPEC members flare so much gas at present.

To appreciate the size of the gas trade relative to the oil trade, gas trade in 1979 amounted to only 3 million barrels per day oil equivalent compared with an oil trade of 31 million barrels per day. OPEC members produced 5 million barrels per day oil equivalent of natural gas but marketed only about two-fifths of that total. Another two-fifths were flared, and the remainder was reinjected to enhance oil recovery. However, OPEC had proven natural gas reserves of 177 billion barrels oil equivalent (see Table 9-2), compared with oil reserves of 435 billion barrels. The reserve-to-production ratio was about 14 for oil but about 34 for natural gas. Thus, natural gas was not used as intensively as oil in comparison with reserves. The primary reason is that natural gas is costly to transport and difficult to handle. However, as oil reserves decline, the relative importance of natural gas will surely increase.

All the natural-gas exporting countries are committed to some form of indexing. Algeria, the hard-liner, advocates indexing to the F.O.B. price of the relatively light Saharan Blend crude. This would yield a U.S. East Coast price of $7.70 per million BTUs using 1980 crude prices. Most of the other gas exporters are willing to accept C.I.F. indexing to the price of a light crude, gas oil, or fuel oil.

Position of the Natural-Gas Importing Countries.   None of the natural-gas importing countries has accepted indexing to F.O.B. prices, since the cost of alternative fuels at the point of consumption is what determines fuel choice. Natural gas commands a small premium over

TABLE 9-2
Proven Reserves of Natural Gas for the Principal Natural-Gas Producers, January 1, 1980

Region	Trillion Cubic Feet	Billion Barrels Oil Equivalent	Percentage of: World	Percentage of: Free World
FREE WORLD				
OPEC	996	177	39	61
United States	194	35	8	12
Canada & Mexico	145	26	6	9
Western Europe & Japan	136	24	5	8
Other	168	30	7	10
Total Free World	1,638	291	64	100
COMMUNIST COUNTRIES				
USSR & East Europe	910	162	35	—
People's Republic of China	25	4	1	—
TOTAL WORLD	2,573	457	100	—

SOURCE: OPEC, *Annual Report, 1979,* Vienna: 1980, p. 73.

the C.I.F. price of alternative fuels because it burns clean, but the premium does not appear to be on the order of $1 per million BTUs.

Whether or not a country will accept the indexing of natural gas prices to those of light crudes depends on the end use to which the country intends to put incremental natural gas supplies. In Japan, the next best alternative to LNG is imported residual fuel oil. In the United States, it is additional natural gas from domestic sources. The U.S. Department of Energy officials who are responsible for issuing licenses to import natural gas and LNG are convinced that additional domestic supplies can be obtained for less than the BTU-equivalent price of light crudes. The Japanese have been inclined to accept high prices, but U.S. officials and natural gas distributors have balked. A principal reason is the Natural Gas Policy Act of 1978. The Act stipulates that industrial users must pay the incremental cost of imported gas. Prior to passage of the Act, distributors were allowed to "roll-in" or "average" high-cost foreign with cheap and regulated domestic supplies. Thus, industrial users are encouraged to use fuel oil in place of imported natural gas.

Incremental pricing produced dramatic results in trade between Canada and the United States during 1980. In February of that year, export prices of Canadian natural gas increased from $3.97 to $4.47 per million BTUs. By April, exports to the United States had declined by 34 percent from the previous year's level. Industrial buyers were simply switching from natural gas to residual fuel oil. The wholesale price of "resid" in April was $25.16 per barrel, which works out to an equivalent natural gas price of $4.32 per million BTUs. This seemingly small cost advantage was enough to tip the scales in favor of residual for many users. A lesson is that the demand for imported gas is highly elastic around the equivalent price of residual fuel oil. This implies that even C.I.F. indexing of natural gas to light crude oil prices can be accomplished only at the expense of sharp reductions in the quantity demanded of natural gas. Indexing to F.O.B. prices of light crudes is out of the question.

Position of the Natural Gas Exporting Countries.   From OPEC's point of view, a sharp reduction in the quantity demanded of natural gas may be quite acceptable. OPEC members have 61 percent of free world natural gas reserves, but most of their current income is derived from oil. When OPEC members sell natural gas at prices below the BTU equivalent price of residual fuel oil they weaken the demand for oil, because natural gas is directly competitive with residual fuel oil. However, member countries flare about 2 million barrels per day oil equivalent of associated natural gas as an undesirable by-product in order to produce oil. The alternatives to flaring are exporting it, using it internally, and reinjecting it into the oil reservoirs. Exporting LNG requires expensive capital equipment, and shipping costs around the Cape of Good Hope are on the order of $3 per million BTUs. The "netback" to Persian Gulf sellers at delivered prices of around $4 per million BTUs is therefore very low. Internal usage offers a better alternative but also yields only $1 to $2 per million BTUs in most present applications. Reinjection to enhance oil recovery is an acceptable alternative under appropriate reservoir and technical conditions.

The countries with the largest natural gas reserves are Iran and Algeria, which together account for 62 percent of proven OPEC reserves (see Table 9-3). Since Algeria has more oil-equivalent natural gas than oil, it is particularly important for Algeria to produce and export natural gas. Iran has explored the possibility of supplying the USSR and Western Europe with natural gas via pipeline, and Algeria is developing a pipeline under the Mediterranean Sea to Italy. The natural-gas pricing issue is therefore relatively more important to Iran and Algeria, but all OPEC member countries have a stake in the outcome.

TABLE 9-3
Proven Reserves of Natural Gas for OPEC Member Countries, January 1, 1980

Country	Trillion Cubic Feet	Billion Barrels Oil Equivalent	Percent of Total	Cumulative Percent of Total[1]
Iran	490	87	49	49
Algeria	132	23	13	62
Saudi Arabia	96	17	10	72
Qatar	60	11	6	78
Venezuela	43	8	4	82
Nigeria	41	7	4	86
Kuwait	34	6	3	90
Iraq	28	5	3	93
Libya	24	4	2	95
Indonesia	24	4	2	97
United Arab Emirates[2]	21	4	2	99
Ecuador	4	1	1	100
Gabon	1	—	—	100
Total OPEC	996	177	100	100

[1]Columns may not add to total due to rounding.
[2]No figures available for Sharjah.
SOURCE: OPEC, *Annual Report, 1979,* Vienna: 1979, p. 74.

Capacity, Production, and Stockpiling Issues

Decisions related to the pace of resource development, capacity, and production are left to the individual member countries. None has large, above-ground storage facilities, since it is cheaper to install excess capacity and, in effect, store oil in the ground. However, exploration and development drilling have slowed markedly since 1973, corresponding to the lower growth rate of OPEC production. There is an optimal level of excess capacity within OPEC which depends on peak production and the desire to hold prices down during an emergency. The latter may serve the interests of member countries by reducing consuming-country incentives to find alternative resources.

Capacity.   In 1971 and 1972 it was reported that Saudi officials planned to install enough capacity to produce 16 to 20 million barrels per day by 1980 and that Iraqi officials planned to produce about 6 million barrels per day. More recent appraisals, however, indicate that capacity in 1985 will be 12 million barrels per day in Saudia Arabia and 4 million in Iraq. Other member countries have reduced their plans for expansion correspondingly. Earlier projections of 1985 combined OPEC capacity were in the 45 to 50 million barrels per day range, but these have been scaled back to 30 to 35 million barrels per day.

The reason for these reductions is that the higher oil prices in effect since 1973 have reduced oil consumption and therefore capacity requirements. Most of the capacity reductions have been planned, but in some cases the pace of resource development has been reduced below what is considered optimal by public authorities in the member countries. The primary reason is that, in light of the perceived political and geological risks, the contractual arrangements fail to provide adequate incentives for the companies to prove new reserves. This seems to be the case in Indonesia, Ecuador, and Algeria. In 1979, Algeria "tied" oil sales to a commitment on the part of buyers to undertake additional exploration. In effect, Algerian oil was sold below market prices in an effort to compensate the companies for additional exploratory drilling. Similar incentives and guarantees are now being used in some of the other member countries.

Production.   OPEC members recognize the seasonal and cyclical nature of oil consumption and their consequent role as residual suppliers. However, they do not particularly like that role, and many statements indicate that they heartily resent it. Nevertheless, they have capacity sufficient to produce at least 32 to 34 million barrels per day, which provides a cushion of 5 to 6 million barrels per day to meet seasonal and cyclical swings. An articulate spokesman and former secretary-general of OPEC, Ali Jaidah, has stated the case as follows:

> The oil-producing countries have unwittingly performed the role of buffer in the past. In a paper I delivered to another conference almost two years ago, I warned that OPEC countries neither wanted nor would be able to continue to serve the world as residual supplier. The role they have performed by providing a free stockpile at no charge at all, from which consuming countries chose at will to draw, or to let accumulate, will have to cease soon.[3]

An alternative to present pricing practices, in which OPEC determines prices and crude buyers determine how much is purchased, is market demand prorationing. Under prorationing, OPEC would determine the level of output, but prices would be determined by competitive bidding among buyers. Naturally, OPEC members would not set levels of production independent of target prices. Prorationing, which proved to be a highly stable and effective method of maintaining prices in the United States during the period 1935–1970 and in world markets from 1928 to 1955, has been advocated by Venezuela since the formation of OPEC in 1960. But that country has had little success in persuading other members that the idea has merit.

The major problem the other members have with prorationing is that it would require them to surrender sovereignty over their own production levels. And, indirectly, prorationing would also require them to surrender sovereignty over the pace of new resource development. So far, they have been unwilling to grant this power to the OPEC secretariat or to any other authority which would be empowered to implement a prorationing system. Thus, the more prosaic issues required to implement prorationing, such as determining the basis for quota allocations (for example, reserves, capacity, or population) are largely academic. Prices and levels of output within OPEC are likely to be determined during the 1980s by the same fundamental processes that prevailed in the 1970s. In short, OPEC will continue to serve as the residual supplier because it determines oil prices; and buyers will continue to determine quantities and from whom to take them.

Stockpiling.   OPEC member countries have very little above-ground storage capacity beyond that needed to meet their operational requirements. Holding excess capacity is a better alternative since it is cheaper to "store" oil below ground in natural reservoirs than above ground in

---

[3] Ali Jaidah, "World Energy Outlook: An OPEC Perspective," in Robert Mabro, ed., *World Energy Issues and Policies* (Oxford: Oxford Univ. Press, 1980), p. 219.

metal tanks. Stockpiling by the consuming countries is viewed as "aggressive," or as an attempt to control prices. Throughout the Iranian crisis of 1979–1980, Saudi Arabian officials threatened to reduce their ceiling on production if the United States resumed filling the Strategic Petroleum Reserve. The threat was apparently successful until October, 1980, when the U.S. Congress mandated resumption at a fill rate of 100,000 barrels per day. In early 1981, the Reagan administration boosted funding to permit a 300,000 barrels per day fill rate, and Saudi Arabia did nothing in retaliation.

Stockpiling by the consuming countries and/or carrying excess capacity within OPEC could prevent, or at least mitigate, price increases caused by oil shortages and panic buying. Oil held in storage and capacity held idle are comparable in that both can be used to meet seasonal, cyclical, and emergency swings in consumption; however, spokesmen in the member countries are inconsistent in their views about the two. They simultaneously complain about consumer-country stockpiling and lament OPEC's role as residual supplier. They want control over quantities brought to market but dislike being the residual supplier.

Stockpiles and excess capacity would have to be very large to prevent a crisis if Saudi Arabian production were totally shut down. Any other country, including Iran or Iraq, could be shut down for months or even years without extraordinarily adverse effects, provided stockpiles and excess capacity were managed properly. It was shown in Chapter 7 that stockpiling by the consuming countries has been a destabilizing element. OPEC member countries, on the other hand, get better marks for their handling of idle capacity, since they generally use spare capacity to reduce "shortages at a price." Saudi Arabia in particular has generally been a reluctant follower of spot prices during the upward phase of the ratchet process. But, in general, they all increase production when markets are tight and withhold production when markets are weak. In short, they serve as residual suppliers.

When the relation between excess OPEC capacity, consumer-country stockpiling, and the ratchet process becomes more clearly understood, there may emerge a more firm basis for consumer–producer cooperation. However, the inherent conflict of interest among buyers and sellers over the proper price makes anything more than an implicit form of "live and let live" cooperation appear unlikely.

Relations with Other International Actors

Actors other than OPEC involved in the world petroleum market include the international oil companies, international banks, consumer-country governments, and non-OPEC less developed countries (LDCs). There are harmonies as well as conflicts of interest within and among these groups. Each participant seeks a degree of control in the determination of output, prices, and the distribution of revenue; but each is interested in continuing trade.

The most direct, recurrent, and important interrelations among the principal actors are those that take place between public officials in the Ministry of Petroleum in a producing country and representatives of the international oil companies. Financial relations with international banks are also important but are not directly related to petroleum markets, since the way in which revenues are invested is largely independent of the basis on which they are received. The framework within which the oil companies and banks operate is provided by governments in the consuming and producing countries. OPEC relations with non-OPEC LDCs are less important from the standpoint of petroleum markets, but OPEC members lay great store in their special relations with them.

International Oil Companies.   When a major dispute interrupts the flow of oil, relations between the exporting countries and the oil companies may appear chaotic and capricious. In reality, they are quite orderly and well structured within the context of international law. From a legal point of view, petroleum arrangements fall into two basic categories—concessions and contracts. Concessions are granted for vast areas to promote exploration and development. Contracts are commonly of the following varieties: (1) production sharing, (2) risk service, and (3) straight service. In addition, there are joint ventures between two or more companies or between companies and governments; but these are simply partnerships and do not alter the basic contractual relations.

Concessions are used in all member countries as well as in more than 100 other countries, but exclusive reliance on concessions has become the exception. Four key provisions are contained in every concession—those governing area, duration, royalty rates, and taxes. OPEC members collect a uniform income tax of 85 percent on the concession's net income. Royalty rates worldwide vary from zero to 20 percent, but the standard royalty to a member of OPEC is 20 percent.

Contract Types.   Exploration and development contracts include "production sharing," "risk," and "straight" service contracts. Production sharing is analogous to "share cropping" and in fact was adopted from agricultural agreements first made in Indonesia. It involves splitting production between the company and the country, with the percentage split depending on both costs and production levels. The company is typically allowed 40 percent of all output until costs are recovered and 20 percent thereafter, but these figures vary from one country to another.

For example, Libya uses an 81 percent government to 19 percent company split (or 81/19), Indonesia uses 66/33, Peru 50/50, and Chile 15/85. In general, the more prolific the output of the producing country, the smaller the split going to the company. In fact, the most highly productive countries no longer enter into production sharing agreements.

Risk service contracts place the burden of making original investments and taking risks on the company, or "contractor." For successful efforts, the contractor brings the discovery on stream and then turns operations over to the country. The contractor is then reimbursed in cash from revenues derived from the sale of any oil discovered. Total reimbursement includes payment of financial capital plus interest plus a payment called the "risk fee." It is from this risk fee that the contractor is expected to recover capital losses incurred in unsuccessful efforts. The risk service contract is used extensively by LDCs such as Brazil, Peru, and Argentina, but it is not generally used by OPEC members.

Service contracts provide the contractor with a flat fee for services rendered. This is the type of contract used by the most prolific oil producers. An important example is the arrangement between Saudi Arabia and Aramco. Aramco produces oil from established facilities for a net tax-free fee of 15 cents per barrel. Exploration is carried out on the basis of a "participating risk and service" contract. Aramco provides part of the risk capital and receives additional crude from new discoveries plus 6 cents per barrel on "new" oil production. This is in addition to the 15-cent service fee.

Destination and Resale Restrictions.   In addition to normal provisions concerning terms, conditions, and price, most contracts provide for restrictions on destination and resale. Following is a portion of the Saudi Arabian(SELLER)–Aramco(BUYER) contract, which illustrates the intent and flavor of the provision with respect to destination requirements.

> ARTICLE 8: BUYER/USER REQUIREMENT AND DESTINATION[4]
> 8.1 It is expressly understood that BUYER will process Crude Oil sold under this Contract in its own processing facilities or under processing arrangements with other refineries for BUYER's own account. BUYER undertakes that under no circumstances shall BUYER resell the said Crude Oil in its original form or blend it with any other crude oil or crude oil deliveries for purposes of resale . . . . The following exceptions to the foregoing principles will be permitted:
> (1) BUYER may transfer Crude Oil sold under this Contract to Buyer Affiliates at cost;

---

[4]Reproduced from *Petroleum Intelligence Weekly*, 25 Aug. 1980, Supplement, by permission of Petroleum and Energy Intelligence Weekly, Inc. Emphasis added.

(2) BUYER may exchange Crude Oil sold under this Contract with Buyer Affiliates; and

(3) provided SELLER's written consent is first obtained (which consent will not unreasonably be withheld), BUYER may make Crude Oil exchanges with companies other than Buyer Affiliates. ([However,] if SELLER requests, *BUYER shall provide documentation with regard to the terms of such exchanges.*)

8.2 BUYER shall comply with the *Laws of Saudi Arabia concerning the country of destination* of Crude Oil sold under the terms of this Contract.

8.3 In the event of any breach by BUYER of paragraphs 1 and 2 of this Article, SELLER shall have the right to terminate this Contract at its sole discretion without any notice or responsibility for compensation or payment and/or any claim from BUYER.

"Documentation" is clearly the key word, since restrictions on destination and resale must be monitored. In practice, however, because SELLER stipulates that BUYER must provide a "bill of lading" at destination, a brisk trade is done in forged bill of lading documents when oil markets are tight. Furthermore, SELLER has no control over the oil after it reaches its first destination. This means that transshipment after unloading and reloading is possible, permissible, and surely done when price differentials become sufficiently great to cover added handling costs. Although OPEC members may devise increasingly complex procedures to prevent resales (thus increasing costs to all concerned), it is virtually impossible for them to preclude such practices.

Force Majeure.   The Iranian revolution in January, 1979, brought about forced reductions in deliveries to the international oil companies. Yet even such contingencies as this are covered in the contract by a provision called *force majeure*. Again, the intent and flavor of the provision is best captured by quoting directly from the Saudi contract:

11.1 In the event of SELLER and/or BUYER being rendered unable by Force Majeure to carry out its obligations under this contract, it is agreed that the obligations of the party shall be suspended. The term "Force Majeure" is hereby defined to include acts of God, strikes, lockouts, work stoppage or other industrial disturbances, acts of the public enemy, wars, blockades, insurrections, riots, epidemics, landslides, lightning, earthquakes, fires, storms, floods, arrests, and restraints of government, ruler and people, civil disturbances, explosions, partial or entire failure of wells or production facilities, failure of refining facilities being used to refine Crude Oil purchased under this Contract, governmental regulations or temporary failure of Crude Oil supply facilities or electric power used in making and/or receiving delivery of Crude Oil hereunder and other causes, whether of the kind herein enumerated or otherwise, not within the reasonable control of the party claiming suspension, all of which by the exercise of reasonable diligence such party is unable to prevent or overcome.

11.2 Nothing contained in this Article shall relieve BUYER of the obligation to pay in full in United States currency for all Crude Oil sold and delivered hereunder and for all other amounts due SELLER by BUYER under this Contract.[5]

National Oil Companies (NOCs).   National oil companies (NOCs) have been established in all OPEC member countries to participate with the international companies in oil exploration, development, production, and refining. Member countries are eager to move away from their position as exporters of a single raw material and to become more involved in such downstream activities as refining, marketing, and the manufacturing of petrochemicals. Industrialization necessitates involvement in these petroleum-industry activities as well as the development of ancillary industries, such as construction, manufacture, trade, and finance. An expanded role for the NOCs is considered desirable because downstream and industrial activities require the development of human capital within the indigenous populations. Additionally, it is thought that increased downstream involvement and industrialization will provide member countries larger overall returns on their investments, less dependence on foreign nationals, and greater sovereignty over the income derived from their petroleum reserves.

The development of NOCs poses both a threat to the established companies and a challenge for OPEC. Any move to rapidly displace the international companies will send them to remote and less promising regions of the world in search of oil; and any successful efforts there will yield output directly competitive with oil from the member countries and make OPEC's task of controlling prices more difficult. Similarly, greater downstream involvement by the NOCs in refining and in petrochemical manufacture will serve to increase quantities available and thus lower their rates of return. The issue of how much downstream involvement the NOCs should undertake is now being resolved by the individual member countries. Thus, a competitive rather than a cartel solution appears probable.

Major Consuming Countries.   The individual OPEC members interact with the consuming countries at a variety of levels—diplomatic, economic, and cultural. Some interactions are of a more personal nature, as when nationals from OPEC countries take degrees in higher education from Western institutions. Saudi Arabia's oil minister, Sheik Ahmed Zaki Yamani, for example, studied economics at Harvard. The University of Colorado and Oxford University in England are particularly active in promoting advanced study for Middle Eastern students. Tech-

[5]Ibid.

nical training in petroleum geology, engineering, management, economics, and finance is particularly coveted.

The economic and political relations between producing and consuming countries depend both on historical developments and on the leaders in power. For example, Algeria and France, Saudi Arabia and the United States, and Libya and the Soviet Union have particularly close ties because of their political ideologies and their diplomatic and economic relations. While an economic connection between two countries does not necessarily reflect close political and cultural ties, neither is it totally independent of these relations.

Economic activities related to the exporting of oil and those related to the importing of other commodities and durable goods need not and often do not develop in tandem. Patterns of oil trade were discussed in Chapter 7, but it bears reemphasizing that oil trade patterns are based largely on the desire to minimize transport costs within the constraints that require matching crudes to specific refineries and to end-use requirements. Thus, while diplomatic relations between Libya and the United States have been notably strained since 1969 when Colonel Qadhafi gained control, Libya nevertheless typically exports over 30 percent of its output to the United States. The reason is that Libyan crude is low in sulfur and has a high API gravity, characteristics ideally suited for U.S. markets, where the refinery slate is tilted toward production of gasoline and where automobile emissions standards are relatively strict. Naturally, these trade patterns emerged from the desire to make profits. U.S. refiners are willing to pay a premium for Libyan crudes, and Libyan authorities are eager to sell wherever their oil will fetch the highest price.

The Libyan example is not an isolated case. Trade relations generally tend to follow established patterns. For example, U.S. buyers purchase a large proportion of African and South American crudes; Japanese importers receive a relatively large proportion of their oil from the Middle East and Indonesia; and the Germans draw primarily upon the Middle East and Africa. These basic trade relationships can be detected by looking at the data in the right-hand column of Table 9-4.

Trade patterns for imports of non-oil products by OPEC members follow educational and cultural ties more closely than do their oil export patterns. Table 9-4 indicates that most OPEC members are running a substantial trade surplus with the three leading oil importing countries—the U.S., Japan, and Germany. The ratio of exports to imports may be interpreted as the number of dollars received per dollar spent in the specific consuming country. The total OPEC ratio is greatest for the U.S. and lowest for West Germany, but it is greater than 1.0 even for the latter. Some OPEC members, however, import more from a specific oil importing country than they export. In such cases, the export to import ratio is less than 1.0.

TABLE 9-4
Value of Exports and Imports for the Principal Oil Exporting Countries in Relation to the Major Oil Importing Countries, 1979

Exporting Region and Country	Exports (C.I.F.) Destination	Imports (F.O.B.) Shipping Point (*millions of U.S. dollars*)	Trade Balance	Ratio Exports to Imports
UNITED STATES				
MIDDLE EAST				
Saudi Arabia	8,730	4,875	3,855	1.8
Iran	2,978	1,020	1,958	2.9
UAE	2,155	667	1,488	3.2
Iraq	671	442	229	1.5
Qatar	291	138	153	2.1
Kuwait	95	764	(669)	0.1
AFRICA				
Nigeria	8,650	632	8,018	13.7
Libya	5,544	468	5,076	11.8
Algeria	5,462	404	5,058	13.5
Gabon	342	32	310	10.7
SOUTH AMERICA				
Venezuela	5,452	3,931	1,521	1.4
Ecuador	894	696	198	1.3
Indonesia	3,925	981	2,944	4.0
Total OPEC	45,190	15,051	30,139	3.0
JAPAN				
MIDDLE EAST				
Saudi Arabia	12,037	3,802	8,235	3.2
Kuwait	4,280	879	3,401	4.9
Iran	4,239	921	3,318	4.6
UAE	3,612	1,038	2,574	3.5
Iraq	1,799	1,600	199	1.1
Qatar	967	240	727	4.0
AFRICA				
Libya	100	544	(444)	0.2
Algeria	57	343	(286)	0.2
Nigeria	42	801	(759)	0.1
Gabon	13	17	(4)	0.8

TABLE 9-4 *(continued)*
Value of Exports and Imports for the Principal Oil Exporting Countries in Relation to the Major Oil Importing Countries, 1979

Exporting Region and Country	Exports (C.I.F.) Destination	Imports (F.O.B.) Shipping Point *(millions of U.S. dollars)*	Trade Balance	Ratio Exports to Imports
		JAPAN *(continued)*		
SOUTH AMERICA				
Venezuela	141	779	(638)	0.2
Ecuador	36	201	(165)	0.2
Indonesia	8,725	2,110	6,615	4.1
Total OPEC	36,049	13,272	22,777	2.7
		GERMANY		
MIDDLE EAST				
Saudi Arabia	2,360	2,412	(52)	1.0
Iran	2,320	1,285	1,035	1.8
UAE	1,155	470	685	2.5
Kuwait	548	1,177	(629)	0.5
Iraq	333	1,143	(810)	0.3
Qatar	84	83	1	1.0
AFRICA				
Libya	3,037	1,177	1,860	2.6
Nigeria	2,369	1,145	1,224	2.1
Algeria	1,698	1,242	456	1.4
Gabon	158	24	134	6.6
SOUTH AMERICA				
Venezuela	245	585	(340)	0.4
Ecuador	81	134	(53)	0.6
Indonesia	400	409	(9)	1.0
Total OPEC	14,787	10,486	4,301	1.4

SOURCE: U.S. Central Intelligence Agency, *International Energy Statistical Review,* 30 December, 1980.
NOTE: Due to rounding, columns may not total exactly.

The economic significance of trade balances is often overemphasized by government authorities and private citizens. In reality, the flexibility of exchange rates and international financial flows minimize the importance of trade balances between any two countries. Kuwait, for example, can export oil to Japan, receive U.S. dollars in payment, and purchase goods from the United States; or, it may exchange the dollars for Deutsche Marks to facilitate the purchase of stocks, bonds, or real estate in Germany. There is an almost endless range of possibilities.

OPEC leaders' willingness to buy, or "revealed preference" for, financial and real tangible assets in the consuming countries is indicative of their belief that the consuming countries are desirable places in which to hold wealth. Consequently, they are anxious that the importing countries remain friendly and stable enough to continue to provide a safe haven for their financial "surplus."

Non-OPEC LDCs.   Although higher oil prices have placed a severe financial strain on many LDCs, their attitude toward OPEC has generally remained favorable. The anomaly can be explained by the fact that OPEC is perceived as a model which many non-OPEC LDCs would like to emulate. Countries that produce coffee, cocoa, sugar, pineapple, rubber, and tin would be delighted to have an organization that could do for them what OPEC has done for the oil exporting countries. Thus, there is little if any animosity toward OPEC members and much admiration for their accomplishments and solidarity.

On the other hand, while OPEC members generally seek to strengthen ties or "solidarity" with the LDCs, the relative commitment varies among countries. Wealthy OPEC members tend to be more generous than their less wealthy counterparts. A useful measure of the sacrifice made by a donor country is the ratio of aid to gross domestic product (aid/GDP), usually expressed as a percent. Using this measure, oil-rich countries such as the UAE, Qatar, Kuwait, and Saudi Arabia generally rank among the top four donors, and Iran, Iraq, and Libya frequently appear among the top ten. Of the developed countries, Sweden, the Netherlands, Denmark, France, and Norway are among the top ten donors, with relative positions varying from year to year.

But any single measure such as the aid/GDP ratio should be evaluated with care. Spokesmen for OPEC contend that the United States and the major European countries are not giving as much to the "truly deserving, poorer LDCs" as might appear from raw figures, because much of their aid is tied to purchases in the donor country and a disproportionate share goes to Israel. These are valid criticisms, but it is also true that many member country loans are for the purpose of financing oil, and a disproportionate share of their aid goes to Arab countries.

Similarly, Venezuelan aid and loans are concentrated among countries in the Caribbean and in South America; and Saudi Arabia has traditionally supported Egypt, Syria, and Jordan in their struggles with Israel. It is clear that aid is not given strictly for altruistic reasons: It is used in varying degrees to promote the political and economic interests of elite groups in the donor countries.

A critical issue influencing OPEC's attitude toward aid to LDCs is the fact that oil is a depletable resource. As such, current revenues from oil may be viewed as the realized "value" of a capital asset, or as a current return on investment. The issue is essentially whether current income should be regarded as a gross or a net return, and it matters a great deal which point of view is adopted. If the capitalized value of oil is to be maintained intact, it would call for the bulk of all revenues to be invested in other earning assets and for the producing countries to live off income derived from their investments. The alternative view would allow the producing country to spend or give away current revenues without replacing the depletable asset.

Leaders within member countries are increasingly adopting the point of view that asset values should be maintained. Thus, their policies toward the LDCs are unlikely to change radically. If anything, there may be retrenchment in the level of aid relative to GDP. The oil-rich OPEC nations are aware that their standard of living, and that of future generations, is dependent on how they use revenue derived from oil. Aid to the LDCs is one alternative, but a balance must be struck. Current gross income is not a good indicator of the ability of the oil exporting countries to support foreign aid, since a large proportion must be reinvested if asset values are to be maintained.

A final issue concerns the form in which aid could be, should be, and is in fact given. Those uninitiated in how markets function are inclined to believe that an OPEC nation could provide aid simply by discriminating among buyers with respect to the price they charge for oil. However, even if price discrimination could work, the amount of aid would tend to be proportional to the level of oil imported. This turns out to be a moot point, since it is so difficult and costly to discriminate that OPEC members generally do not attempt to do so. The basic problem is that when oil is sold to private companies on favorable terms there is an incentive to transship cargoes and otherwise take advantage of the situation. In addition, unless the buyer is the sole distributor in the importing country, the company will charge the going market price. Thus, the subsidy embedded in discriminatory prices would accrue to the company rather than to the ultimate consumers. The same problem exists in government-to-government deals. The result is that OPEC members charge a market price for crude and then offer loans on favorable terms and grant aid on a direct government-to-government basis.

Political Issues

The primary political issue between some of the oil exporting and importing countries concerns the question of Israel's right to exist. This long-standing controversy is an Arab and OAPEC problem, and does not involve OPEC per se. Nevertheless, the Middle Eastern conflicts, the insecurity over oil supplies, and the embargo actions cannot be comprehended without some knowledge of the dispute between Israel and its Arab neighbors.

Arab–Israeli Conflict

The modern conflict between Arabs and Jews is a direct result of the Zionist movement and the subsequent creation of Israel as a soveriegn state. On November 29, 1947, the United Nations voted to end the British mandate over Palestine and to divide the territory in two. The Palestinian Jews were designated an area of 15,655 square miles, and the Arabs were given an area of 14,580 square miles. However, while Jewish leaders agreed to the division, Arab leaders both in Palestine and in nearby Arab countries refused to recognize the split and vowed to destroy the new Jewish state.

British control of Palestine formally ended on May 14, 1948, and Israel officially came into existence. On the very next day, troops from Egypt, Syria, Jordan, Lebanon, and Iraq invaded Israeli land. With British and American aid, the Israelis successfully defended the territory designated to them by the U.N.; and by the end of 1948 they also occupied 2,362 square miles of the territory that had been designated to the Arabs. The remaining area was controlled by Jordan and Egypt. Jordan also controlled the eastern half of Jerusalem, and Israel had the western half. In 1949, a team of United Nations peacemakers negotiated an armistice, and there were hopes for a lasting peace.

But the nearby Arab nations never recognized Israel's right to exist, and hostilities erupted again in July, 1956, when Egypt seized control of the Suez Canal from the British and French, denied Israeli ships access to the Canal, and stopped Israel from using the Gulf of Aqaba. On October 29, 1956, Israel retaliated by invading Egypt. Two days later, seeking to regain control of the Suez, Britain and France joined the attack against Egypt. All of the disputed territory seized by Egypt was reoccupied by November 5, and Israel had also gained control of the Gaza Strip and Sinai Peninsula.

Hostilities and border conflicts continued, but there was a stalemate until Egypt again took the initiative by denying Israel access to the Gulf of Aqaba, causing the outbreak of the "Six-Day War" on June 5, 1967. The war was brief owing to Israel's strategic attack on Egyptian, Jordanian, and Syrian airfields, which destroyed most of their air capabilities while still on the ground. Then, having eliminated the Arabs' strategic air support, Israel defeated their armies, reoccupied the Gaza Strip and Sinai Peninsula, and extended its control to an additional 2,270 square miles of Jordanian territory. Israel's occupied territories then included lands west of the Jordan River, the eastern half of Jerusalem, 444 square miles of Syrian lands, the Golan Heights, and 23,622 square miles in Egypt's Negev–Sinai Desert and Sinai Highlands. Israeli conquests extended to the Gulf of Suez and the Suez Canal. By June 13, 1967, Israeli-occupied Arab territories totaled 26,476 square miles. The "Six-Day War" was the most spectacular of the military victories achieved by the Israelis over their Arab neighbors. Legal and diplomatic scholars still debate the legality of Israel's extensive takeover of Arab lands, but the fact is that Israel captured them and would not relinquish control.

The military conflicts between Israel and the Arab countries were financed by the great world powers. Egypt and Syria were backed by the Soviet Union, whereas the United States supported Israel. And despite Israel's refusal to comply with U.S. requests to give up occupied Arab territories, the United States continued to provide the nation with military and economic assistance. This was to become an increasingly important bone of contention between the Arab oil exporting countries and the United States.

The long-standing Arab–Israeli conflict erupted again on October 6, 1973, along the cease-fire lines of the Suez Canal and Golan Heights. Egypt and Syria claimed Israel launched a two-pronged attack against them, but a United Nations observer agreed that it was Syria and Egypt who launched coordinated attacks against Israel. Israel again used its air superiority to strike deep inside Egypt and Syria, crippling Syrian air defense capabilities and destroying nine of eleven Egyptian bridges across the Suez Canal. On October 10, 1973, a report was received by the Nixon administration that the Soviet Union was airlifting military equipment to Egypt and Syria. Within five days the U.S. State Department announced that the United States had begun to supply Israel with aircraft and equipment to replace its losses. On October 17th, the Pentagon announced it would ask Congress for $2 billion to replace arms shipments being rushed to Israel.

The Arab response was swift and sure. They announced a cut in oil production and declared a complete and total embargo against the United States and the Netherlands. The oil embargo announced on October 17, 1973, and described in detail in Chapter 7 of this book, was thus a retaliation for Western (primarily American) military and economic support of Israel in its ongoing conflict with the Arab nations. Although the success of the embargo in denying supplies to selected nations has been seriously questioned, the production cutback did result in panic buying on spot markets and cause prices to be driven to unprecedented levels. The embargo unquestionably demonstrated the latent power of the producing countries to determine oil prices, and in this sense it may be viewed as a success. However, the action did not seriously reduce the amount of oil flowing to the United States and the Netherlands as compared with other oil importing countries, because the companies simply diverted shipments from non-Arab countries to the embargoed nations. In this sense the embargo was indeed a failure.

More important, from OPEC's standpoint, the embargo and the higher oil prices apparently had some influence on foreign policy. United States support of Israel remains strong, but there is mounting pressure on Israel to withdraw from Arab-occupied territories and limited support for the idea that Israel should recognize the rights of the Palestinians. In addition, in March, 1981, the Reagan administration announced plans to provide "defensive" F-15 fighter planes to Saudi Arabia. This indicates a likelihood that the United States will increase its military support to friendly Arab countries, such as Saudi Arabia, Qatar, and the UAE, and that there will be a firm commitment to defend important U.S. oil interests through cooperation with the Middle Eastern oil exporting countries.

Conclusion

Changes in world petroleum markets since the 1950s have altered the role of the international oil companies. Both the international majors and the independent oil companies are experiencing greater competition from the national oil companies (NOCs). The NOCs, which represent the producing governments, seek to expand their role in refining, transportation, marketing, processing, and manufacture of petrochemicals. The critical issue concerning the role that private companies and the NOCs will play in the future is one that will be resolved through an evolutionary process and that will depend on policies adopted by the producing and consuming countries as well as by the individual companies themselves. Their relations will never be settled once and for all; rather, they will evolve continuously in light of changed circumstances.

Individual member countries of OPEC own the bulk of petroleum reserves and control the rates of exploration, drilling, development, and production. On the other hand, the international companies are well established as refiners and marketers; they have the technical capability and political influence required to deliver about 50 million barrels of refined products throughout the free world each day. This is no mean feat; it requires advanced technology as well as highly specialized human capital from the wellhead to the gasoline pump. The international companies are particularly adept at exploring inhospitable regions, such as deep-water offshore areas, and they are also experienced in secondary and tertiary recovery and in the liquefaction of petroleum gases.

The producing governments recognize the strategic position of the companies and are willing to utilize them as service contractors or limited partners. At the same time, the countries seek to expand the downstream activities of the NOCs while acquiring the technical and managerial knowledge required to compete with, if not "displace," the companies. But the producing governments are constrained by a lack of trained personnel and by the competitive nature of downstream activities. Once oil is lifted and traded, it is processed and sold in highly competitive markets. This is particularly true at the refinery level, where facilities were constructed in the late 1960s and early 1970s on the assumption that world demand would continue to expand by about 7 percent annually. The sharp decline in the rate of increase has resulted in overcapacity and low utilization rates in the refinery sector.

More generally, leaders in the oil exporting countries recognize the companies as potential competitors and are constrained by the knowledge that displacing them too rapidly will drive them into a wide range of competitive activities—from coal gasification and oil shale development to increased offshore drilling and additional exploration in the LDCs. In addition, the companies have political advantages which give them "access" to markets in the consuming countries. At the very least, a concerted effort to directly compete with the companies will lower marketing margins. At most, their efforts will evoke protectionist sentiments and result in denial of access to important markets. More extreme protectionist measures may even limit investment opportunities in the consuming countries. Thus, the NOCs and the international companies will more than likely continue to be partners as well as rivals in world petroleum markets. The NOCs seem destined to improve their relative position in nearly all phases of the petroleum industry, but the majors will remain an important force, especially in downstream activities and in the development of alternative energy resources.

Further Readings

Abdel-Fabil, ed. *Papers on the Economics of Oil.* Published for the State of Kuwait on behalf of OAPEC. Oxford: Oxford Univ. Press, 1979.

Dawisha, Adeed. *Saudi Arabia's Search for Security.* London: The International Institute for Strategic Studies, 1979.

Mabro, Robert, ed. *World Energy Issues and Policies.* Proceedings of the First Oxford Energy Seminar. Oxford: Oxford Univ. Press, 1980.

Mikdashi, Zuhayr M. *The Community of Oil Exporting Countries.* London: George Allen & Unwin Ltd., 1972.

OPEC. *Official Resolutions and Press Releases, 1960–1980.* New York: Pergamon Press, 1980.

———————. *OPEC at a Glance.* Vienna: OPEC Secretariat, 1981.

Segal, Jeffrey and Frank E. Niering, Jr. "Special Report on World Natural Gas Pricing." *Petroleum Economist,* September 1980, 374–378.

Shwadran, Benjamin. *Middle East Oil Issues and Problems.* Cambridge: Schedkman Publishing Company, 1977.

Current Periodicals

Middle East Economic Survey. Middle East Petroleum and Economics Publications, Nicosia, Cyprus. A weekly review of news and views in Middle East oil.

OPEC Bulletin. OPEC, Vienna. Monthly publication prepared by the OPEC Secretariat.

OPEC Review, An Energy and Economic Forum. OPEC, Vienna. Quarterly.

Petroleum Economist, The International Energy Journal. Petroleum Press Bureau, Ltd., London. Monthly trade publication.

Petroleum Intelligence Weekly. Petroleum & Energy Intelligence Weekly, Inc., London. Weekly trade publication.

Outlook **10**

Introduction.

Economic Variables:
Oil Reserves; Energy Consumption; Oil Production by Region; Oil Prices; Prediction of Future Price Movements.

OPEC Stability.

Appendix:
Primary Energy Demand and Sources of Supply (Exxon Projections).

READER'S GUIDE TO CHAPTER 10.
The materials covered in Chapters 2 and 3 were largely theoretical, those in Chapters 4 through 7 were historical and analytical, and those in Chapters 8 and 9 were oriented toward policy. This final chapter of the book condenses the materials of Chapters 2 through 9 to present a broad assessment of the future of OPEC and of its role in the world petroleum market.

Introduction

The outlook for OPEC can be assessed with varying degrees of certainty. As is usual, events near at hand can be forecast with greater confidence than can those in the distant future. Similarly, some variables are easier to assess than others: Estimates of proved reserves are more reliable than are those of probable reserves; the rate of primary energy consumption can be anticipated with a higher degree of certainty than can the rate of utilization of a single resource, such as coal or oil; and it is even harder to predict nominal energy prices. Most difficult of all is an assessment of political variables, which largely determine when an embargo might be imposed. While an analysis of political variables is beyond the scope of this book, it is well to know that they can have important consequences during relatively short time periods. However, in the long run, it is the economic variables which predominate and which themselves influence political decisions.

Economic Variables

Oil Reserves

Naïve observers of world petroleum markets have been led to believe that the age of oil is about over. The basis for that belief is often a simplistic ratio analysis, or an examination of reserves relative to current production. A central problem in assessing when oil will be depleted centers around the definition of reserves. Is the analyst referring to proved, probable, ultimately recoverable reserves—or to oil in place? In round numbers, annual consumption worldwide is 20 billion barrels, and proved reserves amount to about 400 billion barrels. Simple arithmetic shows that proved reserves will be used up in about 20 years at present utilization rates. It should be remembered that proved reserves are comparable to a business' current inventories—they will naturally be depleted if not augmented by new discoveries. Probable reserves represent a broader concept, and when included with proved reserves, amount to about 700 billion barrels. In this view, the time horizon for depletion of oil resources is extended another 15 years. Ultimately recoverable reserves represent a broader category yet. These are between 1,300 and 1,700 billion barrels, which sets the time horizon at between 65 and 85 years at present utilization rates. Recovery rates, however, are only 30–40 percent of "oil in place." So if recovery rates could be increased to 60–80 percent, ultimately recoverable reserves would about double. One thing stands clear from these simple figures: Depending on one's definition of reserves and on future utilization rates, it is possible to conclude either that oil will be exhausted in twenty years or that it will remain an important resource for more than a century.

The preceding discussion combined with the law of demand should be sufficient to allay fears that oil will be depleted any time soon. According to the law of demand, scarce resources command higher prices than abundant ones; so, as oil (a scarce resource) is depleted, its price will rise. Higher prices will then cause a decrease in the quantity of oil demanded (and an increase in the quantity demanded of cheaper energy resources, such as coal and natural gas). The day will surely come when worldwide oil consumption is less than 5 billion barrels a year. But this is not meant to imply there will be an end to civilization as we know it. Rather, it indicates a need to develop alternative energy resources, like nuclear or solar power. In the meantime, oil utilization rates and prices will depend on recovery rates from oil in place and on how rapidly alternative technologies are developed.

Energy Consumption

Primary Energy.   The Exxon projections of primary energy consumption appear fairly reasonable compared with many others available. They imply that while oil will remain an important energy resource in the year 2000, its relative importance will decline from 47 to 31 percent of total primary energy consumption (see Figure 10-1). The regional composition of total primary energy consumption is expected to change significantly in relative but not in absolute terms. In general, consumption will increase slowly in the United States, Western Europe, and Japan; somewhat more rapidly in the centrally planned economies; and most rapidly in the OPEC and non-OPEC less developed countries (see Figure 10-2). A consolidated view of Exxon's projections of primary energy demand and sources of supply by region is contained in Appendix 10–A to this chapter.

Oil Consumption.   Assessments of future oil consumption vary among forecasting groups and over time for the same forecasting group. For instance, in 1977 the U.S. Department of Energy projected that annual free world consumption would be 30 billion barrels in 1990. Two years later the Department lowered its estimate to 19 billion barrels. In 1980, however, Exxon projected that oil consumption would be 20 and 22 billion barrels per year in 1990 and 2000, respectively, but cautioned that the use of alternative energy resources will probably increase if oil prices rise by more than the inflation rate. An analyst from the University of Virginia, S. Fred Singer, went way out on a limb in 1981 by asserting that free world consumption *may be* on the order of only 7 billion barrels by 1990.[1] This figure appears extraordinarily low in view of OPEC's reserves and non-OPEC production potentials.

---

[1]See S. Fred Singer, "The Coming Revolution in World Oil Markets," *The Wall Street Journal,* 4 February 1981, p. 36.

Oil Consumption: Regional Distribution.   Total annual oil consumption in the major industrial countries is expected to decline from 14.6 to about 12.8 billion barrels during the period 1979–2000. This decrease will result from "conservation," efficiency improvements, and substitution of alternative fuels for oil. The United States is expected to

FIGURE 10-1
World Primary Energy Consumption by Source of Supply, 1965–2000.

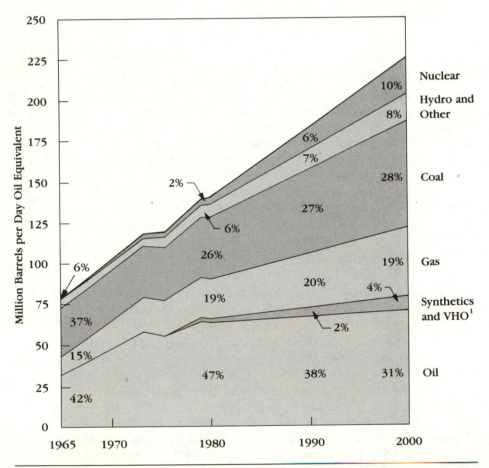

show the steepest decline in consumption, from 6.6 to 5.5 billion barrels; European consumption is projected to decline from 5.5 to 4.7 billion barrels during the 1980s and then to level off during the 1990s; and consumption in Japan is expected to remain roughly constant at about 1.8 billion barrels per year.

FIGURE 10-2
World Primary Energy Consumption by Country and Region, 1965–2000

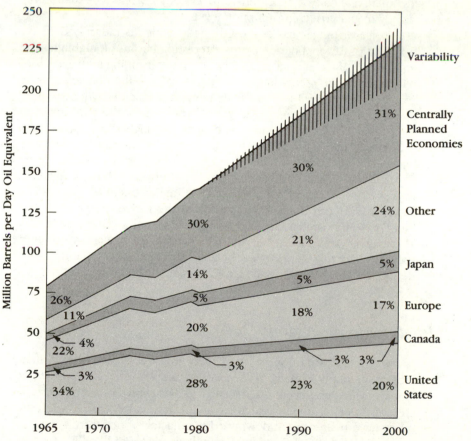

SOURCE: Exxon, *World Energy Outlook*, December 1980, p. 9. © 1980, Exxon Corporation. Reprinted with Permission.

Oil consumption in the developing countries, on the other hand, is projected to grow about 4 percent annually, reaching 9.1 billion barrels by the end of the century. Seventy-five percent of this growth is expected to take place in the oil exporting countries, many of which are pursuing industrialization policies designed to use a larger share of their energy resources at home.

Consumption in communist bloc countries is expected to increase about 1 percent annually, or from 4.7 billion barrels in 1979 to 5.9 billion barrels by 2000. Consumption in the People's Republic of China is expected to expand at a rate of almost 4 percent per year; the USSR at less than one-half of 1 percent; and Eastern Europe to decline only slightly from current consumption levels.

Professor Singer has espoused a view which is radically different from that of Exxon, but one that is interesting because it highlights the importance of technology and oil prices in determining future levels of oil consumption.[2] According to Singer, only 7.3 billion barrels will be consumed each year by 1990, but 75 percent of that total will be refined into motor fuels (as compared with 25 percent of the total going to gasoline in 1980). Singer adds that natural gas, nuclear energy, and coal will be used in place of fuel oil to produce heat and steam. He maintains that the factors which will affect world demand for oil, and thus bring about these radical changes, include: (1) new coal technologies, (2) improved refinery technologies, and (3) higher crude oil prices. The latter will induce consumers to substitute alternative energy resources for oil as well as such nonenergy resources as labor and physical capital. This may be viewed as the "optimistic" scenario. Most analysts, however, do not believe that oil prices will be pushed as high, or new technologies developed as rapidly, as Professor Singer anticipates.

Oil Production by Region

Assessments of where oil will be produced are less controversial than those concerning where it will be consumed; but even here there is a high degree of uncertainty. In the early 1970s, it was thought that annual OPEC production might reach 16 billion barrels by 1980. These estimates have been revised downward by a factor of one-third, and it is now believed that OPEC production will never exceed 12 billion barrels in a single year. Exxon projects OPEC production in the neighborhood of 11 billion barrels in the years 1990 and 2000. Substantial increases are expected in non-OPEC LDCs, with more modest increases in Europe

---

[2]Ibid.

and in the centrally planned economies. Oil production is expected to decline in the United States and Canada. Synthetic oil is not produced in commercial quantities at present, but it is expected to account for 1 or 2 billion barrels by 1990 and 2000 (see Figure 10-3).

The U.S. Central Intelligence Agency presents a more pessimistic scenario, one emphasizing the specter of communism. According to its 1977 report, the CIA expects annual worldwide oil consumption to be 25 to 27 billion barrels in 1985. It estimates non-OPEC production at 7 to 8 billion barrels, which means OPEC would be "called upon" to produce 17 to 20 billion barrels. (Included in this total is an extra 1.3 to 1.6 billion barrels demanded by the Soviet Bloc; but subsequent analysis led the CIA to lower the bloc estimate to 0.7 and later to 0.4 billion barrels.)

The CIA analysis, however, is not as reliable as that of Exxon because, for one thing, it is based on "gap methodology" and, for another, political motives may underlie its pessimistic forecast. In fact, the CIA estimates were used effectively by the Nixon, Ford, and Carter administrations to rally support for Project Independence, creation of the U.S. Department of Energy, and various so-called "conservation" programs. The CIA analysis may indeed be devoid of political motives, but many analysts outside government remain skeptical, and discount its conclusions accordingly.

Oil Prices

The Value Versus Cost of Oil Issue.   The upper limit of real oil prices in the long run is the cost of the next best alternative fuel. The lower limit is the cost of the human and capital resources used to explore, develop, and extract the last barrel that is consumed or stored. However, these upper and lower limits bear no particular relation to *actual* market prices under conditions other than pure competition or monopoly.

The traditional Western view of oil prices, one that is embodied in neo-classical cartel theory, is that oil prices will, or at least should, approximate production costs. In contrast, the view of oil prices espoused by the OPEC secretariat and spokesmen in the member countries is that they ought to, and eventually will, approximate the cost of the next best alternative energy resource at the margin of usage. Neither view corresponds with reality. Alternative energy resources are available at costs ranging from, at the low end, that of oil produced in Saudi Arabia, to that of potential resources which cost so much they are unable to find a market. Actual prices depend on alternative technologies and production levels within and outside of OPEC. Without information on future technologies, OPEC production levels, and the pace of develop-

FIGURE 10-3
World Oil Production by Region, 1979, 1990, and 2000.

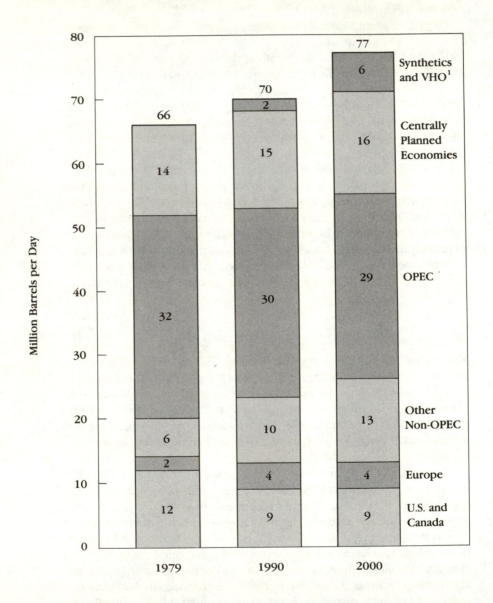

[1]VHO: Very Heavy Oils (10°–15° API gravity).
SOURCE: Exxon, *World Energy Outlook,* December 1980, p. 23. © 1980, Exxon Corporation.
Reprinted with Permission.

ment for non-OPEC reserves, it is impossible to predict real oil prices ten or twenty years into the future. Therefore, it is almost meaningless to forecast real or nominal oil prices in the year 1990 or 2000. There are simply too many imponderables. However, a knowledge of price movements in the recent past is useful in assessing probable prices in the fairly near future. Even here, we are on firmer ground if we emphasize probable long-term *trends* rather than timing and absolute magnitudes.

Review of the Ratchet Process.   The continuous decline of oil prices during the 1960s stands in sharp contrast to the periodic upward ratcheting of prices that took place during the 1970s. Even a cursory examination of price movements during these two decades shows that a different process was in operation during the two periods. The divergent trends cannot be explained by the fact that oil is a depletable resource, since this was true both before and after 1970. It may be tempting to attribute the upward price movements of the 1970s to a perfectly collusive cartel, or to assign exclusive weight to "unpredictable" events, such as those in Iran, or to contend "demand" has periodically outstripped "supply" because of economic growth; but the process is more complicated than implied by these simple explanations.

The process operative since 1970 may be reiterated in general terms. First, a substantial price increase was instigated by a major political event (or act of terrorism) that caused oil production and deliveries to fall sharply. At this point, member countries of OPEC were as much in the dark about the proper price to charge for oil as were the major oil companies or refiner-buyers in the importing countries. However, as spot prices increased, the individual member countries experimented with higher contract prices, and a new pattern of contract prices was established. Each country charged what they thought the market would tolerate, which resulted in a sharp upward thrust of contract prices. The ultimate price level cannot be predicted, but the trend has been for OPEC members to view whatever prices are current as the minimum acceptable. This places a floor on nominal contract prices at whatever level has been attained.

The market structure, or delivery system, contributes to the magnitude of upward price movements. The delivery system was designed to accommodate an uninterrupted flow of oil from the wellhead to the final consumer. And there is sufficient excess capacity at all levels of the system to meet seasonal variations in demand and to allow for modest levels of inventory speculation. However, there is relatively little slack in the overall system, so that virtually any interruption in supply is sufficient to provoke a short-term supply crisis.

This lack of storage capacity is an important contributing factor in the periodic upward thrust of prices. Privately held stocks reduce price fluctuations associated with seasonal variations in demand, but they have accentuated upward price movements during crises. Inventory build-ups and draw-downs have also destabilized OPEC production levels. The reason is basically economic rather than political. Since oil inventory accumulation only pays when oil prices rise by more than inventory carrying costs, inventories are built up during times of crisis and drawn down when supplies become more abundant. Prices do not retract when the crisis passes, because OPEC validates price increases by reducing output. An important conclusion is that private inventory speculation serves to permanently raise oil prices.

OPEC Perception of the Pricing Problem.   The member countries of OPEC are concerned with spot prices when they soar far above or sink much below contract prices. However, it is not clear that important leaders within OPEC, as opposed to a few oil market analysts within OPEC member countries, have a clear understanding of the ratchet process. For example, in June, 1979, when oil prices on the spot market were soaring beyond $40 per barrel, the OPEC conference announced that steps would be taken to limit transactions in the spot market. The oil companies were also called upon to play "a more constructive role" in guaranteeing supplies to developing countries, and they were told that OPEC would not tolerate speculation on the spot market. An oil market expert, commenting on these policies in the trade journal *Petroleum Intelligence Weekly,* quipped that the logic of trying to bring spot prices down by "starving" the spot market is elusive. Indeed, the way to mitigate spot-price increases is for a very large supplier, such as Saudi Arabia, or group of suppliers, such as OPEC, to sell additional quantities on the spot market. When spot prices are weak and sink below contract prices, they should withdraw supplies from the spot market to hold prices up. But it is not clear that the OPEC conference perceives the problem in this way. Consequently, there have been no organized efforts, other than moral suasion and admonition, to control spot prices. And these efforts have been almost totally ineffectual.

Prediction of Future Price Movements

Predicting prices much beyond five years is a dubious pastime. Oil prices depend on technology and on policy-induced changes in production and consumption. And these variables are shrouded in uncertainty. Assessments of near-term price movements are less hazardous, since it is highly probable that the ratchet process will continue to operate.

The periodic upward ratcheting of oil prices may not be in the long-term interests of the producing countries; it almost assuredly is not in the interests of the consuming countries. Price ratcheting is likely to result in isolationist policies designed to achieve energy independence and to similar ill-conceived consumer-country policies that could lead to the development of alternative technologies and to the use of high-cost alternative resources long before they would be implemented if a more gradual price path were followed. If such policies are adopted, the costs to consumers will be higher and benefits for producers lower.

Whether producers and consumers will be made better or worse off by sharp or gradual price movements is largely irrelevant in predicting probable price movements. The history of OPEC seems long enough to make it possible to predict with reasonable confidence the general pattern of price movements. The more probable course is that nominal oil prices will increase, but that the path will not be gradual. Oil consumption worldwide is currently exceeding production (October, 1981). Consumption can be expected to exceed production in 1982 and 1983, with accompanying inventory draw-downs. This will perpetuate problems for OPEC regarding who shall take production cuts. It will also give OPEC members the "false" signal that additional capacity should not be developed, and thus set the stage for another upward ratcheting of oil prices whenever another "crisis" develops.

The probability of another oil crisis occurring during the period 1984–1986 is very great. Because of time lags, the probability of importing-country governments properly perceiving the nature of the problem prior to about 1984 is very low; and the probability of an effective buffer-stock policy prior to 1985 is negligible. Thus, it is highly probable that there will be another doubling of nominal oil prices through the ratchet process between 1984 and 1986. Spot prices around the range of $80–$90 per barrel, with contract prices some $20 lower, would not be at all surprising.

OPEC Stability

A question of vital concern to individuals in both the importing and exporting countries is whether OPEC will remain a viable price-setting and output-restricting institution. The conclusion, based on the analysis of this book, is that OPEC will be around for a long, long time. If OPEC develops like other institutions in world petroleum markets, such as the international corporate cartel and the state regulatory authorities in the United States, OPEC will devise a better system to regulate output and prices than they have at present. A comprehensive system of prorationing would not be surprising by around 1990 or 2000. This is not a prediction, only a possibility. It took the state regulatory authorities in the United States over 20 years (between 1915 and 1938) to devise an effective system of prorationing; and for the international majors it was an ongoing battle from the early 1900s through the middle 1950s, with major agreements occurring in 1914 and 1928. It is not possible to determine the degree to which the international majors limited output, but whatever limit they imposed was sufficient to ensure that the U.S. Gulf price prevailed worldwide until the late 1950s. The effects of prorationing in the United States are more easily documented. So strong was the U.S. system of prorationing, that in 1959, wells in Texas that were subject to the system were producing at only 28 percent of capacity.

Prorationing would be a good alternative to present pricing practices within OPEC because its use would facilitate the achievement of target pricing. It is an indisputable fact that levels of output can be monitored more accurately than can prices and contractual matters related to terms of delivery, cash discounts, and terms of credit. This is important because OPEC experiences the same problems as any other "cartel" (i.e., how to share production cutbacks required to maintain or increase prices). The present system of establishing "differentials" around the Saudi marker crude price promotes instability of market shares and is therefore an inefficient system of price maintenance. Establishing production quotas based on maximum efficient rates of production or a criterion related to reserves would be more efficient. To one who believes in the notion that individuals and groups discard less-efficient practices when more efficient ones become known and understood, it would not be surprising if OPEC were to opt in favor of prorationing.

Venezuela has been advocating such a system since the early 1960s. The main problem is the need for each country to relinquish a degree of sovereignty over its pace of exploration, development, and production. The sovereignty issue is critical and may well be sufficient to preclude the development of a prorationing system within OPEC. However, the international majors experienced the same basic problems and were able to surmount them. A difference is that OPEC already has a procedure that works tolerably well, so it may continue to establish prices in 1990 and 2000 much as it does today. One thing is certain: OPEC is not about to crumble.

Appendix 10-A

Exxon Projections of Primary Energy Demand and Sources of Supply:

United States
Western Europe
Japan
Centrally Planned Economies
Developing Countries*

---

*By region, but not by source of supply.

TABLE 10A-1
United States Energy Demand and Sources of Supply, 1965–2000

	1965	1979	1990	2000
ENERGY SOURCE	*(percentage distribution)*			
Nuclear	—	3	8	11
Hydropower and Other	4	4	6	6
Coal	22	19	24	31
Gas, Domestic Production	30	25	18	15
Oil, Domestic Production	35	27	18	17
Synthetics	—	—	2	9
Oil and Gas Imports	9	22	24	11
Total	100	100	100	100
TOTAL EQUIVALENT DEMAND				
Million Barrels per Day	26	39	41	46
Billion Barrels per Year	9.5	14.2	15.0	16.8

SOURCE: Figures for Tables 10A-1 through 10A-5 have been adapted from Exxon, *World Energy Outlook,* December 1980, pp. 31, 33, 35, 37, and 39. © 1980, Exxon Corporation. Reprinted with Permission.

TABLE 10A-2
European Energy Demand and Sources of Supply, 1965–2000

	1965	1979	1990	2000
ENERGY SOURCE	*(percentage distribution)*			
Nuclear	1	3	11	16
Hydropower and Other	9	8	8	8
Coal, Domestic Production	39	16	16	15
Gas, Domestic Production	2	12	10	8
Oil, Domestic Production	2	9	12	10
Oil Imports	44	46	28	24
Gas and Coal Imports	3	6	15	19
Total	100	100	100	100
TOTAL OIL EQUIVALENT DEMAND				
Million Barrels per Day	18	27	32	37
Billion Barrels per Year	6.6	9.9	11.7	13.5

TABLE 10A-3
Japanese Energy Demand and Sources of Supply, 1965–2000

	1965	1979	1990	2000
ENERGY SOURCE	*(percentage distribution)*			
Nuclear	—	4	10	18
Hydropower and Domestic Fossil Fuels Production	34	8	8	8
Oil Imports	60	73	54	43
Gas and Coal Imports	6	15	28	31
Total	100	100	100	100
TOTAL OIL EQUIVALENT DEMAND				
Million Barrels per Day	3	7.5	9.5	11.5
Billion Barrels per Year	1.1	2.7	3.5	4.2

TABLE 10A-4
Centrally Planned Economies
Energy Demand and Sources of Supply, 1965–2000

	1965	1979	1990	2000
ENERGY SOURCE	*(percentage distribution)*			
Nuclear	—	1	5	9
Hydropower and Other	3	3	3	4
Coal	63	45	41	39
Gas	12	19	23	25
Oil	22	32	28	23
Total	100	100	100	100
TOTAL OIL EQUIVALENT DEMAND				
Million Barrels per Day	20	40	55	69
Billion Barrels per Year	7.3	14.6	20.0	25.2

TABLE 10A-5
Energy Demand in the Developing Countries[1], 1965–2000

	1965	1979	1990	2000
ENERGY SOURCE	*(percentage distribution)*			
Low-Growth Countries	47	31	28	25
High-Growth Countries	23	28	25	25
Non-OPEC Oil Exporters	16	17	17	20
OPEC	14	24	30	30
Total	100	100	100	100
TOTAL OIL EQUIVALENT DEMAND				
Million Barrels per Day	7.5	18	32.5	48
Billion Barrels per Year	2.7	6.6	11.8	17.5

[1]DEVELOPING COUNTRIES
  Oil Exporting Countries
  OPEC (13 countries).
  Non-OPEC (Angola, Bahrain, Bolivia, Brunei, Burma, Congo, Egypt, Malaysia, Mexico, Oman, Peru, Syria, Trinidad, Tunisia, Zaïre).

  Other Developing Countries
  High-Growth (Argentina, Brazil, Chile, Colombia, Hong Kong, Singapore, South Korea, Taiwan, Uruguay).
  Low-Growth (All other countries).

Further Readings

British Petroleum. *BP Statistical Review of the World Oil Industry, 1980*. London: Britannic House.

Central Intelligence Agency. National Foreign Assessment Center. *The World Oil Market in the Years Ahead*. Washington, D.C.: National Technical Information Service, August 1979.

Conoco. *World Energy Outlook Through 1990*. Stanford, Conn.: Coordinating and Planning Dept., Conoco Inc.*

Exxon. *World Energy Outlook*. Exxon Background Series. New York: Corporate Planning Dept., Public Affairs Dept. et al. Exxon Corporation, 1981.

Levy, Walter. "A Warning to the Oil Importing Nations." *Fortune*, 21 May 1979, 48–51.

*Annual update; copies available on request.

Appendix
A

**Statistical Summary
of World and OPEC
Reserves, Production,
and Downstream
Activities:
1979–1980**

TABLE A-1
OPEC Crude Oil and Natural Gas Reserves[1]

	Crude Oil (*million barrels*)	Ratio: Oil Reserves to Production	Natural Gas (*billion cubic meters*)
Algeria	8,440	20	3,738
Ecuador	1,100	14	113
Gabon	500	7	14
Indonesia	9,600	17	680
Iran	58,000	50	13,877
Iraq	31,000	24	779
Kuwait[2]	68,530	75	949
Libya	23,500	31	680
Nigeria	17,400	21	1,172
Qatar	3,760	20	1,699
Saudi Arabia[2]	166,480	48	2,711
United Arab Emirates[3]	29,411	44	581
Venezuela	17,870	21	1,212
Total OPEC	435,591	39	28,205
Total World	641,623	28	72,876
Percent OPEC	67.9		38.7

[1]As of January 1, 1980.
[2]Including 50 percent of Neutral Zone's reserves
[3]Figures for Sharjah are not available
SOURCE: OPEC, *Annual Report, 1979,* Vienna: 1980, p. 147.

TABLE A-2
OPEC Statistical Summary and Indicators, 1979

	OPEC	Total World	OPEC Share of Total World (*percent*)
I. RESERVES[1] AT YEAR'S END			
A. Crude oil (billion barrels)	436	642	67.9
Ratio (reserves/production)	39	28	
B. Natural gas (trillion cubic meters)	28	73	38.7
Ratio (reserves/net production[2])	111	42	
II. CRUDE OIL PRODUCTION (THOUSAND BARRELS PER DAY)			
A. Total	30,928	63,185	48.9
B. National oil companies' entitlement in OPEC crude oil production	23,371		
Percentage of entitlement	75.6		
C. Major oil companies' supply of crude oil[3]	24,400		38.6
III. NATURAL GAS GROSS PRODUCTION (BILLION CUBIC METERS)	303	1,853[a]	16.4
A. Net production (utilization)	119	1,540[a]	7.7
B. Re-injection	50	97[a]	51.5
C. Flared (billion cubic meters)	134	216[a]	62.0
(million barrels oil equivalent per day)	2.3	3.7	
Percentage of Natural Gas Gross Production			
Net Production	39	83	
Re-injection	16	5	
Flared	45	12	
IV. REFINING			
A. Capacity (thousand barrels per calendar day)	5,320	80,035	6.6
B. Throughput (thousand barrels per calendar day)	3,662[b]	62,160[c]	5.9

(continued)

	OPEC	Total World	OPEC Share of Total World
Percentage throughput/capacity	68.8	77.7	
Percentage throughput/crude oil production	11.8	98.4	
V. CONSUMPTION OF REFINED PRODUCTS (THOUSAND BARRELS PER DAY)	2,217	64,125[c]	3.5
Consumption of main products, in percentage:			
Gasoline	46[d,e]	30[f]	
Middle distillates	29[d]	30[f]	
Fuel oil	17[d]	25[f]	
Others	8[d]	15[f]	
Percentage consumption/refinery throughput	60.5	103.2[g]	
Percentage consumption/crude oil production	7.2	97.6[g]	
VI. EXPORTS (THOUSAND BARRELS PER DAY)			
A. Crude oil	26,842	32,022[h]	83.8
B. Refined products	2,026	8,982[h]	22.6
VII. TRANSPORTATION			
A. Oil tanker fleet Unit: million DWT	11.4	327.9	3.5
B. LNG-carriers[4] Unit: thousand cubic meters	424	4,769	8.9
C. LPG-carriers[4] Unit: thousand cubic meters	406	5,958	6.8

[1] *Oil and Gas Journal.*

[2] Gross production minus re-injection.

[3] *Petroleum Economist,* May 1980. The major oil companies are Exxon, Gulf, Mobil, Socal, BP, Shell, and CFP. CFP Correspondence.

[4] *Liquid Gas Carrier Register, 1980.* London: H. Clarkson & Co. Ltd.

[a] Cedigaz, Centre International d'Information sur le Gaz Naturel et tous Hydrocarbures Gazeux.

[b] Excluding natural gas liquids for Saudi Arabia as well as processing deals of Indonesia and Algeria.

[c] *BP Statistical Review of the World Oil Industry, 1979,* World Oil Consumption.

[d] Based on the available data from OPEC member countries.

[e] Gasoline and kerosene.

[f] Excluding USSR, Eastern Europe, and China.

[g] Based on data taken from *BP Statistical Review of the World Oil Industry, 1979.*

[h] Including re-exports.

SOURCE: OPEC, *Annual Report, 1979,* Vienna: 1980, pp. 144-146.

Appendix B

Organizations Involved in International Energy Analysis

This appendix offers an outline of the organizations that are involved in the analysis of international energy issues. In each group one finds a large bureaucracy, an orientation toward a limited aspect of international energy analysis, and myriad issues deemed important to the leadership. Very little of the work of these organizations is exposed to close public scrutiny, although many of them have public information offices which issue publications designed to promote an understanding of their point of view. Each has its idiosyncrasies, and power may wax or wane depending on the characteristics of those who assume control or on the external events that thrust the group to center stage. However, size is important: The views of large organizations tend to predominate because they devote more resources to the development and presentation of their ideas. In any case, the following organizations are potential employers of individuals who have gained expertise in the analysis of world petroleum markets.

I. International Organizations
A. Producer-Country Organizations
  1. OPEC—Organization of the Petroleum Exporting Countries
  2. OAPEC—Organization of Arab Petroleum Exporting Countries
  3. OLADE—Organization Latinoamericana de Energia[1]

B. Consumer-Country Organizations
  1. OECD—Organization for Economic Cooperation and Development
  2. IEA—International Energy Agency
  3. EEC—European Economic Community
  4. IAEA—International Atomic Energy Agency
  5. IIASA—International Institute for Applied Systems Analysis

C. International Financial Corporations
  1. World Bank (aid and developmental loans)
  2. IMF—International Monetary Fund (financial stability)

D. United Nations Organizations
  1. UNCTAD—United Nations Conference on Trade and Development
  2. UNDP—United Nations Development Programme
  3. UNEP—United Nations Environment Programme
  4. UNITAR—United Nations Institute for Training and Research
  5. UNIDO—United Nations Industrial Development Organization

---

[1]This is an organization of Latin American "Departments of Energy"—it is producer-oriented.

II. Domestic Organizations in the Consuming Countries

A. United States (Government)
   1. Cabinet-Level Departments
      a. Department of Energy
      b. Department of State
      c. Department of Treasury
      d. Department of Commerce
   2. Executive Agencies
      a. Office of Managment and Budget
      b. Council of Economic Advisers
      c. Central Intelligence Agency
   3. Congressional Offices
      a. Congressional Research Service
      b. Office of Technology Assessment
   4. National Laboratories
      a. Oak Ridge National Lab
      b. Argonne National Lab
      c. Brookhaven National Lab
      d. Lawrence Livermore National Laboratory

B. United States (Private)
   1. Research Institutes
      a. Brookings Institution
      b. Resources for the Future
      c. Petroleum Industry Research Foundation
   2. Private Funding Agencies
      a. Ford Foundation
      b. Rockefeller Foundation
      c. National Science Foundation
      d. Electric Power Research Institute
   3. Consulting Groups
      a. Data Resources Incorporated
      b. Institute for Energy Analysis
      c. Levy, Walter J.
      d. Mitre Corp.
      e. Petroleum Industry Research Foundation
      f. Rand Corp.
      g. SRI International (formerly, Stanford Research Institute)
      h. Wharton Econometric Forecasting Associates

III. National Oil Companies of OPEC Member Countries, 1979

Country	National Oil Company	Designation
Algeria	Société Nationale pour la Recherche, la Production, le Transport, la Transformation et la Commercialisation des Hydrocarbures	SONATRACH
Ecuador	Corporation Estatal Petrolera Ecuatoriana	CEPE
Gabon	National Oil Company of Gabon	PETROGAB
Indonesia	Perusahaan Pertambangan Minyak & Gas Bumi Negara	PERTAMINA
Iran	National Iranian Oil Company	NIOC
Iraq	Iraq National Oil Company	INOC
Kuwait	Kuwait Oil Company	KOC
Libya	National Oil Corporation	NOC
Nigeria	Nigerian National Petroleum Corporation	NNPC
Qatar	Qatar General Petroleum Corporation	QGPC
Saudi Arabia	General Petroleum and Mineral Organization of Saudi Arabia	PETROMIN
United Arab Emirates	Abu Dhabi National Oil Company	ADNOC
Venezuela	Petroleos de Venezuela S.A.	PDVSA

SOURCE: OPEC, *Annual Report, 1979,* Vienna: 1979, pp. 185–186.

IV. Leading Petroleum Corporations in the United States, 1980

Rank Among U.S. Oil Companies	Name of Company (*headquarters*)	Net Sales (*billions of U.S. dollars*)	Rank among All U.S. Corporations
1	Exxon (New York)	103.1	1
2	Mobil (New York)	59.5	2
3	Texaco (Harrison, New York)	51.2	4
4	Standard Oil of California (San Francisco)	40.5	5
5	Gulf Oil (Pittsburgh)	26.5	7
6	Standard Oil of Indiana (Chicago)	26.1	9
7	Atlantic Richfield (Los Angeles)	23.7	11
8	Shell Oil (Houston)	19.8	12
9	Conoco (Stanford, Connecticut)	18.3	14
10	Phillips Petroleum (Bartlesville, Oklahoma)	13.4	16
11	Tenneco (Houston)	13.2	17
12	Sun (Radner, Pennsylvania)	12.9	18
13	Occidental Petroleum (Los Angeles)	12.5	20
14	Standard Oil of Ohio (Cleveland)	11.0	23
15	Getty Oil (Los Angeles)	10.2	26
16	Union Oil of California (Los Angeles)	10.0	28
17	Marathon Oil (Findley, Ohio)	8.2	39
18	Ashland Oil (Russell, Kentucky)	8.1	40
19	Amerada Hess (New York)	7.9	43
20	Cities Service (Tulsa)	7.8	44

SOURCE: "The 500 Largest Industrial Corporations," *Fortune,* 4 May 1981, pp. 324–327.

V. Leading Petroleum Corporations Outside the United States, 1980

Rank among Oil Companies Outside the U.S.	Name of Corporation (Outside U.S.)	Country	Net Sales (*billions of U.S. dollars*)	Rank among Foreign Corporations
1	Royal Dutch-Shell Group	Netherlands–Britain	79.4	1
2	British Petroleum	Britain	49.5	2
3	ENI	Italy	25.0	3
4	Cie. Française des Pétroles	France	27.3	5
5	Petroleos de Venezuela	Venezuela	18.8	7
6	ELF Aquitaine	France	16.9	12
7	Nippon Oil	Japan	16.2	14
8	Petrofina	Belgium	10.7	23

SOURCE: "The Year the Red Ink Flowed Deeply," *Business Week,* 20 July 1981, pp. 86–124.

VI. Leading Petroleum Corporations Outside the United States by Country of Origin, 1980

Country and Company	1980 Sales (*billions of U.S. dollars*)
NETHERLANDS	
Royal Dutch-Shell	79.4
GREAT BRITAIN	
British Petroleum	49.5
Burmah Oil	2.9
Ultramar	2.3
FRANCE	
Compagnie Française des Pétroles	22.3
ELF Aquitaine	16.9
ITALY	
ENI	25.0

VI. Leading Petroleum Corporations Outside the United States by Country of Origin, 1980 *(continued)*

Country and Company	1980 Sales (*billions of U.S. dollars*)
JAPAN	
Nippon Oil	16.2
Maruzen Oil	8.2
Mitsubishi Oil	6.3
Toa Nenryo Kogyo	5.5
Daikyo Oil	5.2
Showa Oil	4.6
Koa Oil	2.9
VENEZUELA	
Petroleos de Venezuela	18.8
MEXICO	
PEMEX	14.5
BRAZIL	
Petrobras	12.2
BELGIUM	
Petrofina	10.7
CANADA	
Imperial Oil	5.1
Total Petroleum of North America	1.6
Husky Oil	1.1
Dome Petroleum	1.0
SPAIN	
Enpetrol	4.8
Compañia Española de Petroleos	3.3
Union Expl.	1.7
Petroliber	1.0
INDIA	
Indian Oil	5.6

(continued)

VI. Leading Petroleum Corporations Outside the United States by Country of Origin, 1980 *(continued)*

Country and Company	1980 Sales *(billions of U.S. dollars)*
FINLAND	
Neste	3.5
AUSTRIA	
OMV	3.4
KOREA	
Korea Oil	3.0
PHILIPPINES	
Philippine National Oil	2.6
PORTUGAL	
Petrogal	2.0
NORWAY	
Statoil	1.7
CHILE	
Compañia de Petroleos de Chile	1.1

SOURCE: "The Year the Red Ink Flowed Deeply," *Business Week,* 20 July 1981, pp. 86–124.

Index

Page numbers in italics indicate illustrations.

A

B

C

301